'A welcome historical study of behaviour that often divides everyday opinion – public drinking, obscenity, vice and immorality – some of which is prosecuted in court, some ends up in the newspapers, and much of which is discussed in the pub. Not least, the book reminds students, legal researchers, historians, and sociologists that a great deal of human behaviour is often regarded as "offensive".'

Barry Godfrey, Professor of Social Justice,
University of Liverpool, UK

'How often is one's conduct in private unacceptable behaviour outside the home? If instinctively the conduct evokes a ready answer, it is far from obvious in infinite situations. Occupancy of the audience, visually or imagined, is everything. Once it was the obscenity of the language – written or uttered vocally in a crowded scene is one way. Social attitudes are another. The authors choose the period 1857 to 1960 to pose the societal problems, which reminds one that only after the Matrimonial Causes Act of 1857 was a divorce granted judicially for the first time, and then only in cases where one spouse was litigiously at fault by way of adultery, desertion, or cruelty. The myriad problems of conflicting moral values are fascinatingly expounded by the authors in a sample of sociological material that is, literally, all too rare a publication.'

Sir Louis Blom-Cooper, QC

Public Indecency in England 1857–1960

Throughout the nineteenth century and twentieth century, various attempts were made to define and control problematic behaviour in public by legal and legislative means through the use of a somewhat nebulous concept of 'indecency'. Remarkably however, public indecency remains a much under-researched aspect of English legal, social, and criminal justice history.

Covering a period of just over a century, from 1857 (the date of the passing of the first Obscene Publications Act) to 1960 (the date of the famous trial of Penguin Books over their publication of *Lady Chatterley's Lover* following the introduction of a new Obscene Publications Act in the previous year), *Public Indecency in England 1857–1960* investigates the social and cultural obsession with various forms of indecency and how public perceptions of different types of indecent behaviour led to legal definitions of such behaviour in both common law and statute.

This truly interdisciplinary book utilizes socio-legal, historical, and criminological research to discuss the practical response of both the police and the judiciary to those caught engaging in public indecency, as well as to highlight the increasing problems faced by moralists during a period of unprecedented technological developments in the fields of visual and aural mass entertainment. It is written in a lively and approachable style and, as such, is of interest to academics and students engaged in the study of deviance, law, criminology, sociology, criminal justice, socio-legal studies, and history. It will also be of interest to the general reader.

David J. Cox is Reader in Criminal Justice History at the University of Wolverhampton, an Honorary Research Fellow of Keele University, and a fellow of the Royal Historical Society. His research interests include Victorian prisons, eighteenth-century policing (with particular emphasis on the Bow Street 'Runners'), and the role of the magistracy in dispensing informal justice. He has published widely in the field of criminal justice history. Recent publications include *Crime in England, 1688–1815* (Routledge, 2014), *Policing the Factory: Theft, Private Policing and the Law in Modern England 1777–1968*, with B. Godfrey (Bloomsbury Academic, 2013), and *'A Certain Share of Low Cunning': A History of the Bow Street Runners, 1792–1839* (Routledge, 2012).

Kim Stevenson is a Professor in Socio-Legal History at Plymouth University, a co-founder and director of SOLON, and one of the general editors of the Routledge SOLON series. Her research interests focus on the historical and contemporary aspects of the criminal law with particular emphasis on sexual offences and sexuality. She has published numerous books in her field, with recent publications including *Crime News in Modern Britain: Press Reporting and Responsibility, 1820–2010*, with J. Rowbotham and S. Pegg (Palgrave, 2013), and an edited collection entitled *Gender, Sexualities and Law* (Routledge, 2011).

Candida Harris is a Visiting Research Fellow at Plymouth University. Her research interests include constitutional law and human rights, historical perspectives on contemporary problems, and the Mental Deficiency Act 1913 and the control of deviant behaviour. Her publications include 'Inaccessible and Unknowable: Accretion and Uncertainty in Modern Criminal Law', with K. Stevenson, in *Liverpool Law Review* 29 (2008) and 'Truth, law and hate in the virtual marketplace of ideas: perspectives on the regulation of Internet content', with J. Rowbotham and K. Stevenson, in *Information & Communications Technology Law* 18, no. 2 (June 2009).

Judith Rowbotham is a full-time independent scholar based in London, a co-founder and director of SOLON, one of the general editors of the Routledge SOLON series, and Honorary Research Fellow at Plymouth University in the Plymouth Law School. Her research interests include the presentation or reportage of the legal process, including the criminal justice system, in various nonfiction and fiction formats, and issues of gender, violence, and cultural comprehensions of the law in action, from the late eighteenth century to the present. Recent publications include the aforementioned *Crime News in Modern Britain: Press Reporting & Responsibility, 1820–2010* (Palgrave, 2013) and *Shame, Blame, and Culpability: Crime and Violence in the Modern State*, edited with Marianna Muravyeva and David Nash (Routledge, 2012).

Routledge SOLON Explorations in Crime and Criminal Justice Histories

Edited by Kim Stevenson, University of Plymouth; Judith Rowbotham, University of Plymouth; David Nash, Oxford Brookes University and David J. Cox, University of Wolverhampton

This series is a collaboration between Routledge and the SOLON consortium (promoting studies in law, crime and history), to present cutting edge interdisciplinary research in crime and criminal justice history, through monographs and thematic collected editions which reflect on key issues and dilemmas in criminology and socio-legal studies by locating them within a historical dimension. The emphasis here is on inspiring use of historical and historiographical methodological approaches to the contextualising and understanding of current priorities and problems. This series aims to highlight the best, most innovative interdisciplinary work from both new and established scholars in the field, through focusing on the enduring historical resonances to current core criminological and socio-legal issues.

Public Indecency in England 1857–1960

'A serious and growing evil'

David J. Cox, Kim Stevenson, Candida Harris, and Judith Rowbotham

Routledge
Taylor & Francis Group

LONDON AND NEW YORK

First published 2015
by Routledge
2 Park Square, Milton Park, Abingdon, Oxon, OX14 4RN

Simultaneously published in the USA and Canada
by Routledge
711 Third Avenue, New York, NY 10017

First issued in paperback 2018

*Routledge is an imprint of the Taylor & Francis Group, an informa
business*

British Library Cataloguing in Publication Data
A catalogue record for this book is available from the British Library

Library of Congress Cataloging-in-Publication Data
Cox, David J.
    Public indecency in England 1857–1960 : "a serious and
growing evil" / David J. Cox, Kim Stevenson, Candida Harris
and Judith Rowbotham. — First Edition.
        pages cm. — (Routledge SOLON explorations in crime
and criminal justice histories ; 6)
    1. Criminology—Great Britain—History—19th
century.   2. Criminology—Great Britain—History—20th
century.   3. Indecent assault—Great Britain.   I. Title.
    HV9647.C69 2015
    364.1'74094209041—dc23
    2014049118

ISBN 13: 978-1-138-49928-7 (pbk)
ISBN 13: 978-0-415-52471-1 (hbk)

Typeset in Times New Roman
by Apex CoVantage, LLC

Contents

Tables

Preface and acknowledgements

This book is not intended as a straightforward narrative history of public indecency between 1857 and 1960. Neither is it a dry tome concerned only with the passing of Acts of Parliament and other legal paraphernalia. It most emphatically is *not* an edited collection; instead it was written in a truly cross-disciplinary fashion, with all of the authors contributing their various areas of expertise to each of the chapters. Consequently, it includes aspects of socio-legal studies, criminology, history, and law.

The book introduces our definition of public indecency before going on to provide a brief historical background to such indecency before 1857 in order to contextualize the later chapters. It then broadly follows a chronological route, dealing with three periods: 1857–1885, 1885–1908, and 1908–1960. The first period is bookended by the Obscene Publications Act 1857 and the Criminal Law Amendment Act 1885 (the latter year also seeing the creation of the National Vigilance Association), whilst the second ends with the publication of the *Report of the Joint Select Committee on Lotteries and Indecent Advertisements*. The final period ends with the infamous trial of Penguin Books concerning the publication of *Lady Chatterley's Lover*. The book then looks at an extended case study of how one provincial English town (Crewe in Cheshire) dealt with those caught and punished for practising public indecency.

Within the three chronological periods the book discusses a panoply of themes, including the rise of moral activism and its effects on governmental responses to public indecency; the concept of 'decency' as a British (English) trait; how new technologies (especially with regard to the visual and aural arts) proved problematical for the moralists; and the practical responses of both the police and the judiciary to public indecency.

No book is simply the result of the sole knowledge of its author(s); rather such a publication emanates from its authors having consulted the combined wealth of experience, expertise, and publications of a wide variety of academic and other specialist sources. The authors would therefore like to take this opportunity to thank the many colleagues and fellow academics who have provided food for thought in the writing of this book, and would especially like to thank the staff at the National Archives (especially Liz Hore) for their unfailingly helpful attitude and tremendous archival knowledge. We also say a sincere 'Thank you' to

Professor Barry Godfrey (University of Liverpool) and Professor Stephen Farrall (University of Sheffield) for their allowing us (in Chapters Six and Seven) to extrapolate data from the Crewe database originally created by them together with David J. Cox as part of a Leverhulme Trust–funded project, and would also recommend the two books which resulted from that project: Godfrey *et al.*, *Criminal Lives: Family Life, Employment, and Offending* (Oxford University Press, 2007), and Godfrey *et al., Serious Offenders: A Historical Study of Habitual Criminals* (Oxford University Press, 2010). We would also like to thank Heidi Lee at Routledge for her unfailing assistance, good humour, and patience.

Abbreviations

BBFC	British Board of Film Classification (formerly British Board of Film Censorship)
BMA	British Medical Association
BMJ	British Medical Journal
CORR	Correspondence
CS	Criminal Statistics
DPP	Director of Public Prosecutions
HC	House of Commons
HL	House of Lords
JS	Judicial Statistics
LCO	Lord Chamberlain's Office
LCP	Lord Chamberlain's Papers
LCPPM	London Council for the Promotion of Public Morality
L&NWR	London & North Western Railway
NCPM	National Council for Public Morals
NVA	National Vigilance Association
OBP	Old Bailey Proceedings
OPA 1857	Obscene Publications Act 1857
PMC	Public Morality Council
PP	Parliamentary Papers
SRM	Society for the Reformation of Manners
SSV	Society for the Suppression of Vice and the Encouragement of Religion and Virtue
TNA	The National Archives

List of Cases

For most of the cases, page numbers are followed by the footnote (fn) number.

Associated Provincial Picture Houses Ltd v Wednesbury Corporation [1947] 1 KB 223124 fn94

Ellis v Dubowski [1921] 3 KB 621 128 fn115

Gough v UK [2014] ECHR 1156 1 fn1

London County Council v Bermondsey Bioscope Co., Ltd. [1911] 1 KB 445 124 fn93

McGowan v Langmuir [1931] SLT 94 33

Mills v London County Council [1925] 1 KB 213 128 fn116

R v Avery, (unreported) *The Times,* 4 October 1900 61 fn73

R v Bocca, (unreported) *The Times,* 14 April 19 61 fn73

R v Gray [1900] 2 QB 36 54

R v Hicklin [1868] 3 QB 360 28, 29, 31, 33, 43, 60, 64, 78, 101

R v Jacombe, (unreported) *The Times,* 4 October 1906 61 fn73

R v Knuller (Publishing etc.) [1973] AC 435, 457–8 140 fn13

R v Marsham et al., (unreported) *The Times,* 17 February 1902 61 fn 73

R v Wegel, (unreported) *The Times,* 3 August 1905 61 fn73

Reg v Martin Secker & Warburg Ltd. [1954] 1 WLR 1138; [1954] 2 All ER 683 99 fn140

Scott v Scott [1913] AC 417 80

Theatre de Luxe (Halifax) Ltd v Gledhill [1915] 2 KB 49 124 fn94

Thomson v Chain Libraries [1954] 1 WLR 999 98 fn130

List of Statutes

Beer Act 1830 161–2

Children and Young Persons (Harmful Publications) Act 1955 98
Children and Young Persons Act 1909 165
Cinematograph Act 1909 123–4, 131
Criminal Law Amendment Act 1885 31, 34, 45, 81, 142
Customs Consolidation Act 1876 61–2

Habitual Drunkards Act 1879 171

Incest Act 1908 81
Indecent Advertisements Act 1889 55, 57, 62, 67–8, 69, 81, 180
Indecent Displays Act 1909 180
Inebriates Act 1888 171
Inebriates Act 1898 171–2
Infant Life Preservation Act 1929 141
Intoxicating Liquors (Sale to Children) Act 1901 165

Mental Deficiency Act 1913 45–46, 49
Metropolitan Police Act 1829 25
Metropolitan Police Act 1839 40, 74, 96
Municipal Corporations Act 1835 26, 31

Obscene Publications Act 1857 (OPA) 11, 28–9, 31, 33, 40, 44, 57,
    59–61, 64, 71, 77, 81, 90, 95, 100–1
Obscene Publications Act 1959 101, 180
Offences Against the Person Act 1828 142
Offences Against the Person Act 1861 56, 69, 140, 142

Post Office Act 1870 62
Post Office Act 1908 62
Profane Oaths Act 1746 153–4
Public Libraries Act 1850 178–9

Series editor introduction

The volumes in this series contribute to the unashamedly interdisciplinary exercise in which SOLON has engaged since its inception in 2000, something now enhanced by the collaboration with Routledge to present cutting-edge interdisciplinary research in crime and criminal justice history. The focus is on issues which, while rooted in the past, also have a crucial current resonance, and so the volumes reflect on key issues and dilemmas which persist in terms of contemporary priorities.

This volume constitutes an engaging addition to the series, being particularly valuable because it explores a diverse range of activities which have, in the past, amounted to public indecency – but which have rarely been studied in any depth because so much of the behaviour amounting to public indecency involved low-level offending. Examined in this work are the historical cultural contexts out of which conceptualizations of public indecency between 1857 and 1960 arose. These are valuable in that they are used to frame and explain the levels of public demand that the phenomenon be managed legislatively and through the criminal justice process as well as through the pressure of social disapproval. But the volume also provides contemporary explanations of public indecency which have current resonances and can encourage reassessments of the practical legacy of attempted censure of people's private tastes and individual conduct.

The text explores how fears about the ability of certain 'liberal' ideas (particularly those relating to sexual matters manifesting themselves in print and art), as well as overindulgence in drink or drugs and activities like gambling, have been used to create alarm and despondency amongst the population. A belief that a strong and healthy society is one not corrupted by immoral ideas is far from new. But the responsibility in the medieval and early modern periods rested substantially with religion to identify and provide remedies against immorality and indecency, both public and private. The public indecency agenda that began to emerge in the UK towards the end of the seventeenth century was driven as much by secular as by religious concerns – and where there were religious motivations, they were increasingly driven by high-minded individuals rather than by established religious hierarchy. What is explored here, in effect, is the practical secularization of the public indecency agenda – where the secular, rather than the religious, courts took on the management process, aided by secular institutions such as the police.

This accounts for the chronological choice which bookends this volume: the passage of the Obscene Publications Act 1857 at the start, and the rethinking of the standards of public indecency encapsulated in the Obscene Publications Act 1959 at the close. Within this time frame, the wider phenomenon of public conduct adjudged to be 'indecent' is shown to extend to activities which were never, in themselves, identified as either sexual or obscene. However, what this volume demonstrates is that performers of any activities held to disgust or annoy observers were understood by contemporaries in a context of fear that the very visibility of these actions could incite others to imitation and to an escalation of levels of both public and private indecency, including the sexual and the obscene. Consequently, the authors demonstrate how drunkenness needs to be understood as a form of public indecency because of its association with other forms of low-level offending, which in turn threatened the health and stability of communities and the nation as a whole.

The national interest is a constant theme underpinning these explorations, especially as fears about the global pre-eminence of Britain and her Empire grew. It was seen as essential that the British conduct themselves decently if they were to continue to deserve that level of divine favour which had made the nation a Greater Britain – and can it be thought to be coincidence that the passage of the Obscene Publications Act 1959 comes at a time when that Greater British identity was being rethought against a background of the end of Empire, amongst other things. The British were reinventing themselves, and consequently revisiting their conceptualizations of what amounted to the threat of public indecency. However, the legacy of this initial secularization of the public indecency agenda continues to underpin much legislation governing the continuing criminalization of public conduct which is held to breach the standards of everyday decency within the community. What this detailed study reveals are the origins of the twenty-first century agenda of public indecency, which include aiding a better understanding of phenomena like the tellingly named Anti-Social Behaviour Orders for instance, as well as the continuing high level of fears over public drunkenness and its impact on the moral as well as physical health of the nation. As such, this volume fits well into a series which illustrates how a historically framed comprehension of the present criminal justice process and its cultural context leads to greater insights and the potential for policy improvement.

Introduction

Defining public indecency

This is a book about public indecency in the century between 1857 and 1960, how worries about increasing levels of such indecency manifested themselves in English society in the modern era, and the ways in which such concerns framed the legal management of public indecency. *Public indecency* is a broad and often an apparently vague term; it is one that is capable of being stretched and broadly applied to cover a range of visible and perceived behaviours, especially by those with particular perspectives about the 'acceptability' of certain actions and conduct whether in the public mind or in the courtroom. For the purposes of this book, the focus is on the concept of public indecency in the shape of acts and behaviour which may or may not be illegal according to the prevailing legal provisions but which become so when they are visible in the public domain instead of being confined to a private place, where that behaviour could not directly harm the public. It was the public knowledge and awareness of the existence of those acts which made them indecent rather than the actual conduct itself. As the contemporary example of the so-called Naked Rambler, Stephen Gough, arrested on numerous occasions for being naked in public, confirms, being naked was and is not a problem in the confines of an appropriate location such as one's own bedroom or bathroom, but public nudity was, and is still regarded as, unacceptable behaviour.[1] Equally, it was generally not a criminal act to create or manufacture pornographic material involving adults, but it was unlawful to seek to disseminate it to the public in some form.[2]

---

1 Between 2003 and 2014 Stephen Gough was arrested in England and Scotland for appearing naked in public and prosecuted for breach of the peace as there is no criminal offence of being naked in public; section 66 Sexual Offences Act 2003 only criminalizes the intentional exposure of the genitals provided there is an intent to cause alarm or distress. When sentenced to prison Gough was segregated for refusing to wear any clothes. He claimed that his right to freedom of privacy under Article 8 European Convention on Human Rights and freedom of expression under Article 10 had been violated by such repressive measures. The European Court of Human Rights dismissed his application confirming that there was no disproportionate interference by the UK in the performance of its duty to protect the public from public nuisances, in this case his antisocial conduct. See *Gough v UK* [2014] ECHR 1156.
2 The creation, distribution, and possession of child pornography is controlled by the Protection of Children Act 1978 and the Criminal Justice Act 1988 as amended by s45 Sexual Offences Act 2003. Extreme pornography is governed by ss63–67 Criminal Justice and Immigration Act 2008; both are, however, outside the remit of this book.

Clearly, the concept of public indecency was wide-ranging, with many activities which were perfectly legal in private having the potential to offend morally when publicly visible. This volume seeks to explore the phenomenon of increasing concern over inappropriate conduct which was believed to damage the welfare of the nation by vitiating its moral standards. In order to understand this for the period considered here, a starting point must be the recollection that not only were the majority of those expressing concern typically adherents of Protestant Christianity, but they were also classically educated. This manifested an understanding of decency and its antonym, *in*decency, which interpreted the morality that decency represented something which went beyond the strictly sexual and the religious. To be 'decent' was to behave, in public at least, in ways that attested to an inner sound moral character by demonstrating the modesty appropriate to one's social station as well as appropriate good manners, especially respect for other members of the community according to social norms which took account of class, age, and gender. This was observed behaviour underpinned by the demonstration of an appropriately refined taste in the consumption associated with it. For the social and political elites of the country, this amounted to civilization; for the rising middle classes the term increasingly used to represent decency was *respectability*.[3] By contrast then, indecency was uncivilized and unrespectable – and that covered quite a wide potential remit of everyday conduct.

One long-standing and key aspect of such everyday manifestation which could be classed by onlookers as public indecency was solicitation for prostitution, together with engaging in sexual activity in public (street-located prostitution). Prostitution itself, of course, was not and is not a criminalized activity, though legal management of the practice by labelling behaviour accompanying commercial sexual activity as offensive was achieved under catch-all legislation such as the Vagrancy Act 1824. Such conduct was traditionally dealt with in the courts as a form of disorderly behaviour rather than an expression of immorality.[4] As much for this reason as for the fact that a substantial amount has already been written on the legal management of prostitution, the simple rehearsal of which in summary form would add little to the existing literature, prostitution is not included as a core theme in this

3   The discussions about respectability as a governor of public behaviour were initiated by Thompson (1988), and subject to considerable debate subsequently. It is acknowledged that respectability as a concept was frequently far from cohesive in communities, and was instead often divisive and diverse in how it worked. In the legal process and the criminal justice system, there was, however, less flexibility. So, for the purposes of a discussion on the legal management of public indecency, the ways in which respectability was generally reduced to a common denominator makes it a useful concept. See F. M. L. Thompson, *The Rise of Respectable Society: A Social History of Victorian Britain, 1830–1900* (London: Fontana Press, 1988). For contemporary support for use of respectability as a concept in the legal process, see E. Cox, *Reports of Criminal Cases Argued and Determined in All the Courts in England and Ireland* (London: Law Times Office, 1855), especially p. 11 and pp. 153–5.

4   On the tradition of managing prostitution through imaginative use of the law in England and Wales, see R. M. Karrass, *Common Women: Prostitution and Sexuality in England* (Oxford: Oxford University Press, 1996).

volume.[5] On occasion and, in association with other headline themes, including indecent images or performances, the issue of prostitution and indecency usefully coincide, but otherwise this volume does not directly engage with prostitution as an expression of public indecency. Instead, the focus here is to offer a contextualization of a much broader phenomenon: a long-standing battle to define and impose moral boundaries on everyday public expression and behaviour through the use of the law. As such, this analysis examines public indecency in its least-definable sense, as a term used almost indiscriminately in condemnation of the behaviour of 'the other'.

It is often said that criminal law is rooted in the 'harm principle' first articulated by J. S. Mill in 1859, whereby (in simplistic terms) the intrusion of the law into the lives of citizens is constrained by an assumption that it is justified only by the prevention of harm to others.[6] This book explores the complexities which arise from this notion when strong moral convictions are confronted with changing popular values. During the period reviewed, the assertion of indecency was a consistent battle cry for moral activists who assiduously sought to maintain and extend the argument that if behaviour offended *their* sensibilities, it was therefore harmful, and thus merited and even required legal intervention. Consequently, between 1857 and 1960, the landscape of English culture and society was significantly shaped by such concerns.

Law and the management of public indecency

It is the fact that, during this period, indecency began to be labelled as a 'serious' as well as a growing evil in ways that were both enduring and essentially secular that is so telling and justifies this examination. The principle of the secular law, *de minimis non curat lex* (the law does not notice trifling matters) is the one upon which the criminalization of actions and types of personal conduct has taken place in English legal history. Traditionally, matters of morality were the concern of the ecclesiastical courts. As these had declined and disappeared during the long eighteenth century (1688–1815), there had been an expansion in matters brought before the secular courts, with greater or lesser success. But despite the best efforts of initiatives such as that of the Society for the Reformation of Manners (hereafter SRM), these early attempts to 'improve' the public landscape had been more an ecclesiastical than a popular concern, and they had not resulted in any significant changes in legislation and prosecution practices. The argument presented in this volume is that between the middle of the nineteenth century and the middle of the twentieth century, there was a level of popular (though often still minority) concern about a range of so-called indecent behaviours which in turn generated pressure on politicians and legislators to respond and react to those demands.

---

5 See, for example, N. J. Ringdal, *Love for Sale: A World History of Prostitution* (New York: Grove Press, 2004); P. Bartley, *Prostitution: Prevention and Reform in England 1860–1914* (London: Routledge, 2000); J. Peakman, *The Pleasure's All Mine – A History of Perverse Sex* (London: Reaktion, 2013).

6 J. S. Mill, *On Liberty* (London: Longman, Roberts and Green, 1859).

This serves to reveal that various forms of indecency, previously largely over-looked, were no longer considered either trifling or inconsequential in the eyes of the law. 'Indecent behaviour' was no longer something to be resolved (sometimes legally as an action in tort) between the individuals concerned. Instead, it was a matter of national concern, affecting the welfare of the whole community. This raises, from the start, the need for insights into the ways in which contemporaries sought to evolve strategies to measure and identify indecency. It is crucial to understand why a generic, overarching term like *indecency* was used in the legal management of expressions of offensive behaviour rather than the more strictly specific, and legally precise, terminologies such as obscenity. A key issue here is that indecency was not only considered to be a serious challenge to national welfare, but also a growing *evil* – utilizing a metaphoric terminology strongly associated with immorality and sin, and thus suggesting continuation of a traditional perspective rooted in the management of immoral conduct through the ecclesiastical courts or community-based shaming punishments. All of this serves to underline that while it was perceived as a serious and growing evil,[7] public indecency was being identified as something which was a genuine threat to the national character – to 'Britishness'.

Indecency, decency, and Britishness[8]

As well as having an individual aspect, decency has always represented conformity to the dominant morality within a culture or a society. Essentially, the attribute of *decent* ascribes to communities as well as individuals within them, those cultural and behavioural attitudes which sustain certain agreed moral principles. Identification and adherence to standards of decency amount to a form of community management tool, ensuring compliance with the principles agreed to be a matter of morality with a national consequence. In origin, morality represented 'good' behaviour in the sense of being pleasing to higher powers such as the gods, as Aristotle expressed it in works such as his *Nichomachean Ethics*, where he refers to *eu zên* (living well) and two types of virtue, intellectual *and* ethical.[9] Aeschylus insisted that the greatest gift of the gods to humanity was what is

---

7 The phrase 'A serious and growing evil' is taken from Parliamentary Papers, *Report from the Joint Select Committee on Lotteries and Indecent Advertisements, together with the proceedings of the committee, minutes of evidence, and appendices* (London: HMSO, 1908), HC Paper 275, para.40.

8 It is, at this point, worth explaining that while the focus of this volume is necessarily only on England and Wales, because of Scotland's possession of a separate legal system, the terms *British* and *Britishness* are still being used because, historically, they are appropriate and more widely used by contemporaries. In reality, Britishness was something deeply rooted in a dominant English culture, but the wider terminology was used positively and with substantial consent throughout the United Kingdom in the period examined by this volume. We have therefore decided to use it in that sense. For discussions about Britishness, see L. Colley, *Britons: Forging the Nation 1707–1837* (New Haven, CT: Yale University Press: 2005).

9 Aristotle, *Nicomachean Ethics*, trans. J. Sachs (London: Focus Philosophical Library, Pullins Press, 2002).

frequently translated as 'decency of mind' or virtue.[10] Such virtue was, he argued, the outcome of being trained or educated into a consciousness of what constituted living well and then making a deliberate choice to do so. This involved learning to identify what was ethical – and so for the greater happiness of individuals and communities – through use of an intellectually grounded use of reason to make those choices. The combination of both led to decent behaviour. For Aristotle, behaving virtuously or decently created a state of inner virtue.

In England, as elsewhere in the Christian West, outward decency of demeanour and conduct was seen rather as a measure of one's inner state of Christian morality that was reflected outwards. Chaucer's Parson talks of the importance of imitating that *honestee* (decency) which Christ and his 'friends' (disciples) showed in their lives but the point was made that he was a man 'rich in holy thought', which manifested itself in his life and work.[11] Decency of inner mind and honesty of behaviour were also linked by Shakespeare in *Henry VIII*. Increasingly, during the eighteenth century, the two came together in the interpretation of the concept of good-natured 'fair play' which the English (or British, to use the terminology of the day) now prided themselves on.[12] The emphasis on decency as an intrinsic element in the national character has been stressed regularly since the eighteenth century, being perhaps most memorably expressed in the repeated last line of each stanza of Henry Newbolt's 1892 poem, 'Vitaï Lampada': 'Play up! play up! and play the game!'[13] This sense of fair play is still one of the traits by which British people appear to define themselves; for example, during a recent debate about 'Britishness', former Prime Minister Gordon Brown remarked in an article in *The Guardian* that 'liberty, tolerance, fair play – these are the core values of Britishness.'[14] Equally it is since the eighteenth century that the definition and control of *in*decency was to become so important to the regulators of society.

This helps to explain why secular governance was willing to accept responsibility for moral regulation of public indecency while it left untouched other areas of ecclesiastical regulation of private indecencies, unless and until they also became in some way issues of 'public' concern. It undoubtedly helped the mid-Victorian statesmen in their decisions to make increasing use of the law and criminal justice processes to manage public indecency that they had an overtly secular tradition

10 Aeschylus, *Agamemnon*, trans. R. Lattimore, (Chicago: University of Chicago Press, 1952). Agamemnon demands to be respected as a man, not a god, and insists this sense of proportion is mankind's greatest gift from the gods. Other translations use phrases such as the avoidance of folly, or honesty, further emphasizing the virtuous nature of the concept.

11 G. Chaucer, 'Parson's Tale', lines 426–7, *Canterbury Tales*, (London: Penguin Classics, 2005).

12 P. Langford, *Englishness Identified. Manners and Character 1650–1850* (Oxford: Oxford University Press, 2000), especially Chapter 3, 'Decency'; Colley, *Britons*. Its continued resonance is visible in Gordon Brown's speech, deliberately invoking the historical echoes touched on here, which talked of Britishness being rooted in a shared sense of what constitutes 'fair play' as well as a value for tolerance and liberty.

13 For full poem, see http://exhibits.lib.byu.edu/wwi/influences/vitai.html.

14 See *The Guardian,* 8 July 2004: www.theguardian.com/politics/2004/jul/08/britishidentity.economy.

to guide and inspire them. Such men were well educated in classical history and drew very direct parallels between the ancient Roman Empire and that of Britain, including the sense that Britain would only retain her empire so long as she continued to deserve it.[15] The word *decency* derived from the Latin *decentum*, meaning that which was fitting and appropriate in human behaviour; it was used by the Romans to summarize their core public virtue.[16] Cicero, for instance, insisted that the main value of decency was that it ensured a man gave no offence to others.[17] But such mid-Victorian statesmen were, as Boyd Hilton has pointed out, also powerfully affected by evangelical thought and theology.[18]

The rise of Romanized Christianity had added a powerful religious dimension to the thinking on which Roman law could draw, and after the withdrawal of Rome, that combination had survived, as already touched on here. Essentially, in the medieval and early modern periods, it had been the Christian Churches (Roman Catholic and Protestant) which had identified the parameters of public decency at national and local levels. The stance of Christian theology (broadly in line with Aristotle's thinking also) was that while mankind had a degree of intrinsic 'natural' morality there was also a need to learn, or be trained in, what constituted the highest standards of virtue and decency for individuals. This gave the Christian Churches the right to, and the duty of, identifying the influences which caused or sustained decency predominantly by highlighting the challenges to it in the shape of indecency. Churchmen identified the materials from which humanity might acceptably learn the right standards, and also those which challenged them. For the most part, these threats to decency were characterized by being thought to be of a heretical nature initially, but with sexual chastity and modesty becoming increasingly important to Christianity from the eleventh century on, conduct of an obscene nature was also held to be of the nature of the devil, and thereby to invite indecency of thought and so of public behaviour.[19] This involved management partly by religious warnings of the post-mortem consequences of indecency but partly also by use of the law, essentially canon law and the ecclesiastical courts.

The beginnings of print provided new challenges for the Christian Churches, Roman Catholic and Protestant, because this enabled the production of a growing number of indecent works as well as those promoting decency and piety. As a result, for instance, in 1559 Pope Paul IV authorized publication of the *Index Librorum Prohibitorum*, censoring works of literature (including their illustrations) which often featured inappropriately explicit material, often of an obscene

15 For a discussion of obscenity regulations throughout the British Empire, see D. Heath, *Purifying Empire: Obscenity and the Politics of Moral Regulation in Britain, India and Australia* (Cambridge: Cambridge University Press, 2014).

16 *Decorum* has a similar root, for instance.

17 Cicero, M. T. *De Officiis* (London: Heinemann, 1913), 1.99.

18 B. Hilton, *The Age of Atonement: The Influence of Evangelicalism on Social and Economic Thought, 1795–1865* (Oxford: Clarendon Press, Oxford University Press, 1988).

19 See, for instance, J. Brundage, *Law, Sex and Society in Medieval Europe* (Chicago: University of Chicago Press, 2009); C. Olson, ed., *Celibacy and Religious Traditions* (Oxford: Oxford University Press, 2007).

or sexual nature. Nor were Protestants far behind in such censorship. The problem for most Protestant denominations was that the reliance on self-conscious acceptance of salvation put the emphasis on aiding the personal path to that goal and increasingly, printed works of piety, from the Bible itself to collections of sermons and prayers, so the development of a printing industry was more likely to be encouraged. In England and Wales, small printing establishments became widespread during the seventeenth century and so, practically speaking, less susceptible to a strict and State-managed censorship regime.[20] But the interest of the State (headed by a monarch who combined responsibilities as Supreme Governor of the Anglican Church with secular ones) in providing a sound core of available printed materials is underlined by royal sanction for both a standard or authorized translated version of the Bible commissioned by James I and the revised edition of the Book of Common Prayer sanctioned by Charles II in 1662.

However, the aftermath of the Glorious Revolution of 1688 saw a decline in the authority and importance of the ecclesiastical establishment, partly as a result of the gradual rise in practical everyday toleration for Protestant (though not yet Roman Catholic) dissent from Anglicanism. It is telling that Evangelicalism and the associated rise of the reformist movement which became Methodism were essentially grass-roots movements. The Evangelical-inspired Protestant Foreign Missionary movement also emerged at the end of the eighteenth century as a grass-roots initiative. Neither manifestation of religious enthusiasm was received positively by the Anglican establishment; indeed there was a real will to *dis*courage such initiatives, but with a singular lack of success. As Boyd Hilton notes, the appeal of Evangelicalism had an increasing impact on the ideas and understandings of numbers of men in Parliament, helping to shape policy on a number of fronts.[21] Evangelicalism and Enlightenment thought and scientific explorations challenged some old certainties or made them less relevant and this shifted – or expanded – the grounds on which moral judgments were made.

Helping to create this reality was the Puritan legacy of independence of moral and religious thought from the exhortations and rulings of the senior figures of the Anglican Church, which tended to manifest itself at local and parish level in a greater willingness to assert local decisions and feelings. Another expression of this was the increasing willingness of Anglican clergy to look to the secular courts to prosecute cases which could have been conducted (arguably more appropriately) in the ecclesiastical courts rather than via a tweak of existing secular legislation to redefine moral wrongdoing as, for example, a breach of the peace. For instance, as will be discussed in more detail in Chapter One, the SRM, though substantially supported by Anglican parish clergy, was very ready to use the secular courts for their prosecutions because of the greater speed and the potential

20 The Commonwealth period is something of an exception. See H. Love, *The Culture and Commerce of Texts: Scribal Publications in Seventeenth Century England* (Boston: University of Massachusetts Press, 1998); S. Jung, ed., *British Literature and Print Culture* (Martlesham: Boydell & Brewer, 2013).
21 Hilton, *Age of Atonement*.

for more substantial punishments. The effect of this was to undermine the direct ability of the Christian Churches to take action which would promote decency by regulating indecency. It was not automatic that the secular State should take on the role previously considered the province of the Church, but, as Samuel Johnson was to point out, thanks to Enlightenment thought, the concept of decency had become also a marker of public order and civilization in a secular sense. It was that which the State considered that the law was committed to preserving.[22] Statutes on vagrancy, for instance, relied on an understanding that such nuisance offences amounted to an affront to public decency because of the inappropriate behaviour of those criminalized under its provisions.[23]

Thus the background premise to this work is that decency and virtue were so intertwined in English thinking, and so central to the welfare of the nation, and not simply of the individual, by the middle of the nineteenth century that there was an entrenched expectation that the law could and should be used to ensure the highest standards of decency in public, where its preservation relied on tackling the assaults on virtue provided by indecency. As will be discussed in Chapter Five, new technologies ensured that, at that point, the 'decency' of the nation was being assaulted in ways never before considered possible.

The perception of indecency

Decency and indecency remain, in the early twenty-first century, widely invoked concepts, but the words now hold a different meaning to that of the period being examined here. A work such as E. L. James' *Fifty Shades of Grey* can now be read in public by individuals sitting on Clapham omnibuses. It is, though, also true that the American Library Association placed the book at number four on its Top Ten 'Most Challenged' list for 2013 on the basis of its offensive language and sexually explicit content, suggesting a survival of older standards.[24] But this only underlines the complexities involved in estimating how a society views the issue of public decency and its opposite. History suggests that there has always been a disjunction between that which was judged to be indecent by elites and that which was seen as indecent by the masses. Humour, for instance, has always provided a problematically 'grey' area, inflected by considerations of the vulnerabilities of gender, age, and race. Dealing with the propensity of the 'vulgar' (the ordinary people) to laugh at jokes displeasing to elites, Quintilian insisted that 'laugher cost too much' if it was obtained 'at the sacrifice of decency'.[25] Victorian critics of, for example, music hall jokes and innuendo-laden comic songs shared a similar perspective.

22 S. Johnson, *The Rambler* 55 (25 September 1750).

23 See, for instance, Parliamentary Papers, *Report from the Select Committee on the Existing Laws Relating to Vagrants*, vol. 543 (1821).

24 American Libraries Association, 'Frequently challenged books of the 21st century': www.ala.org/advocacy/banned/frequentlychallenged/21stcenturychallenged, accessed 18 April 2013.

25 Quintilian, *Institutio Oratoria* (New York: HardPress Publishing, 2012); see Book VIII, Chapter Two, in which the issue of indecency and humour is discussed in depth.

There was, perhaps, wider agreement when it came to literature. Again, here the association between the positive aspects of the national character and decency were intrinsic to the general description of texts considered dubious because of their sexual and moral content as 'French' novels, even if they were not in the least French in origin, such as those by Ouida (1839–1908).[26] But a decline in (or cosmopolitanization of) the idea of decency as a quintessentially English characteristic has meant a greater toleration for such works of literature. The romance novel, as published by firms such as Mills and Boon, now features sexual detail which would have been unthinkable in their productions in the middle of the twentieth century.[27] Returning to the concept of the 'shades of grey' in estimating public indecency, a century earlier society would have been scandalized both by such an 'indecent' text as that written by E. L. James and the fact that such a text could be considered 'mainstream' literature.[28] As has already been stressed, the identification of behaviour or activity which constitutes indecency once it becomes public has always been a highly subjective concept. For this reason, the law and the application of the law remained confused and even contradictory during the period of our study, despite a general agreement that public indecency was a serious threat to individual happiness and the welfare of the nation. Previous generations had expressed the secular regulation of public indecency in terms of a 'reform of manners', the 'suppression of vice', or the promotion of 'purity'. However, the Roman terminology of decency was preferred by the Victorians and their successors. Partly this was for practical reasons – 'bad manners' and vice amounted to concepts which had too often proved intractable when dragged into a court for enforcement of types of behaviour. There was also a need to assess the basis for successful prosecutions, which saw a narrowing of the Victorian focus in terms of public indecency onto matters relating to inappropriate or immodest activity with the sexual dimension of vice. Even so, when vice was raised in Parliament as a topic for legal reform, the disagreements over definition proved insurmountable. Decency versus indecency provided a more concrete and manageable trope because it was one with a pedigree in Roman regulation of society which was broadly familiar to all grammar and public school educated men. This enabled the 'indecency agenda' to become more than the simple rhetoric it had largely been in the eighteenth century. So labelled, it developed into a legally effective weapon (or set of weapons) that could be utilized against perceived offending and offensive behaviours.

26 J. Rignall, 'One great confederation? Europe in the Victorian novel', in F. O'Gorman (ed.), *A Concise Companion to the Victorian Novel* (Oxford: Blackwell Publishing, 2005), 244–5.

27 See J. McAleer, *Passions Fortune: The Story of Mills and Boon* (Oxford, Oxford University Press, 1999).

28 It is worth remembering that a mid-Victorian masculine elite certainly did *not* worry about 'indecent' writing when circulated privately amongst that elite. One of the authors, when carrying out PhD research on Edward Knatchbull Hugessen, sought out a private Parliamentary production, *The Owl*, and found that it was a mix of political comment and pornographic humour. Equally sexually explicit works such as *The Autobiography of a Flea* (1887) or *My Secret Life* by 'Walter' (1888) were published and known at least to a restricted and largely male 'cognoscenti', but they were not widely available.

Methodology and interdisciplinary approaches

The development of this legal effectiveness cannot be taken too far: confusion and contradiction still complicated both the application of the law and its popular reception, as this volume will explore. In law, 'indecency' remains neither a single moral principle nor a defined legal concept, but rather something framed by perceptions of behaviour or feelings that certain actions and beliefs represent an impropriety that give rise to some measure of psychological discomfort or offence in those bringing or adjudging a prosecution. The challenge is the jumble of common law and statutory offences capable of being brought into service to combat those discomforting behaviours. Our aim is to examine both the legal conceptualizations of public indecency and those popular conceptualizations of it which framed its management. We investigate the social and cultural obsession with various forms of 'indecency', how public perceptions of various types of indecent behaviour led to legal definitions and responses in both the common law and statute law, and how the police and magistracy dealt with such behaviour in practical terms. We argue that broad categorizations of the types of behaviour that were regarded as constituting 'indecency' operated by reference to a core lexicography that on one hand underpinned a significant and strident morality-based legal activism, and on the other related to long-established familiarity with an appeal to decency as a patriotic virtue in order to justify that activism.

This volume is the product of the combined cross-disciplinary expertise of four authors, and realistically could not have been produced otherwise. It draws on law and history, but also on literature and theology as well as the social sciences (notably criminology). The aim is to advance understanding of the processes through which a type of behaviour was managed by being criminalized, with varying degrees of popular support over time, and in particular, to explore the demands on the State from groups within society to inflict sanctions in order to safeguard national 'decency'. 'Indecency' relates to forms of behaviour and popular culture which are often regarded by concerned elements as inappropriate for a 'modern' State framework, because they are held to impede a supposedly inexorable 'civilizing process'. But as this study reveals, the reality has been more complex and far less in line with a simple interpretation of Elias' conceptualization of the civilizing would suggest.[29] As such, this volume complements the work being done on the survival of shame and shaming punishments in the nineteenth and twentieth centuries by scholars such as Nash and Kilday. What further frames this volume are the deeper questions that need to be asked about the State and the nature of its relationship to its citizens – especially in terms of its willingness and ability to respond to popular pressures. How the State conceptualized itself, and how the ordinary citizenry regarded the appropriate role, reach, content, and authority of the State has, naturally, changed and

---

29 For a fuller discussion of Elias, see S. D'Cruze, E. Avdela, and J. Rowbotham, eds., *Problems of Crime and Violence in Europe 1750–2000*, (New York: Edward Mellen Press, 2010).

evolved over time.[30] The period under study here represents a transitional period in terms of the ways in which State authority has been regarded and invoked. We believe that a historically shaped examination of the criminalization process used to manage public indecency and its ultimate failure is revealing both of the ability and willingness of the State to respond to popular concerns and the extent to which the citizenry look to the State and its legal powers to set the standards of public decency. This volume suggests that it is by no means clear that there has been a linear development, amounting to modernity, in attitudes towards what came to be labelled as 'public indecency' over the century of this study. Instead, the chapters show how complex and fluid such conceptualizations have been over time, and how complex the supporting reasoning has been also.

The context in which this is explored is that of the 'modern' State and its laws, broadly comprehended. This takes us back to those stock figures in legal history, Foucault and Elias, and their advertised responsibility for identifying the modern State as the core promoter of 'civilized' or 'decent' conduct.[31] Consideration of how useful this frame is for public indecency is reflected on throughout. The period reviewed is bookended with the Obscene Publications Act 1857 (hereafter OPA 1857) and the famous trial of Penguin Books over their publication of *Lady Chatterley's Lover* in 1960. We take the subtitle of this book from a comment midway through the period, when in 1908 the Joint Select Committee on Lotteries and Indecent Advertisements recommended that the existing law relating to 'indecent literature, pictures, and advertisements relating to things indecent and immoral' should be amended and consolidated to tackle this 'serious and growing evil'.[32] The OPA 1857 represented growing unease (or even 'moral panic') over new levels of availability of indecent or 'obscene' material. It is not coincidental that the 1850s were also a period when the preservation of public decency as a matter of national importance was much discussed, especially in the context of the Crimean War. It was a matter of approval that the most-read book in 1853, by British officers at least, was Charlotte Yonge's *The Heir of Redclyffe*, whose hero was the ultimate in British decency.[33] In 1908, the sense of threat from 'things indecent and immoral' also echoed a time of national unease and rising patriotism. In that year, scouting for boys as a way of enhancing both their decency and their patriotism was being widely lauded.[34] By 1960, however, that link between

30 See, for example, A. Doig, *State Crime* (Cullompton: Willan, 2010); D. Faulkner, *Crime, State and Citizen: A Field Full of Folk* (Hook: Waterside Press, 2006); N. Lacey, *State Punishment: Political Principles and Community Values* (London: Routledge, 1994); D. Gibbons, *Society, Crime and Criminal Behavior* (Upper Saddle River: Prentice Hall, 1992).

31 See, for example, C. Pierson, *The Modern State* (London: Routledge, 1996); J. Carter Wood, *Violence and Crime in Nineteenth-Century England: The Shadow of Our Refinement* (London: Routledge, 2004).

32 Parliamentary Papers, *Report from the Joint Select Committee on Lotteries and Indecent Advertisements, together with the proceedings of the committee, minutes of evidence, and appendices* (London: HMSO, 1908) HC Paper 275, para. 40.

33 C. Yonge, *The Heir of Redclyffe* (London: Macmillan, 1853).

34 'Practical Patriotism', Letter to the Editor, *The Spectator*, 11 April 1908.

Englishness and decency was heavily obscured by the debates and dilemmas of a post-war and increasingly multicultural society where what constituted indecency was even less clear-cut and certainly less valued than it had been at the height of Empire. Thus, we end the volume at that point, because while indecency continues to trouble the courts, it now needs to be assessed in different ways and as part of a very different cultural landscape.

1 The historical background

Indecency and the rise of moral activism

Introduction

In focusing on the period between 1857 and the 1960s, account needs to be taken of the reality that attempts to define and control 'indecency' by use of the English legal process clearly predate our starting point and left a legacy which framed the later efforts. Consequently, the picture of events in this crucial century for the management of public indecency can be well understood only after a brief consideration of the legacy of earlier efforts, especially in terms of how this shaped contemporary comprehensions of indecency (and decency). In England and Wales, as outlined in the Introduction, one result of the Protestant Reformation and the setting up of a State church in the shape of the Church of England, was a slow but increasingly substantial secularization of the moral management of communities.[1] It was part of a process which was to affect all of Europe, including Catholic States, but the creation of an established Church gave an authority to Anglicanism which mirrored the ecclesiastical authority of the papacy and yet incorporated a secular dimension from the start because the head, or Supreme Governor, of the Church of England was also the monarch or head of the secular State.[2] There was also, given the quasi-nationalist dimension that was intrinsic to that Church, a will to revisit canon law and reject those elements which were seen as too 'Catholic' and so challenging to English monarchical authority as well as to Protestant theology. While Church Courts survived the Reformation, their legal processes tended to reflect the values and expectations of medieval society as well as one which was Roman Catholic.[3] To an increasingly urbanizing and capitalist society, as well as a Protestant one, the Church Courts were seen as clumsy and inflexible. Both informal control in the shape of opprobrium from the parish priest and formal attempts by spiritual authority to regulate public indecency through the Church

---

1 J. Spurr, *The Post Reformation: Religion, Politics and Society in Britain, 1603–1714* (London: Routledge, 2006).
2 Ibid.
3 It is worth pointing out that the Church of England also claims the label of being 'catholic' or all-embracing, and that it was in many ways closer to Roman Catholicism in its theology and practices than to Protestantism as practiced by Scottish, as well as many European, denominations.

Courts (irreligiously also known as 'Bawdy Courts') had diminished. This had been obvious to those in government; as Langford states, 'generations of politicians had learned to treat religion as a matter of private conviction and public indifference.'[4] Numerous Acts, collectively known as the Ecclesiastical Courts Acts, enacted between 1787 and 1860, severely curtailed and emasculated the power and role of the Church Courts.[5]

One thing which underlines this is the reliance of the SRM on the secular magistrates' courts as the locus for their prosecutions, rather than the ecclesiastical courts. The ambition of the SRM was to reform the nation through eradicating from it indecent and 'unmannerly' behaviour of the type considered to have become all too prevalent since the Restoration of 1660. The Glorious Revolution of 1689 had alerted the nation's moralists to how well-established the Devil's work was, and spurred a will to stern action in the campaign for reform. It was no longer considered sufficient to exhort and persuade through sermons and good example. Instead, the SRM, through its various branches, paid informers to seek out examples of public indecency and bring prosecutions against the offenders.[6] Though officially interdenominational and with a strong membership among dissenting ministers, in fact many of the prominent supporters and even members of the SRM were Anglican clergy. Men like Thomas Tennison (Archbishop of Canterbury), for instance, as well as figures like Gilbert Burnet (Bishop of Salisbury) and prominent local clergy like the Reverend Thomas Caryll of Nottingham, might have been expected to seek remedies for the perceived disorder and indecency of the nation through the courts that particularly belonged to the national Church, but they preferred the secular courts because of the relatively greater speed of the processes there as well as their capacity to inflict heavier punishments such as floggings.[7] As a result, the ecclesiastical courts became identified even by their natural supporters as increasingly redundant, especially as numbers of clergymen were amongst those acting as Justices of the Peace or Magistrates. Practically, they could thus ensure that a Bench was alert to the need to combat sin by use of the law.

The SRM effectively died out by the 1730s (though there were attempts in subsequent years to revive it, and the late eighteenth-century Society for the Suppression of Vice and the Encouragement of Religion and Virtue [hereafter SSV], was a clear inheritor of its principles) but it acted as a catalyst for the previously slow process of decline in the use of the ecclesiastical courts.[8] In terms of their impact

---

4 P. Langford, *Public Life and Propertied Englishmen 1689–1798* (Oxford: Oxford University Press, 1991), 586.

5 For details of the work of Church Courts, see, M. Ingram, *Church Courts, Sex and Marriage in England, 1570–1640*, Past & Present Series (Cambridge: Cambridge University Press, 1990); and P. Hair, ed., *Before the Bawdy Court: Selections from Church Court and Other Records Relating to the Correction of Moral Offences in England, Scotland and New England, 1300–1800*, (New York: Barnes & Noble, 1972).

6 Spurr, *The Post Reformation*.

7 Ibid. See also T. Claydon, *William III and the Godly Revolution* (Cambridge: Cambridge University Press, 2004).

8 See A. Hunt, *Governing Morals: A Social History of Moral Regulation* (Cambridge: Cambridge University Press, 1999) for a history of the SSV.

on everyday life, this was largely concluded by the end of the eighteenth century. In practice, what this also meant is that while Anglican clergy and dissenting ministers continued to promote both morality and public propriety, the regulation of public decency was also increasingly a secular matter. There was a readiness to accept this because there was already a strong tradition of community management of inappropriate behaviour of various kinds, as David Nash and Anne-Marie Kilday have shown in their work on shame and shaming punishments.[9] This covered offenders such as female scolds and nags, but also immoral behaviour such as adultery and prostitution, especially where these were particularly blatant and so a matter of community gossip. This was capitalized on by elements in the educated elite who took upon themselves the responsibility of civilizing and managing those popular efforts at promoting public decency within communities, which could often be 'uncivilized' in themselves.[10]

As discussed in the Introduction, it was during the eighteenth century that ideas linking Britishness and civilization were firmly established. These ideas had a popular appeal, but also an intellectual one, manifesting itself as a corollary to Enlightenment thought in Britain. Unsurprisingly, therefore, this also had its effects on jurisprudential thought. Amongst others, the lawyer Sir William Blackstone reveals how practice and intellectual justifications combined in Enlightenment legal thinking. The point of Blackstone's renowned *Commentaries on the Laws of England* was to explore the contemporary state of the law through its historical evolution (he held the Regius Chair of Legal History in Cambridge) in order to show how superior those laws then were to all previous systems.[11] As part of this exercise in nationalist jurisprudence, Blackstone took care to comment on matters of public decency and challenges to these. Interestingly, he was clearly conscious of the core ambiguity surrounding the sharing of responsibility between Church and State, recognizing it as something difficult to resolve in a State headed by a figure who was head of the secular arm of governance and the ecclesiastical as well. But also, this ambiguity did justify and explain the feeling of responsibility that legislators and lawyers as well as religious leaders felt for promoting the agenda for eradicating public indecency. Writing in 1769 and reiterating earlier pronouncements, Blackstone confirmed that he considered 'open and notorious lewdness: either by frequenting houses of ill-fame . . . or by some grossly scandalous and public indecency'[12] to belong in the category of 'offences against God and religion'. This located indecency alongside (amongst other transgressions) drunkenness, swearing, and profanation of the Sabbath. But Blackstone also made it plain that while the legal position was that responsibility for regulating and shaping the behaviour of individuals and the moral standards of society did not lie primarily with the secular State and the law as its arm of enforcement, there was a duty to act in the national interest.

---

9 D. Nash and A. Kilday, *Cultures of Shame: Exploring Crime and Morality in Britain 1600–1900* (London: Palgrave Macmillan, 2010).
10 Ibid.
11 W. Blackstone, *Commentaries on the Laws of England*, vol. 6 (Chicago: University of Chicago Press, 1979b).
12 Blackstone, *Commentaries*, vol. 6, 64.

This is the context in which the shift towards a more criminalizing secular management of what was becoming identified as indecent behaviour became visible in the rise in organized – and sometimes highly influential – morality campaigns generated by the rapidly expanding voluntary sector of political society.

This was also a period when the law was, itself, evolving and becoming more formalized in many of its processes through a growing reliance on statute law. A discrete criminal law emerged in this period as a result of the use of statutes to identify individual conduct which was held to be so threatening to the moral welfare of the community that it deserved to be called 'criminal'. In the eighteenth century, the core preoccupation was with legal protection of property, epitomized in its most simplistic sense by the 'Black Acts'.[13] Taken together, these Acts were, in effect, a catalogue or code of felonies and capital crimes and accompanying legal responses or 'punishments'. But – as was already established in the common law tradition – reputation or character was counted as property, both for individuals and communities. This helps to account for the readiness of the emerging criminal justice process to accept as criminal those acts or wrongdoings which were interpreted and recognized as immoral and therefore illicit behaviour.

The focus for this volume is the development of a sophisticated conceptualization of indecency as a problem for the nation, instead of a predominantly lower-class manifestation of 'bad behaviour' with no wider than local or individual implications. While it is not yet fully evolved, it is clearly rooted in this period. What was not yet present was the wider comprehension of indecency as a product of circumstance and not individual volition or sin. The associations between deprivation and crime began to emerge only in the late eighteenth century, when the concept of indecency in broad terms became part of a new way of framing responses to low-level everyday criminality. The focus became more directed toward *changing* and *civilizing* behaviour rather than imposing automatic punishment, through aids such as the emerging Sunday School movement and Hannah More's *Cheap Repository Tracts*. The moral crusaders of the late eighteenth and early nineteenth century were effectively the first to link crime with social welfare reform by seeing crime as a manifestation of an inner sinfulness and lack of moral fibre.

This approach repeated itself in the late nineteenth and early twentieth century. In Edwardian England, fears of radicalism among the working classes and a rising perception of 'national degeneration' (a term which is an interesting Social Darwinist twist on the earlier ecclesiastically based notions of immorality) appear to have resulted in a pervasive sense of crisis, or loss of control, amongst both middle and upper classes. This is at least part of the context for a renewal of moral campaigns against indecency and of determined (and partially successful) attempts to incorporate this particular world view into a legal framework. By way

---

13 Waltham Black Act 9 Geo.1 ch.22 was the first of a series of statutes (1723–1758) that codified virtually every form of criminal activity against persons and property including entering woods (to go poaching) with a blackened face. P. Rogers, 'The Waltham Blacks and the Black Acts,' *The Historical Journal* 17 (1974): 465–86.

of historiographic introduction this chapter explores in more detail how earlier attempts to delineate and 'manage' indecency underwent a shift from ecclesiastical control to State control. By the mid nineteenth century social and cultural obsessions with indecent behaviour which had gradually assumed a stronger profile within the common law at the start of the eighteenth century had a range of statutory provisions on which to draw, even though much of which was not explicitly characterized as indecency legislation.

Encouraging piety and virtue

A national dimension to moral thinking about individual conduct was a constant undercurrent in the various campaigns for the improvement of society that manifested themselves from the late seventeenth century on. Efforts were made to deal legally with affronts to virtue and national morality, and as already mentioned, this resulted in a will to shift away from an exclusive ecclesiastic control of matters of morality and an acceptance by the secular State of an assumption of responsibility for management of such issues. However, it should not be thought that these eighteenth-century campaigns were consistent in terms of their targets when seeking to improve the nation, or that the manifestations of public indecency that moralists were concerned about were linked to vice in the shape of sexual immorality, as was the case in the post-1857 period.[14] In a reaction that partook substantially of what later became identified as moral panic about the dangers of behaviour linked to a 'Satanic' view of Roman Catholicism in the wake of the Glorious Revolution of 1688, the SRM emerged in London during 1690.[15] There, its strongest manifestation was in Tower Hamlets, but it spread more widely and attracted the support of William and Mary (both known as personally devout and godly in their habits) and leading politicians as well as some leading Anglican figures like the future Archbishop of Canterbury, Thomas Tennison. Consciousness of the narrow escape from the religious persecution that, it was believed, would inevitably have followed in the wake of leaving a Roman Catholic dynasty on the throne helped to give it a national dimension. Branches were set up in a number of provincial towns and cities, including Bristol and Nottingham. While sharing the name, these branches were largely independent of any central organizing policy or individuals. The Nottingham branch, for instance, one of the earliest and most active, being certainly in operation by 1692, attracted – to the disapproval of the Archbishop of York – a considerable number of dissenting ministers to it. Propaganda for the cause of reformation of manners took the shape of both secular lectures and sermons from the pulpit. But as well as this campaign of persuasion to good behaviour, the SRM took an original initiative in that its adherents decided, from the start, that persuasion alone would not

---

14 E. Bristow, *Vice and Vigilance: Purity Movements in Britain Since 1700* (Dublin: Gill and Macmillan, 1977), 2.
15 M. Roberts, *Making English Morals: Voluntary Association and Moral Reform in England 1787–1886* (Cambridge: Cambridge University Press, 2004), 20.

be sufficient – and sufficiently speedy – to achieve the urgent national reform needed to safeguard the nation from danger. It thus took advantage of the way in which the court processes worked (which required private citizens to initiate even criminal prosecutions) to agree that a core tactic would be the enforcement of moral behaviour through a campaign of prosecutions.[16] Thanks almost certainly to the endorsement of men like Tennison, the SRM soon had a signal of State approval for their strategy: in 1691 a Royal Proclamation was issued which formally required Justices of the Peace to actively enforce laws against profanity and immorality.[17] Initially, there was substantial momentum behind the SRM and enough money was gathered to enable the employment by branches of the SRM of informers who would report profane and immoral behaviour. These men acted as observers, looking to identify significant levels of public indecency and use their observations as evidence in prosecutions brought against the individuals concerned. The strategy generally used to enable prosecutions was that the 'indecent' conduct observed amounted to a breach of the peace. This legal sleight of hand was widely welcomed by magistrates up to the end of Queen Anne's reign, with reissuance of the Royal Proclamation to Justices of the Peace coming in 1702 and again in 1708.[18]

However, the levels of support for the SRM eventually dwindled, especially after the Hanoverian succession seemed to guarantee a Protestant dynasty and the safety of religion in England and Wales. It was more or less dead by 1730. There were various discussions, almost amounting to attempts to reinvigorate the SRM, in succeeding decades by figures including the Wesleys. It was not until a mood of alarm and a widespread consciousness of national danger took hold in the 1780s that the issue of the moral reform of society once more gripped the public imagination. The loss of the war with the American colonies and the continuing threat to the British grip on its Indian territories seemed, to many contemporaries, to be 'proof' of Divine displeasure with the state of things. It all gave fuel for the hitherto relatively small, but growing, evangelical movement within both the Church of England and Nonconformity, which had long been warning of the need for national, as well as individual, reformation. Men like Reverend John Newton and his successor in the cure of souls at Olney, Reverend Thomas Scott, were powerful and popular preachers who used their sermons (including the printed versions of them) to arouse and enhance that sense of alarm. They had a range of targets in sight, including – most famously – the moral evil of slavery and the slave trade.

---

16 For further discussion of the work of the seventeenth century SRMs see Hunt, *Governing Morals*, 28–56.

17 Royal Proclamation to Middlesex Justices of the Peace, 2 Mary 21 January 1690/1, quoted in R. Shoemaker, *Prosecution and Punishment: Petty Crime and the Law in London and Rural Middlesex, c. 1660–1725* (Cambridge: Cambridge University Press, 1991), 239.

18 Royal Proclamation for the Encouragement of Piety and Virtue, 1 Anne, 25 February 1702/3, quoted in T. B. Howell, *A Complete Collection of State Trials and Proceedings for High Treason, and other Crimes and Misdemeanors from the earliest period to the year 1783*, Vol. 5 (London: Hansard, 1816), 361.

But a sense of national moral decay, held to account for the continuation of such evils, was also a major theme. Evangelical preachers from the Wesleys and Isaac Watts, in their old age, to newcomers like Scott and, particularly, Henry Venn of Holy Trinity Church in Clapham all agreed in warning against the 'bad' or 'evil' manners of the day.[19]

This was the background to the personal crusade of that noted Anglican moralist and activist in the slave trade abolitionist cause, William Wilberforce. In 1786, he began to shape a campaign for the improvement of the state of the national morality and, as part of that, to lobby at the highest level for support for his cause. Influenced by Dr Josiah Woodward's account of the SRM,[20] Wilberforce wanted to revive use of the legal process to control current levels of bad behaviour, moving beyond the current tactics of evangelicalism in the shape of exhortation through sermons and similar aids to personal reformation. He had, as a result, very little interest in developing the popular appeal of such reformation, and instead turned his attention to gaining the support of those in positions of local and national authority who were in a position to fund and implement a more forcible approach to the improvement of society. The small Clapham-based group of which he was a part, later dubbed the Clapham Sect, had clear links to many socially prominent figures, and Wilberforce used his own social standing to get access not only to the Archbishop of Canterbury but also the Queen. They joined with him in persuading George III, in the shape of the King in Privy Council, to reissue Queen Anne's Proclamation 'for the Encouragement of Piety and Virtue, and for the Preventing and Punishing of Vice and Profaneness and Immorality', with its message that leading citizens, especially Justices of the Peace, had a civic duty to take action to enforce the goals of that Proclamation on the intractable elements in society through the petty sessions. To support this initiative, Wilberforce founded, that same year, his Proclamation Society.[21] From the start, Wilberforce concentrated on persuading the nation's elite to support his cause, and the initiative gained rhetorical support from many of the 'great and the good', including prominent aristocrats, MPs, judges, and nineteen of the twenty-six English bishops.

Like its predecessors, this Proclamation asserted 'Our indispensable Duty to exert the Authority committed to us for the Suppression of these spreading Evils' in order to maintain the protection of the Almighty to ensure a happy and prosperous reign.[22] Hunt asserts that its demands for enforcement 'invoked a traditional

---

19 See Hilton, *Age of Atonement*, and M. Noll, *The Rise of Evangelicalism: The Age of Edwards, Whitfield and the Wesleys* (Downers Grove, IL: Intervarsity Press, 2003).

20 J. Woodward, *An Account of the Societies for the Reformation of Manners in London and Westminster and other parts of the country* (London: Defoe, 1699).

21 S. Tompkins, *The Clapham Sect: How Wilberforce's Circle Transformed Britain* (London: Lion Books, 2010).

22 Royal Proclamation For the Encouragement of Piety and Virtue, and for the Preventing and Punishing of Vice, Profaneness and Immorality, 27 Geo. III, 1 June 1787, reproduced in T. Burgess, *A charge delivered to the clergy of the diocese of Salisbury, at the primary visitation of the diocese in August MDCCCXXVI* (London: C. and J. Rivington, 1828).

providential doctrine on the necessity to avoid divine wrath and to secure divine pleasure by suppressing immorality.'[23] Persons of piety and virtue would be marked by royal favour as exemplars of model citizens to encourage morality and religious respect. However, miscreants (i.e. those living 'dissolute and debauched lives'), were to be punished, shamed, or held in contempt irrespective of their social standing or respectable status. The 'evil' behaviour identified as needing to be curtailed included, once again, a wide range, including the 'playing on the Lord's Day at Dice, Cards or any other Game whatsoever, either in Publick or private Houses, or other Place'. Instead of such pastimes, everyone was commanded to attend Church on pain of prosecution. Judges, Mayors, Sheriffs, Justices of the Peace, and all other officers and ministers were called upon to prosecute and punish, either through ecclesiastical law or the civil law, anyone found drinking, blaspheming, swearing, cursing, acting lewdly, or guilty of any 'other dissolute, immoral, or disorderly Practices'. As *The Times* lamented, drinking was a 'dangerous and pernicious vice to be avoided,' but it acknowledged that 'There is no greater fun than intoxication with liquor; for the Scripture informs us, that drunkenness is the root of all evil.' Only if men 'could observe the foolish expressions, the obscene behaviour, and the indecent postures which too frequently happen when alcohol dethrones reason and sense' would there be a likelihood of reform, and court proceedings and the rehearsal of evidence of drunkenness in that public forum might achieve that end.[24]

Public officials were criticized, particularly through the medium of newsprint, for not taking harsh action to prevent the current poor state of affairs which was putting the nation in danger. In October 1787 it was held to be 'to the shame and reproach' of the Westminster Magistracy and their neighbours that they had not imposed stricter controls when issuing licences to local hostelries. This laxity meant that, as another title put it, the area from Temple Bar to Exeter Exchange was

> infested with nothing but pickpockets and strumpets. They assemble in such crowds and behave with such indecency and audacity, as makes it dangerous and shocking for any female of character to pass that way. *The Strand* seems to have indeed become the *vortex* of vice and profligacy.[25]

The licensing of public shows and entertainment became more restrictive; the publishers and sellers of 'loose and licentious Prints, Books and Publications,

23 Hunt, *Governing Morals*, 66.
24 *The Times*, 14 October 1785.
25 *World and Fashionable Advertiser*, 15 October 1787. The area around the Bow Street Magistrates' Office was itself surrounded by a number of 'low' public houses (known as 'flash houses'). See J.M. Beattie, *The First English Detectives; the Bow Street Runners and the Policing of London 1750–1840* (Oxford: Oxford University Press, 2013), 69–74 for a discussion of their usefulness as sources of information about the criminal underworld.

dispensing Poison to the Minds of the Young and the Unwary' were also targeted and prosecuted.[26]

The activities so clearly defined by these late eighteenth-century attempts to 'reform manners' were, though only in part of the activities which would later come to be absorbed into the concept of indecency. But again, the breadth of bad behaviour so identified worked against the widespread and long-term success of the Proclamation Society. Despite the membership of many influential figures from both ecclesiastical and political elites, the Proclamation Society failed to achieve the influence of its predecessor. In the end, the supportive rhetoric did not translate itself into local action, as it had at the end of the seventeenth century. In contrast, the Society for the Abolition of the Slave Trade – involving many of the same people, including Wilberforce himself – had grown and flourished, partly because of its greater popular appeal but also, significantly, because its focus on a single moral measure encouraged local as well as national activism, and activism of a kind which did not involve the expense of regular prosecutions.[27] By 1800 the Proclamation Society, although still notionally in existence, was practically inactive. This does not mean that there was no interest in the reform of society – the vacuum left by the effective collapse of the Proclamation Society was filled instead by what Hunt calls a 'new project of moral regulation' – but the project's newness lay largely in the fact that, as he also points out, it emerged 'from a different social base', and no longer relied substantially on a national social elite.[28] Instead, new campaigning societies for the improvement of moral behaviour emerged in the context of the French Revolutionary and Napoleonic Wars. These societies renewed national alarm and the consequent reshaping of a British evangelical vigour in the early years of the nineteenth century. These were more provincial and even more middle class in their inspiration, as well as shaped by concerns over the rise in popular literacy and also in more freely available and potentially dubious printed material, from political pamphlets to obscene literature.[29] The Society for the Diffusion of Pure Literature Among the People (the Pure Literature Society) was founded in 1800 and the SSV in 1802. One correspondent to *The Morning Post* (a title which had a national subscription list and was widely read in libraries and reading rooms, being sent by post to most major towns and cities in the kingdom) outlined the objectives of the Pure Literature

26 Royal Proclamation For the Encouragement of Piety and Virtue, and for the Preventing and Punishing of Vice, Profaneness and Immorality, 27 Geo. III, 1 June 1787, reproduced in T. Burgess, *A charge delivered to the clergy of the diocese of Salisbury, at the primary visitation of the diocese in August MDCCCXXVI* (London: C. and J. Rivington, 1828), and see letter from W. Wilberforce to William Hey, reproduced in R. I. Wilberforce and S. Wilberforce, *The Life of William Wilberforce*, vol. 1 (London: John Murray, 1838), 132–4.

27 J. R. Oldfield, *Popular Politics and British Anti-Slavery: The Mobilisation of Public Opinion* (London: Routledge, 2012).

28 Hunt, *Governing Morals*, 68; Tompkins, *Clapham Sect*.

29 D. Vincent, *Literacy and Popular Culture: England 1750–1914* (Cambridge; Cambridge University Press, 1998), 71–6.

Society. He went on to stress that its membership was already 1,200, 'amongst whom are to be found persons of the first rank and consequence in the country'.[30] Its aims were broadly similar to the original SRM – and so also very broad – being to target indecent behaviour in the shape of Profanation of the Lord's Day; false weights and measures; blasphemous, licentious, and obscene books and prints; illegal insurances in lotteries; keeping of riotous and disorderly houses, brothels, and gaming houses; seductive practices of procurers; profane swearing; cruelty to animals; and 'all other such gross offences as come within His Majesty's most admirable Proclamation against Vice, Profaneness and Immorality'.[31] Once again, the Pure Literature Society did not long endure as a movement.

The Pure Literature Society's near contemporary, the SSV, was a very different entity, and one that had learned lessons from the Society for the Abolition of the Slave Trade. Although its period of influence was chronologically brief it set the tone for much that followed through the nineteenth and into the twentieth century because, in practice, its focus was on conceptualizing public indecency through a much more narrow and focused lens. Like the SRM, it was intended to be a broad-based social movement and to have a strong local basis. It certainly successfully harnessed the energies of volunteer activists rather than wealthy figureheads (although the latter remained vital sources of patronage and funding). At first sight, its narrower and more 'modern' focus does not seem obvious, given that the initial targets for reform were actually expanded from the 1787 Proclamation. They included:

> Profanation of the Lord's Day and profane swearing; publication of blasphemous, licentious and obscene books and prints; selling by false weights and measures; the keeping of disorderly public houses, brothels and gaming houses; procuring; illegal lotteries; and cruelty to animals.[32]

In practice, however, it was sexual immorality which was the key target, and this was rapidly made plain. This kind of immorality was now blamed by the SSV for most of the evils afflicting British society, including the 'idleness and criminality of the lower orders'. Equally responding to a modern reality, sexual immorality was held to be so dangerous because it was 'articulated through discourses of degeneration and demoralization' – particularly the printed matter and illustrations that were now too readily available to the masses.[33] This focus on sexual immorality as the 'real' public indecency gave the clear single focus that was needed for longer-term success in the campaign to combat this increasingly pervasive form of 'bad' manners because it provided a clear and quantifiable target.

---

30 *Morning Post*, Letter to the Editor, 27 September 1804.

31 Ibid.

32 Proposal for Establishing a Society for the Suppression of Vice and the Encouragement of Religion and Virtue, throughout the United Kingdom (1801): 1–2; Vice Society, Address, ii. 44, in Roberts, *Making English Morals*, 67.

33 Hunt, *Governing Morals*, 69.

The 1820s saw the SSV step up its campaign against immorality, targeting libertine pornography published by William Benbow, George Cannon, William Dugdale, John Duncombe, and others.[34] In the five years between 1839 and 1843, for instance, the SSV's officers 'seized 37,186 obscene prints and pictures . . . 4,598 books and pamphlets . . . besides large stocks of letter-press and obscene songs, in sheets, and of snuff-boxes and other articles with infamous devices'.[35]

Legal strategies

The issue for the SSV and its successors was how to use the existing law in order to control, forcibly, the dissemination and availability of this pernicious temptation to corruption. By now, use of breach of the peace legislation had been shown to be less than useful in promoting wholesale control. Instead, what better suited the objectives of the SSV were the terms of vagrancy legislation, especially after the passage of the Vagrancy Act 1824. This was an era when politicians and leading figures in communities nationally had been affected, from its small beginnings, by the perspectives of the Evangelical movement. Rising political figures like William Gladstone, as well as established ones such as Sir Samuel Romilly, were influenced by Evangelical arguments which related the success of Britain globally (including her recent triumph over the forces of evil represented by Napoleon and his generals) to her conscious pursuit of an agenda for moral rectitude.[36] Unsurprisingly, therefore, the early nineteenth century saw the passage of several legislative initiatives which attempted to define and control indecency, drawn up in the light of admitted ambiguities surrounding the common law offences. Statute law now turned its attention to this area of putative criminality and expanded to fill some perceived gaps. In particular the Vagrancy Act 1824 criminalized an impressive range of 'undesirable' behaviours by employing the relatively simple strategy of labelling those convicted as rogues or vagabonds and making them liable to a relatively harsh sanction of up to three months imprisonment with hard labour. Section 4 penalized 'professing to tell fortunes', betting and gaming in the street or other public place, 'wilfully exposing to view . . . any obscene print, picture or other indecent exhibition', as well as 'wilfully exposing the person'. This was the offence of indecent exposure, which could only be committed by a male with his 'person', in other words his penis, in public view.

---

34 William Benbow (1784–unknown) was a Radical and Chartist, as much feared for his seditious sentiments as his occasional forays into pornography. He worked closely with both George Cannon (1789–1854) and William Dugdale (1800–1868), both of whom were prosecuted for pornographic publications on numerous occasions. John Duncombe was a Radical publisher who was prosecuted for publishing an edition of John Cleland's *Fanny Hill*. For further details of the published output and prosecutions of these individuals, see I. McCalman, 'Unrespectable radicalism: Infidels and pornography in early nineteenth-century London,' *Past and Present* 104 (1984), 74–110; and I. McCalman, *Radical Underworld: Prophets, Revolutionaries, and Pornographers in London 1795–1840* (Cambridge: Cambridge University Press 1988), especially Chapter 10.

35 *The Era*, 30 July 1843.

36 Hilton, *The Age of Atonement*.

This latter offence provides an example of the extent to which the new legislation constituted a marked advance in standards of public 'civility' of behaviour and the emphasis on bodily modesty, given the previously common habit of public urination in many places, with trades like fullers who made use of the ammonia extracted from stale urine, actually providing stone jars for the contributions of passing males.[37]

That this mood to associate sexual immorality and public indecency was widespread is demonstrated by several accompanying developments in the first half of the nineteenth century. For example, the Select Committee set up in 1823 under Edward Bulwer Lytton to improve the Stage Licensing Act 1737 soon set its sights not on political matters but rather on issues to do with modesty and propriety when it came to censorship of plays. The legislation which eventually resulted, the Theatre Regulations Act 1843, gave further statutory legitimacy to the role of the Lord Chamberlain for this purpose in censoring plays nationally, and not just in Westminster.[38] Equally, as part of the moves to expand the use of a modern uniformed police nationally and the consequent need to make this development in social regulation acceptable and useful to ratepayers, the Town Police Clauses Act 1847 gave the police new powers to deal with public indecency. In an overt (and in many localities probably substantially successful) appeal to local branches of the SSV, the Act built on the Vagrancy Act 1824 in giving the police a particular responsibility to regulate the streets in order to prevent visible public indecency.[39]

Policing indecency

The passing of the Town Police Clauses Act 1847 was an important development, because as long as legal enforcement remained in the hands of citizen volunteers when it came to regulation of public decency, the pressures of both time and expense ensured that the prospect of controlling the everyday behaviour of the lower classes by utilizing the law would be both unpalatable and impractical. Advertising that the creation of permanent, professional enforcers in the shape of the police marked a watershed in the law's ability to permeate beyond the boundaries of serious property crime and personal violence into the more mundane activities was intended, quite specifically, as a way of capitalizing on the current mood to promote a more decent and modest society but to do so as painlessly as possible.[40]

37 Langford, *Englishness Identified*, 166–9. Public toilets were often provided in larger towns and cities by private speculators; human waste in the form of both excrement and urine had considerable value due to their respective uses in industrial processes such as the fulling of cloth, tanning of leather, manufacture of gunpowder, and dyeing. It was not until the passing of the Public Health Act 1848 that every dwelling in Britain was required by statute to have access to a sanitary facility, be it an earth closet, ash pit, or privy.

38 J. Davis and V. Emeljanow, *Reflecting the Audience: London Theatregoing 1840–1880* (Iowa City, IA: University of Iowa Press, 2005).

39 Heath, *Purifying Empire*, 59.

40 Ibid. See also C. Emsley, *The English Police: A Political and Social History*, 2nd edition, (Abingdon: Routledge, 1996).

The 'professional' police officer is a relatively new concept in English history. Rudimentary (and occasionally relatively effective) policing systems had been in place since at least the Anglo-Saxon period, in the form of various manifestations of a parish constabulary (i.e. each parish having an individual employed on a voluntary basis to help maintain the peace within its boundaries under the direction of a local Magistrate). It was not until the latter half of the eighteenth century that England first experienced a professional police force, with the creation of the Bow Street Public Office and its associated system of police patrols and plain-clothes detectives.[41] With the exception of the Bow Street system and its sister Public Offices created throughout the rest of London by the Middlesex Justices Act 1792, England lagged behind Scotland in the field of professional policing. Glasgow in particular beat London to the creation of a full-time salaried beat constabulary by a number of years.[42]

The Metropolitan Police Act 1829 created the Metropolitan Police, which subsequently proved to be the blueprint for the majority of professional provincial police forces throughout the rest of England, which were created on a somewhat piecemeal basis between 1829 and 1856 following a series of Acts of Parliament which allowed (and eventually forced) counties and boroughs to establish professional and full-time police forces.[43] Such forces, whilst new in the respect that they were 'professional' and salaried, in many ways harked back to the earlier parish constabulary system; as Beattie remarks, 'the Metropolitan Police Act of 1829, which, although forward-looking in some ways, reached back to an older ideal of policing in its total dependence on the prevention of crime by surveillance.' It was this aspect of surveillance which appealed so much to the moralists: a large body of men available to patrol the streets, actively looking for acts of public indecency on which to unleash the full force of the law, was an attractive proposition.[44]

41 For overviews of the development of policing in England, see P. Rawlings, *Policing: A Short History* (Cullompton: Willan, 2002) and Emsley, *The English Police*. For the history of the Bow Street Public Office and its seminal place in the history of both metropolitan and provincial law enforcement, see D. J. Cox, *A Certain Share of Low Cunning: A History of the Bow Street Runners 1792–1839* (London: Routledge, 2012) and Beattie, *The First English Detectives*.

42 For the development of policing in Scotland, see D. G. Barrie, *Police in the Age of Improvement: Police Development and the Civic Tradition in Scotland, 1775–1865* (Cullompton: Willan, 2008); J. McGowan, 'The emergence of modern civil police in Scotland: a case study of the police and systems of policing in Edinburghshire 1800–1833' (unpublished PhD thesis, Open University, 1996); and A. Dinsmor, 'Glasgow police pioneers', *Journal of the Police History Society* 15 (2000), 9–11.

43 The Metropolitan Police did not, however, provide a *universally* popular model for the whole of England – see for example M. Tennant, 'An honourable failure? A reassessment of the police of the First Cheshire Constabulary Force within the wider context of 19th century police reform', paper delivered at the European Centre for Policing Studies, Open University, Milton Keynes, October 2008; and M. Tennant, 'Fields of struggle: A Bourdieusian analysis of conflicts over criminal justice in England, c. 1820–50' *Social History*, 39, no. 1 (2014): 36–55.

44 J.M. Beattie, *Policing and Punishment in London 1660–1750: Urban Crime and the Limits of Terror*, (Oxford: Oxford University Press, 2001), 422.

Consequently, such moralists often attempted to steer the various police forces (both metropolitan and provincial) towards the policing of public morality. Their degree of success in such an aim appears to have been variable. Many of the provincial police forces, of which there were more than 200 by the Edwardian period, were at least initially controlled (under the proviso of the Municipal Corporations Act 1835) by watch committees, whose members often pursued their own short-term interests in maintaining and directing the activities of their employees; they were often more concerned about protecting their own commercial and business interests than providing moralists with a force with which to effectively tackle the serious and growing evil of public indecency. Rawlings remarks that 'the connections between watch committees and employers was reinforced by the practice in some borough forces of drawing part of their funding from local business: for instance, in the mid-1860s 60 per cent of the officers in the Middlesborough force were financed by local firms.'[45]

Despite the passing of the Town Police Clauses Act 1847, which aimed to consolidate many policing powers under one Act which could be enforced under the control of a civic body in the form of a local council, many police forces remained effectively under the direction of a small body of non-elected watch committee members. It was not until 1856 with the introduction of the County and Borough Police Act 1856, by which all counties and boroughs in England were forced to create police forces, that some degree of standardization and a stronger link between police forces and local councils was established. Two further Acts, the Municipal Corporations (New Charters) Act 1877 (which prevented small boroughs of under 20,000 inhabitants from creating police forces) and the Local Government Act 1888 (which forced all such small boroughs to amalgamate any existing forces with their respective county forces), further amalgamated and standardized provincial policing, placing it more firmly within the hands of local authorities rather than a self-appointed and self-selecting few.

Conclusion

Attempts to define and control 'indecency' clearly did not begin in 1857. In the preceding century, responsibility for regulating and shaping the behaviour of individuals and the moral standards of society underwent a significant shift from exclusive ecclesiastic control towards increasingly deliberate efforts at State control coupled with a rise in organized – and sometimes highly influential – morality campaigns generated by the rapidly expanding volunteer sector of political society. By conceptualizing indecency as a problem, moral reformers of the eighteenth and early nineteenth centuries began the process of integrating perceptions of criminality – or at least the criminality of the lower classes – into a more sophisticated understanding of deprivation and crime. The concept of indecency in broad terms became a new way of framing responses to low-level criminality,

---

45 Rawlings, *Policing: A Short History*, 166.

but in these earlier manifestations arguments and activism were more focused on *changing behaviour* rather than mere punishment, and pressure for legislative change was focussed primarily on obscenity laws rather than a wider agenda to criminalize indecency *per se*. From these foundations, the conceptual framework would become considerably more complex and ever more inconsistent after 1857.

2 The intensification of the indecency agenda 1857–1885

Introduction

The seeds of the indecency agenda were sown in the late eighteenth century but struggled to find firm ground for much of the Victorian era. The assorted interests of morality persuasion ebbed and flowed between moral, conscience-based (non-legislative) activism and explicitly legislative activism. Early legal efforts to effect control of indecency were undertaken primarily through the case-by-case use of the common law. This was followed by an expansion of statute law which, although not necessarily framed as such, was driven by the 'indecency agenda' of morality-based behavioural modification. The broad range of undesirable behaviours and offences encapsulated in the Vagrancy Act 1824 became a staple focus of the indecency agenda. During the 1840s, partly because the growing presence of modern uniformed police forces enabled this, a number of Acts had attempted to define and control indecency in essentially urban locations. There was, for instance, the Theatre Regulations Act 1843 which had strengthened the role of the Lord Chamberlain in censoring plays, and where the reliance was on local policing to intervene to ensure that that censorship was put into practice. Equally, the Town Police Clauses Act 1847 conferred new powers on the police when dealing with public indecency.

But this fragmentary approach did not satisfy those who felt themselves surrounded by indecency in the mid-nineteenth century, particularly during the periodic high tides of moral activism when campaigning groups were most active in their attempts to enforce and expand the law. The problem, for campaigners, enforcers, and legislators alike, was to arrive at a legal concept sufficiently broad to meet the perceived need, but sufficiently well-defined to be legally effective. In this, they failed. However, the failure, far from limiting the indecency agenda, proved to be a great advantage. A single legal offence may have been what campaigners wanted, but it was not what they needed in order to pursue their objectives.

The triumph of legislative activism appeared to have won with the passing of the OPA 1857, which provided a sledgehammer with which to attack some high-profile examples of indecent literature. However, despite the expansion beyond its original intentions as a result of the case of *Hicklin*, the OPA 1857 was less suited to the task of modifying indecent behaviour more generally since it clearly was not able to deal with the merely offensive (i.e. short of 'deprave and corrupt').[1] Although hailed by morality campaigners such as the SSV, the OPA 1857 soon became a cause for disillusionment and frustration, perhaps due to what *The Times* referred to in its editorial of 23 July 1857 as 'shallow sophistry'. It is possible that perception of the OPA 1857 as a completed task contributed to a fall-off in active and financial support for campaigners such as the SSV, which appears to have collapsed in 1880 due to lack of funds. The morality campaigns of the late nineteenth century turned to other high-profile causes.[2] Despite the best efforts of moral campaigners, and the propitious expansion of institutions – magistrates courts and police in particular – legal action against indecency in the nineteenth century was a somewhat fitful matter, often overshadowed, and in campaigning terms, crowded out, by higher-profile issues-based campaigning against specific ills such as prostitution, brothels, the Contagious Diseases Act, sexual offences, and establishing an age of consent.

By the 1850s, British society was substantially urban, and by the end of that century, it was overwhelmingly so. This provided a new, and yet essentially anonymous, arena for public indecency, where the scale of the problem was one of the issues faced by those who were determined to manage and control it, in the interests of national welfare. Drunkenness (see Chapter Seven) and sexual immorality were at the core of contemporary concerns, and these were so intrinsically intertwined that both were often seen as interdependent, the one leading to the other in an inevitable way that guaranteed a terrifying descent into irredeemable indecency for the individual unless that progress was halted. The morally improving literature of the day, and even the more marginally moral sensation novels, took for granted this interdependency in working out the fates of their characters – for example, the immensely popular sensational and implicitly moralistic romantic novels of George Payne Rainsford James (1799–1860), in which decency and virtue invariably triumphed over indecency and evil.

At the same time, indecency arguments clearly involved the troubled perceptions of the middle classes when faced with the dramatic changes to the lives of the working classes in terms of political power, education, disposable wealth, and leisure for entertainment. In the 1860s, alongside concerns about the regulation of drink,

> It was the wider range of consumption choices available to a growing proportion of the working population legitimately earning above subsistence wages which attracted new comment. Music halls (from the 1850s in London, the 1860s in the provinces), the popular press (from the early 1870s) and the accompanying spread of commercialized sport and gambling all provided a focus for recurrently obsessive debate around the theme of working-class ability to manage limited resources in an age of commercially promoted temptation.[3]

1 *R v Hicklin* (1868) 3 QB 360.
2 Bristow, *Vice and Vigilance*, 49.
3 See J. Rowbotham, K. Stevenson and S. Pegg, *Crime News in Modern Britain: Press Reporting and Responsibility 1820–2010*, London: Palgrave Macmillan, 2013, Chapter Two; and Roberts, *Making English Morals*, 195.

Indecency in a broad sense included behaviours which in part were condemned (by the objectors) for some ill-defined causative effect in relation to the criminality of the lower classes – thus Sunday trading, gambling in public places, drunkenness, 'disorderly' behaviour, begging, and vagrancy were consistently part of the picture. Indecency at its core may have been an add-on to the obscenity laws and sexual offences laws, but beyond this it was a means of tackling offensive behaviours throughout the public sphere – most notably, those behaviours exhibited by the working classes as they exercised their expanding leisure time (and their literacy) and spent their newly available disposable income.

This chapter focusses on two key factors that were mutually essential in priming the development of the indecency agenda. The first factor was a politico-legal framework which was suited to the task of imposing control over everyday behaviour. With no state prosecutor until 1880 (following the passing of the Prosecution of Offences Act 1879), limited, centralized institutions with scarce enforcement resources lacked the intrusive ability necessary for low-level interference with the behaviour of ordinary people: something more wide-reaching was needed. Police forces assumed the (often unwilling) mantle of quasi-public prosecutors from the mid-1850s onward following the statutory creation of police forces by the County and Borough Police Act 1856. By this time, private prosecution was waning, especially with regard to the various associations for the prosecution of felons.[4] The second factor was a conceptualization of objectionable behaviours as unambiguously criminal and thus a legitimate target for State-enforced coercion. The politico-legal framework emerged sporadically but unquestionably from the major institutional reforms of the early nineteenth century in response to the pressures of urban and industrial expansion. The conceptualization of objectionable behaviors as criminal was already partially in place within the common law and would be ripe for statutory action, but always remained problematic.

The politico-legal framework

Justices of the Peace had been a central pillar of the English legal system at the local level for centuries, but the role of local magistrates courts grew dramatically throughout the eighteenth and nineteenth century with a plethora of legislative measures which expanded the range of summary jurisdiction into almost every aspect of life, and linked magistrates into a complex network of legal regulation and enforcement in conjunction with the increasingly empowered local authorities and (from 1856) the soon-to-be ubiquitous police forces.[5] It was not only the

---

4 See B. Godfrey, D. J. Cox, and S. Farrall, *Criminal Lives: Family Life, Employment, and Offending*, Oxford: Clarendon Criminology Series, Oxford University Press, 2007); and B. Godfrey, D. J. Cox, and S. Farrall, *Serious Offenders: A Historical Study of Habitual Criminals*, Clarendon Criminology Series, (Oxford: Oxford University Press, 2010) for accounts of the changes in prosecutorial agencies.

5 See P. King, *Crime and Law in England 1750–1840: Remaking Justice from the Margins*, (Cambridge: Cambridge University Press, 2006); and D. J. Cox and B. S. Godfrey, (eds.), *Cinderellas and Packhorses: A History of the Shropshire Magistracy* (Almeley: Logaston Press, 2005).

structural measures put in place by Parliament – although these were numerous including the Municipal Corporations Act 1835, Petty Sessions Act 1849, Summary Jurisdiction Act 1879 etc. – but also the extension of summary criminal offences in a wide range of areas such as the Juvenile Offenders Acts 1847 and 1850, and the Criminal Justice Act 1855. Legislation such as the Vagrancy Act 1824 placed old misdemeanours on a statutory footing and also expanded the range of possible offences.

New summary offences with accompanying statutory powers were also created under the Weights and Measures Act 1824, Education Acts, Industrial Schools Amendment Act 1885, Criminal Law Amendment Acts 1885 and 1912, Children Act 1908, etc. The magistrates' role in controlling undesirable behaviour was reinforced by the licensing role in relation to alcohol (e.g. under the Licensing Acts of 1872 and 1874). This growth in summary jurisdiction was 'linked to the emergence of the regulatory state, which extended its influence into ever more aspects of day-to-day life and thus increased the likelihood (especially for young working-class men) of falling foul of the law'.[6] The Church was by now almost completely replaced as the arbiter of 'decency' and 'indecency'; there had been an irreversible shift from spiritual to secular oversight of the behaviour of the English public.

Statute law and indecency in the nineteenth century

Much has been written about the OPA 1857, which gave magistrates the power to issue warrants for the search and seizure of material believed to be obscene (possession then was not illegal), and the consequent landmark ruling of *Hicklin* in 1868[7] introducing the 'deprave and corrupt test' to define 'obscene'.[8] One of the principal objections raised by critics of the Bill as it progressed through Parliament was the problematic lack of definition of 'obscenity'. Lord Lyndhurst argued that he could 'easily conceive that two men will come to entirely different conclusions as to its meaning'.[9] Lord Wensleydale, although sympathetic to the 'proper desire to put an end to the nefarious traffic in indecent publications', believed that

> The common law, as it stood, was quite strong enough to deal with such offences. Any person exposing indecent prints was liable to be indicted for a misdemeanour. The extensive powers sought to be conferred on the police by the Bill required grave consideration, and the definition of what was obscene

6 D. Taylor, *Hooligans, Harlots and Hangmen: Crime and Punishment in Victorian Britain* (Oxford: Praeger, 2010), 21.

7 *R v Hicklin* (1868) 3 QB 360.

8 J. R. Alexander, 'Roth at fifty: Reconsidering the common law antecedents of American obscenity doctrine', *The John Marshall Law Review* 41, no. 393 (2008): 393–433; T. Lewis, 'Legislating morality; Victorian and modern legal responses to pornography,' in J. Rowbotham and K. Stevenson (eds.), *Behaving Badly: Social Panic and Moral Outrage – Victorian and Modern Parallels* (Ashgate: Aldershot, 2003), 143–58.

9 *Hansard* HL Deb, 25 June 1857, vol. 146 cc. 327–38, 331.

was very uncertain. There was not a library in which books could not be found containing passages which a strict-dealing magistrate might consider to bring them within the operation of this Bill.[10]

Although never a catch-all for indecent behaviour more generally, the newly enacted concept of obscenity certainly had a wide scope – too wide, the critics feared.

Curiously this legislation played a comparatively small part in the indecency story of the second half of the nineteenth century, although it did have a high-profile impact in the following case. In March 1873 three men (John Davidson, John Dennison, and Henry Romilly) appeared before Marlborough Street Magistrates' Court charged with 'exhibiting certain indecent and demoralizing representations for the purpose of gain'. There was a second summons calling on them to show cause why the models seized by the police 'should not be destroyed'. The well-known solicitor, George Lewis, who appeared for the defendants, said it was their wish that the magistrate should not pass judgment on this case, but that facilities should be at once given for sending it before a higher tribunal and getting the question finally decided whether models which had been publicly exhibited for twenty-five years really formed the subject of a criminal offence.[11] The magistrates reportedly sent the case to the Central Criminal Court and the models were to be held at Newgate Prison for subsequent inspection by the judge.[12]

This case, prosecuted by the SSV, was the result of an anatomical exhibition held at 'Dr' Kahn's Museum. This museum had been established in 1851 by an Alsatian, Joseph Kahn. Although he left England in 1858 (after several brushes with the law for selling 'quack' remedies for the cure of venereal disease), the museum continued in various guises and through various owners.[13] The 'museum' contained anatomical models (to a varying degree of accuracy) of many human body parts, including reproductive organs, depictions of the effects of sexually transmitted diseases, and the head and face of an 'onanist'. It had been a source of irritation for many years to moralists, and several newspapers clearly held a similar view: *Freeman's Journal & Daily Commercial Advertiser*, on hearing of the closure of the museum by police, remarked 'They have now given the 'coup de grace' to that collection of vulgar horrors known as the Kahn museum.'[14]

---

10 *Hansard* HL Deb, 25 June 1857, vol. 146 cc. 327–38, 336.
11 'Anatomical models', *British Medical Journal* 1, no. 637 (March 15, 1873): 295.
12 It appears that the case never actually reached the Central Criminal Court; there are no records in either newspapers or the Criminal Registers of the defendants appearing at the Old Bailey. It looks instead as though the matter was returned to Marlborough Street Magistrates' Court in mid-December 1873.
13 See A. W. Bates, 'Dr Kahn's Museum: obscene anatomy in Victorian London', *Journal of the Royal Society of Medicine* 99, no. 12 (December 2006): 618–24 for further details of Kahn's 'museum'. There are modern parallels with the furore caused by the exhibition of plasticized human remains displayed in a series of exhibitions entitled "Body Worlds" from 2002 onwards by Gunther von Hagens. Numerous complaints were received over these often troubling but admittedly fascinating exhibits.
14 *Freeman's Journal & Daily Commercial Advertiser*, 3 March 1873.

Whilst the models were clearly designed in part to shock, the defendants argued that the exhibits performed a valuable scientific, medical, and educational function for their audience. However, the defendants must have realized that the writing was on the wall, as in mid-December 1873 they pleaded guilty at Marlborough Street Court to the exhibition of obscene articles under the OPA 1857 and the court decreed that the offending models were to be destroyed. In a rare victory for the SSV, Mr Collette, the SSV's solicitor, claimed the privilege of personally destroying the first model.

The OPA 1857 may have been seen as fulfilling a particular legislative need at the time, but it was only later that the moral activists were able to harness the potential of the statute's interpretative uncertainty against a wider range of literature and visual arts, perhaps helped by fading memories of the original reservations and caveats which had initially accompanied the legislation. The Act was thus increasingly well-used and controversial in the twentieth century with censorship of high-profile 'demoralizing literature' such as D. H. Lawrence's *The Rainbow*, Radclyffe Hall's *The Well of Loneliness*, and Joyce's *Ulysses*.[15] But for the moral activists of the late nineteenth century, it had important limitations.

The concept of obscenity was, in many ways, not sufficiently malleable for moral enforcers to use against indecency. 'Obscenity' was not merely a synonym for 'indecent' (a point made by Lord Sands in *McGowan v Langmuir*, although he agreed the two expressions blurred into one another.[16]) The OPA 1857 and the *Hicklin* test essentially froze the idea of obscenity into a high-level legal standard of harmful expression ('to deprave and corrupt') which merited the full force (and cost) of a jury trial. The concept was too rigid to be used as a tool to police day-to-day behaviour. It could not be used against behaviour or expression which was merely 'offensive' to the sensibilities of those who observed it (or simply knew of its existence). To be obscene implied some measure of harm to the audience – and whilst it was a standard trope of the morality reformers that indecency *was* corrupting and damaging to society, this was an argument that could all too easily fail before a jury if the nature of the objectionable act or material was, by the perhaps less-elevated standards of the man on the Clapham omnibus, somewhat commonplace or trivial. Indecency, by contrast, was a far more accommodating concept – an idea of offence rather than harm which could be modulated and adapted to meet all the diversity of unpleasant behaviours – the 'serious and growing evil' – which the insecure classes perceived around them.

Parallel tracks? Conceptualizing indecency

One of the problems for those who sought to use the law as a mechanism for changing objectionable behaviour was that of finding an overarching concept that could capture the multitude of problematic activities within its net. It was, of

15 See A. Travis, *Bound and Gagged: A Secret History of Obscenity in Britain* (London, Profile Books, 2000).
16 *McGowan v Langmuir* (1931) SLT 94.

course, possible to criminalize each 'micro-act' – to some extent, this was the common law approach whereby a multitude of actions and expressions could fall foul of any one (or more) of the numerous fingers of the law.

But what also concerned the mid-Victorian moralists was this question: given that by now, it was established that the majority of them were naturally decent in their instincts, what forces and factors tempted English men and women from the paths of decency? What induced men and women to take to drink and so wander into sexual immorality, or to fall into that immorality and then take to drink?[17] It was the assessment of this that preoccupied Victorian moral commentators, as they urged their conclusions on politicians who (often moral commentators themselves) felt increasingly impelled to improve the potential of legislation to control not just indecency itself but those things which promoted and increased its spread in the Victorian cities and towns.

Early legal efforts to control indecency had been undertaken primarily through the case-by-case use of common law, as discussed in Chapter One. This had been followed by some expansion of statute law which, although not necessarily framed as such, was driven by the 'indecency agenda' of morality-based behavioural modification, such as the Vagrancy Act 1824 with its extensive powers against 'idle and disorderly persons'. Superficially, at least, 'indecent', in the language of the nineteenth-century campaigners for legal change, was often coterminous with 'sexual', a word which was rarely used but was always implied. Equally, although the State and campaigning groups had particular ideas of exactly what constituted obscenity, these were ultimately subjective views and were often widely and publicly challenged by both individuals and campaigning societies, both in the burgeoning press and the courts. From the 1850s on a great deal of campaigning and legislative effort generating an 'indecency agenda' was spent on issues where this sexual aspect was most apparent, notably the control of prostitution and soliciting particularly through the Contagious Diseases Acts (1864–1869) and campaigns against them; debates about establishing and settling the age of sexual consent, culminating in the Criminal Law Amendment Act 1885 preceded by W. T. Stead's scandal-inducing exposure of child prostitution published in the *Pall Mall Gazette* in July 1885, the 'Maiden Tribute of Modern Babylon'; obscenity in literature, arts, theatre, etc.

The idea of indecency was much wider than these discrete issues and development of the law on indecency can be seen to run on parallel tracks to obscenity laws, sexual offences laws, and anti-prostitution campaigns. Indecent behaviour, particularly for the moral campaigners who sought to extend legal regulation, certainly included explicit sexual activity and expressions of such, but went much further to encompass 'corrupting' literature which was not sufficiently sexually explicit to be considered obscene but nevertheless seemed undesirable. Likewise, street ballads, music hall acts, and later theatre and cinematic

---

17 It is recognized that drunkenness could also lead to non-sexual immorality such as fighting, swearing, and domestic violence.

performances were objectionable as 'corrupting' or 'lewd' rather than obscene. Prohibition (and calls for greater legal repression), frequently extended to medical topics such as birth control, and while 'serious' literature remained under constant threat of prosecution, there were also rising concerns about less literary aspects of the printed genre, notably the expanding popular press with its less-than-reverent portrayal of human foibles. Part of the objection was certainly related to fears about the changing status of women. Thus, one aspect of the indecency agenda (and the reason why obscenity and sexual offences laws were seen as inadequate) lies in an attempt to hold back the tide of female emancipation and protect both the image and the delicate mind of the 'angel of the home' with all that she symbolized, and by so doing, delineate a clear division between Madonna and whore, 'decent' and 'indecent'. The phrase 'angel of the home' seems to have been coined by Reverend John Milton Williams, an ardent opponent of female suffrage:

> While I can conceive of no benefit accruing to women, or to the public in general from the ballot, my unshaken conviction is that almost every human interest would suffer from it. Woman has no call to the ballot-box, but she has a sphere of her own, of amazing responsibility and importance. She is the divinely appointed guardian of the home, where human interests mainly centre, and where human influence reaches farthest and lives longest. She should more fully realize that her position as wife and mother, and angel of the home, is the holiest, most responsible, and queenlike assigned to mortals; and dismiss all ambition for anything higher, as there is nothing else here so high for mortals.[18]

It is also clearly linked with Coventry Patmore's 1854 poem 'The Angel in the House', which similarly praises pious Victorian female domesticity.

At the same time, indecency arguments clearly involved the troubled perceptions of the middle classes when faced with the dramatic changes to the lives of the working classes in terms of political power, education, disposable wealth, and leisure for entertainment. In the 1860s, as Roberts notes, alongside concerns about the regulation of alcohol, 'it was a wider range of consumption choices available to a growing proportion of the working population legitimately earning above subsistence wages which attracted new comment.'[19] These included music hall entertainment, increasing literacy and interest in the popular press,[20] and the addictive attractions of commercialized sport and gambling, which 'all provided a focus for recurrently obsessive debate around the theme of working-class ability to manage limited resources in an age of commercially promoted temptation.'[21]

18 J.M. Williams, 'Woman suffrage', *Bibliotheca Sacra 50* (April 1893): 343.
19 Roberts, *Making English Morals*, 195.
20 See Rowbotham, *et al., Crime News in Modern Britain*, especially Chapter Two.
21 Roberts, *Making English Morals*, 195.

Indecency in a broad sense included behaviours which in part were condemned (by the objectors) for some ill-defined causative effect in relation to the criminality of the lower classes – thus Sunday trading, gambling in public places, drunkenness and 'disorderly' behaviour, and begging and vagrancy were consistently part of the picture.

Civil activism – the rise of the moral campaigners and the development of a sufficient consensus for action

The 'indecency agenda' did not solely depend on moral campaigners to drive it, and low-level prosecutions tended to continue fairly steadily in the years between 'moral panics' or revivalist moral upsurges, but there seems little doubt that moral campaigns and agitation for reform played an important role. While both the rhetoric and the legal actions against indecency continued fitfully throughout the nineteenth century, the challenge of moral reform was taken up with renewed vigour in the later period and achieved something of a 'perfect storm' in the early twentieth century:

> The rise of the Women Question . . . paralleled the revival of the Condition of England question, the onset of the Great Depression, the first serious challenges to Britain's economic and imperial pre-eminence, the rapid extension of the franchise, and the swift emergence of the socialist alternative to bourgeois capitalism. In addition, the moral and intellectual foundations of British culture were under assault by a new generation of critics and writers from the 1880s on.[22]

The moral campaigners would have had little to work with if they had merely been an extremist fringe. The growing preoccupation with indecency is deeply connected to a wider sense of changing identity awareness amongst many social interest groups. F. M. L. Thompson describes a Victorian world in which the rise of 'respectable society' included notions of self-respect which increasingly overlapped with those of the classes above and below.[23] 'Class' is always a somewhat fluid and imprecise concept and by 1857 it refers essentially to a web of interest groups connected internally (strongly at times) through traditional class indicators such as occupation and property ownership, but in a world where some measure of social mobility now existed, in which the boundaries and privileges of class were increasingly fluid – and from some perspectives, under threat. For the first time in England, the idea – and to some extent the reality – of personal choice had entered the social equation.

The Enlightenment paved the philosophical way; the upheavals of the American and French revolutions demonstrated the potentialities and dangers of politics as

22 R. A. Solway, *Demography and Degeneration: Eugenics and the Declining Birthrate in Twentieth Century Britain* (Chapel Hill: University of North Carolina Press, 1995), 111.

23 Thompson, *The Rise of Respectable Society*.

a mechanism of choice; widening education and a growing mass media expanded awareness of the world and its possibilities; and the traditional land-owning aristocratic elite saw economic (and thus political and social) power shifting to the new industrialists as value and profit moved inexorably away from primary agrarian wealth towards secondary industrial production, opening routes of social mobility to anyone who could harness the new technologies (with the proviso that they were male; very few women were able to progress through the 'cast-iron' ceiling of Victorian industry or commerce).[24] In such a world, self-identification became possible: you were who you believed (or projected) yourself to be. By choice of residence, occupation, and the values a person chose to espouse, a social presence could be formed, or at least negotiated, where once it was allocated by birth.

By the mid-nineteenth century, most social groupings had at least relatively more life choices than their ancestors had ever experienced. The exception may have been the traditional aristocrats, still bound by the conventions of hereditary power and expectation. The 'working classes' – those whose place in society depended largely on their ability to sell their own labour – had more choices over the type of work they sought and the employer they worked for, at least in times of economic stability. The censuses of the mid-nineteenth century onwards illustrate that such workers no longer felt tied to their place of birth. This putative freedom was of course greatly facilitated by the invention and growth of means of transport such as railways and bicycles – the latter being especially formative in the creation of wider horizons from the 1880s for women (with regard to both employment and social opportunities). Agricultural depression and the allure of better wages in the mills and foundries of the urban centres made mobility possible, and according to the fluctuations of the market, often essential for survival. However, it was the 'middle classes' (Hoppen's 'middle sort of people') who most dramatically benefited from new choices.[25] This was the ever-changing but always growing category of the 'relatively comfortable' and, from 1832 onwards, newly enfranchised, with some property of their own and/or valuable professional skills to provide a foothold in the economy. This social sphere arguably provided most opportunity for economic and thus social advancement, and with it, an increasing sense of self-identification, and thus a vulnerability to anything that threatened that self-conceived image. The image was consciously not 'upper class' – the preserve of those perceived to be idle landowners – but equally not that of a worker solely dependent on the will of others. The new opportunities were not merely external.

The development of the industrial/urban milieu as a geographical space had its cultural impact as well. By the 1900s 'nearly half the population lived in households

---

24 Examples of remarkable women who did break through the 'cast-iron' ceiling can be found in Eliza Tinsley (1813–1882) of Cradley Heath in the Black Country, who ran her own chain-making firm from 1851 to 1872, employing more than 4,000 people and Eleanor Coade (1733–1821) who managed her ceramic stone business in Lambeth for almost fifty years until her death.

25 K. T. Hoppen, *The Mid-Victorian Generation 1846–1886* (Oxford: Oxford University Press, 2008), 31–49.

where there was only one occupant or less per room, a figure that pointed tentatively towards new possibilities of individualism and privacy within the family circle.'[26] Here, the crucial elements of identity could emerge to include autonomy and respectability in the context of genuine private space in which, for many, a new emphasis on family life would emerge. It was this respectable self-identity, and the experience of the world as a comfortable place of shared values, which was most threatened by the perception of unacceptable behaviour by others. This view of respectable self-identity was of course promoted and strengthened by Victoria and Albert and their plethora of children – the ultimate personification of the respectable 'middle-class' family unit. In such a world, 'respectability', and its evil twin 'indecency', became part of the conceptual terrain over which the low-level cultural battle for status was fought. Thus, the 'enthusiasts and work-horses' of the nineteenth-century moral reform societies 'were much more likely to emerge from social and occupational backgrounds typical of the majority of the members they attracted – that is, from the ranks of the metropolitan business and professional community'.[27]

That is not to say that the moral campaigners necessarily reflected a majority view. In some respects, the indecency agenda, like the previous purity campaigns, may have been uncomfortable, or even deeply abhorrent, to many people in all sections of society. Wilson argues that on the whole, people in the eighteenth century 'took a robust view of the vulgarity of British life' and that what had emerged in the early nineteenth century was in fact a 'false delicacy' or hypocrisy: 'it was not that people were offended, but that they were affecting a claim to virtue.'[28] False or not, by 1857, the delicate sensibilities were able to demand and receive considerable publicity and a significant measure (though in the eyes of many campaigners, not a sufficient measure) of legal protection.

Conceptualizing indecency: The relationship between indecency and immorality

Many of the nineteenth- and early twentieth-century discussions on legislative reform correlate indecency with immorality – at times appearing to equate the two. Blackstone had earlier drawn the clear connection: 'lewdness' was 'against religion and morality' and 'cognizable by the temporal courts'.[29] At times, 'indecent' is little more than a casual term of criticism, with no legal import: in a debate on the Advowsons Bill in 1856, for example, the Earl of Shaftsbury rails against 'disgraceful, blasphemous, and indecent' expressions and 'indecent jokes and badinage'.[30] At other times, in the legal discussion indecency is firmly paired with the idea of immorality, with both being regarded as valid objectives of legal restraint. In 1908, the establishment of a Select Committee to consider the law

26 J. Harris, *Private Lives, Public Spirit: Britain 1870–1914* (London: Penguin Books, 1994), 63.
27 Roberts, *Making English Morals*, 79.
28 B. Wilson, *Decency and Disorder 1789–1837* (London: Faber and Faber, 2007), xviii.
29 W. Blackstone, *Commentaries on the Laws of England*, vol. 4 (Chicago: University of Chicago Press, 1979a), 64.
30 *Hansard* HL Deb, 8 July 1856, vol. 143 cc.491–3: 491.

on lotteries and advertisements was asked, as part of its brief, to inquire into the law 'as to indecent literature and pictures and advertisements relating to things indecent and immoral'; in 1910 the Morality Bill, and subsequently the Prevention of Immorality Bill in 1911, were both designed 'to make further provision for the protection of women and girls, for the suppression of immoral and indecent literature . . . and otherwise for the prevention of immorality and indecency', thus demonstrating that some parliamentarians, at least, had no qualms about including immoral behaviour within the sphere of the law.[31]

However, whilst many campaigners sought to make their case for reform on moral grounds, it seems clear that the distinction between immorality and indecency was a constant presence in the key arguments. In essence, morality (or lack of it) had traditionally been the sole preserve of ecclesiastical jurisdiction, and the established Church had been reluctant to give up this exclusive power. An example of this can be found in Reverend Samuel Marsden's *Female Register* of 1806, in which he listed and therefore condemned women living in Tasmania who were not married in Church of England ceremonies as 'concubines', not including any common-law or other religions' marriage ceremonies. This has been memorably described as 'an inspired piece of creative bigotry'.[32]

To argue for legal regulation of moral behaviour was thus an approach fraught with difficulty. By contrast, if immoral behaviour could also be labelled as indecent, it acquired a penumbra of criminality which legitimized secular authorities taking control. In some respects, indecency had always been the legally enforceable component of immorality. After all, Blackstone himself had already drawn the line when he stated that all crimes should be 'estimated merely according to the mischiefs which they produce in civil society: and, of consequence, private vices . . . are not, cannot be, the object of any municipal law'.[33] To ensure legal enforcement against offending behaviours, it was therefore more effective to argue the case in terms the law already recognized as being legitimate targets because there was some danger of harm. Thus 'with the rise of secular currents and religious heterogeneity, moralizing discourses increasingly linked immorality to utilitarian claims about the personal or social harm associated with the wrong.'[34] But even then, campaigners and reformers needed to make the case that law was the appropriate weapon.

Conceptualizing indecency: Changing offending behaviour by persuasion or coercion

The emergent social/cultural obsession with indecency is part of the wider picture of a rationalist Enlightenment attitude towards the social problems of the industrial age. Gradually, as later chapters will show, this started to translate into

---

31 *Hansard* HC Deb, 20 March 1908, vol. 186 c.992: 992; *Hansard* HC Deb, 14 June 1910. vol. 17 c.1202; *Hansard* HC Deb, 15 February 1911, vol. 21 c.1064.
32 R. Hughes, *The Fatal Shore* (London: Vintage Books, 2003), 263.
33 Blackstone, *Commentaries*, vol. 4, 41.
34 Hunt, *Governing Morals*, 7.

calculated use of law to control behaviour on the grounds of indecency. This was not a straightforward transition. Throughout the period, the question of whether legal enforcement was the appropriate response to morally objectionable behaviour remained a controversial one.

Some groups, such as the Proclamation Society (founded in 1789, eventually changing its name to the Society for Bettering the Condition of the Poor), with its socially elite membership, its first chairman being the Bishop of Salisbury, operated naturally within the established power relationships of the day and thus easily adopted the attitude 'that most good could be done most quickly by using the law to modify the behaviour of individuals'.[35] That such societies often offered financial incentives to promulgate moral and decent behaviour is perhaps less well known; for example a letter written to the *Royal Cornwall Gazette, Falmouth Packet and Plymouth Journal*, 26 November 1814 lists numerous annual awards granted to the poor of Carmarthen County, Wales, who had passed various 'decency' tests.

The Sunday Observance movement established something of a precedent for legitimation of the State as an appropriate agency for the enforcement of moral behaviour as a result of 'the effect produced under the Metropolitan Police Act of 1839 – an Act which introduced a systematically enforced regime of restricted Sunday opening hours for public houses'.[36] Other movements and individuals objected to the prosecutorial efforts of the moral enforcers. Cobbett, for example, argued that the Proclamation Society's activities gave 'the laws . . . an extension and a force which it was never intended they should have'.[37] In 1854 the Pure Literature Society chose persuasion rather than legal force: instead of attempting to suppress by law the corrupting influence of the 'penny press' and other immoral literature, it instead 'set out to use commercial methods to "overcome evil with good" '. For example, in *The Times* (21 May 1856), the society advertised: 'six bookhawkers wanted – strong, unmarried, and with good testimonials'.[38]

By contrast, the SSV of the early nineteenth century and the National Vigilance Association (hereafter NVA) of the late nineteenth and early twentieth century both adopted the strong-arm tactics of legal activism by seeking to initiate prosecutions, or to force others to prosecute and, at times, to expand the grasp of the law by lobbying for new legislation, thus placing themselves firmly in 'the "moral panic" tradition in which the promotion of a public campaign produces demands for greater action to combat the targeted evil which, in turn, results in a combination of institutional expansion and legislative action'.[39] One parliamentary critic of the coercive approach commented of Lord Campbell's Obscenity Bill that it

---

35 Roberts, *Making English Morals*, 49.
36 Ibid, 166–7.
37 Ibid, 87.
38 Ibid, 170.
39 Hunt, *Governing Morals*, 12.

'was an attempt to make people virtuous by Act of Parliament' and that 'there was a great danger of making mischief by an undue interference with the affairs of private life, and by encouraging abuse of power.'[40]

For other parties involved in the enforcement of 'moral standards of behaviour' the question of their appropriate role was particularly acute. As is shown in Chapter Six, local magistrates were frequently under pressure from moral campaigners to more actively enforce the law but also had to negotiate the complex web of the wider interests of both commercial and local community residents of all classes. Thus, in their licensing role, the magistrates found themselves between a 'rock and a hard place' when the interests of the brewers and licensees conflicted with those who sought to place strict limits (or even to completely abolish) the sale and use of alcohol (see Chapter Seven). The extent to which individual magistrates swayed under these conflicting pressures seems in part to have depended on their own preferences, and also on the pressure that members of local councils and other powerful local interests were able and willing to exert. At the same time, magistrates were now dependent on the police forces for enforcement, and these could not necessarily be relied upon to fall in line with a hard-line indecency agenda.

The myriad of police forces throughout England often had their own agendas that did not necessarily coincide with that of magistrates. Joanne Klein's research into the day-to-day activities of the police forces of Liverpool, Manchester, and Birmingham in the first decades of the twentieth century found that 'Constables tended to ignore a multitude of public order laws unless they involved public danger or hazards . . . Offences such as obstructing footpaths, jostling, shouting or using indecent language, were dealt with on a case-by-case basis, getting attention only if someone complained.'[41] As Emsley has stated:

> The police were well aware of the problems that their civilising role might cause and both the first commissioners of the Metropolitan Police, and their senior officers, were rather more cautious in the way that they directed their constables to enforce the law than many middle-class reformers hoped or expected.[42]

The police were in a particularly difficult situation, especially in the mid-to-late nineteenth century. There was by no means universal consensus about the necessity or desirability of professional policing, and there was considerable distrust, particularly at the local level and from working-class communities but also at a higher political level. The stereotype of the European 'secret policeman' spying on citizens was a strong counterbalance to the calls for professionalized law and order

---

40 Mr Roebuck MP *Hansard* HC Deb, 12 August 1857, vol. 147 cc.1475–84: 1475.
41 J. Klein, *Invisible Men: The Secret Lives of Police Constables in Liverpool, Manchester and Birmingham, 1900–39* (Liverpool, Liverpool University Press, 2011), 46.
42 Emsley, *The English Police*, 74.

institutions: 'God forbid that he should mean to countenance a system of espionage.'[43] Despite these early concerns, it seems the new Metropolitan Police force were deployed quickly as enforcers of polite behaviour: 'within days of the creation of the Metropolitan Police, squads of them were seen to be deployed in clearing the streets of "scenes of drunkenness, riot and debauchery",' although it should also be noted that a large number of the newly recruited police officers were themselves sacked within months for drunkenness or other offences of public indecency whilst on duty.[44]

By the later nineteenth century the police 'were able to demonstrate their utility by the enforcement of new levels of order and decorum in the streets'.[45] But as the range of calls for enforcement of old laws and the range and grasp of new laws – national and by-laws – increased into the twentieth century, this role brought them increasingly into potential conflict with the communities they were tasked with patrolling. This problem was recognized by contemporary commentators; Reynolds *et al.* noted in 1911 that:

> The police are charged . . . with the enforcement of a whole mass of petty enactments, which are little more than social regulations bearing almost entirely on working-class life. At the bidding of one class, they attempt to impose a certain social discipline on another.[46]

Many officers, both senior and grass roots, attempted to exercise discretion, but this could bring them into conflict with the morality reformers and even with their local council watch committees (especially where these watch committees included moral reformers). Alternatively, rigorous attempts to enforce behaviour could end up in clashes with more liberal (or more pragmatic) elements in the watch committees or local political hierarchy; Emsley identifies 'notable confrontations' between watch committees and head constables. In Birmingham 1880–1881, Chief Constable Major E. E. B. Bond changed the traditional practice of allowing 'quiet drunkards' to proceed on their way without interference and instructed his men to arrest them. The decision was taken without reference to the watch committee. Bond also decided to prosecute the manager of Day's Concert Hall for improper performances and performing without a licence. The watch committee instructed Bond not to take such action in future without consulting them.[47] Similarly, in Liverpool 1890 the Vigilance Association won a majority on the watch committee and instructed the head constable to prosecute brothels. The head constable advised against this but proceeded. As he had predicted, the

43 Ibid, 25, and see C. Emsley, *The Great British Bobby* (London: Quercus, 2009), 43–5 for dismissal examples and statistics.
44 *The Times*, 14 October 1829.
45 Emsley, *The English Police*, 73–4.
46 S. Reynolds, B. Wooley, and T. Wooley, *Seems So! A Working-Class View of Politics* (London, MacMillan, 1911), 86.
47 Emsley, *The English Police*, 90–1.

result was merely for the brothels to relocate to more respectable areas, leading to protests from local traders.[48]

Conclusion

As will be shown in Chapters Six and Seven, it is apparent that day-to-day suppression of 'indecent behaviour' was not primarily a matter of high-profile prosecutions in jury trials. Where there is a convergence of disparate but reinforcing agendas operating between certain key agents within the legal environment, the use of relatively 'trivial' offences to inhibit behaviour may be particularly effective. From a wider historiographical perspective, the existence of such cases is not necessarily unique nor automatically warrants interest. Free speech has been repressed throughout history and arguably such examples are merely a continuation of the Victorian respectability agenda and imposition of 'morality' and eradication of 'poison, pollution and infestation.'[49] From a legal perspective, the existence of low-level indecency cases may appear insignificant and inconsequential. But it is precisely the 'low-level' nature of indecency law and enforcement which contains the key to understanding its significance. Despite the supposed widespread acceptance of Mill's *On Liberty* and the harm principle mirrored against a backcloth of growing liberalism, the repressive and puritan tendency of the Victorians thrived, endured, and continued until at least the mid-twentieth century.

Why did Britain become a byword for censorship amongst the emerging democracies of the early twentieth century, or as Clive Bell asserted, 'one of the least free countries of the world'?[50] One answer is that a deeply rooted notion of using law as a day-to-day mechanism for the enforcement of moral standards had become established. Compared to the significant discussion and column inches that *Hicklin* and *Vizetelly* generated, the low-level localized clampdown on indecent speech and behaviour flew under the radar of public concern, at least until *The Well of Loneliness* became something of a cause célèbre in 1928.[51] The moral campaigners had some success in changing statute law to include indecency more explicitly in the early twentieth century, but crucially, this was not necessary in order to pursue the indecency agenda against objectionable behaviour: the existing web of common law and statutory offences, left almost unnoticed alongside the OPA 1857, proved very effective in the task of repression of undesirable public activities.

48 Ibid, 91.
49 See Lewis, 'Legislating morality', 145.
50 C. Bell, *On British Freedom* (London: Chatto and Windus, 1923), 1, quoted in C. Froula, 'On French and British Freedoms: Early Bloomsbury and the Brothels of Modernism', *MODERNISM/ modernity* 12, no. 4 (2005): 553.
51 R. Hall, *The Well of Loneliness* (London: Jonathan Cape, 1928).

3 'Demoralization' and moral activism

Fighting the 'serious and growing evil' 1885–1908

Introduction

The late nineteenth century marked the start of a rise in, and convergence of, concerns which would solidify into a nexus of indecency issues in the early twentieth century. Again, the underlying framework related to changes in the availability of material which might be considered indecent due to advances in technology and the commercialization of popular entertainment. 'Social purity' efforts focussed more on education than legislation, although the Criminal Law Amendment Act 1885 was a notable exception. By the Edwardian period, all pretence that non-legal solutions might address the perceived problems appears to have been subsumed by a growing acknowledgement that the control of morality should be a task for the State. Indecency gained a new importance as a target for legislative reform and enforcement of existing law. Legal activism intensified through the stronger organization of groups such as the NVA (founded 1885) and the London Council for the Promotion of Public Morality (hereafter LCPPM), founded 1898, with its first public meeting being held 1 February 1900.[1] Middle-class campaigners enjoyed greater influence, co-opting newly empowered local councils, magistrates, and the now-ubiquitous police to the cause.

Significant legal gains were realized with the prohibition of 'indecent' literature and other material and actions including birth control propaganda, dramatic performances, mail communications, advertisements, lotteries, mental deficiency, and sexual acts and conduct, etc. The indecency agenda reached beyond the criminal law towards eugenics-based provisions such as the Mental Deficiency Act 1913, yet unlike many other countries (particularly the United States and Canada) this approach was never fully accepted: sterilization of the mentally

---

1 *The Times*, 23 January 1900. The wide-ranging and ambitious aims of the LCPPM were reiterated in an article in *The Times*, 7 August 1916: 'It is proposed to deal with suggestive or indecent placards, the suppression of shops selling suggestive literature, the closing of private cinema boxes, the prohibition of undesirable films, the right of entry into suspected houses and flats, and the better control of tea rooms and lounges in the West End, as well as hotels and restaurants which have recently been frequented by people of a certain class.'

disordered was discussed but ultimately rejected.[2] Perhaps most significantly, the indecency agenda played a powerful role in shaping (some might argue neutering) British arts, entertainment, and the mass media, an impact which lingers to the present day as is evident in film classification and broadcast codes and watersheds.

It could, however, (from a liberal perspective) have been much worse. It is apparent that day-to-day suppression of 'indecent behaviour' was not primarily a matter of high-profile prosecutions. This is evidenced by an examination of some of the barely noticed cases of the late nineteenth and early twentieth century. A cluster of reported cases identified in *The Times* for the period 1900–1910 reveals that a number of published items, including books – national, international, scientific, and fiction – advertising material, and postcards, etc., became the subject of prosecution, mainly in the magistrates' courts and with little fanfare. Typically, this censorship on the grounds of 'indecency' in fact invoked a variety of disparate reasons under a generic prohibition rather than a clear-cut legal definition of 'indecent'. The only consistent theme of these cases appears to be that they represent an imposition of 'morality' and eradication of 'immorality', usually in explicit terms.

Attempts to impose legal standards of morality were often thwarted by a complex range of obstacles. Unsurprisingly, in the face of new electoral pressures, fundamental economic shifts, conflicting agendas of moral activists, and the threat and actuality of war, parliamentarians and government ministers often lacked sympathy (or time) for indecency campaigns. In parts of the country campaigners were able to gain some support in local councils but community politics were rarely dominated by them. Although often amongst the loudest voices they were seldom the most listened to or the most politically effective, with other powerful interest groups (the unions, liberal elites, and even the Church) acting as significant countervailing forces. The police were frequently ambivalent in their response to demands for action against indecency: far from embracing a role as morality enforcers, both chief constables and beat officers typically regarded such pressure as at best a distraction from more serious crimes, and at worst a real danger to their status in local communities.

Thus, the story of indecency at the turn of the twentieth century is a narrative of active legal intervention in terms of galvanizing legislative and enforcement action but harnessed by certain constraints. This chapter aims to throw light on this wider legal context and the dangers of too-easy acceptance that enacting legislation was the panacea to perceived immoralities. Despite opposition and the inconvenience of political apathy, the indecency agenda undoubtedly had a major impact on British life. In a combination of the final fling of Victorian moralism and renewed urgency precipitated by the perceived 'Edwardian crisis' of a declining empire, the twentieth-century indecency campaigners launched a wide-ranging

2 See B. Godfrey, *Crime in England 1880–1945: The Rough and the Criminal, the Policed and the Incarcerated* (Abingdon: Routledge, 2013), Chapter Eleven, for a succinct discussion concerning criminality and the eugenics movement in Britain.

assault against the 'demoralization' of British culture which arguably created the most censored democracy in the western world.

Indecency and degeneration: The coalescence of fears

Perhaps one of the most striking features of the early twentieth-century zeitgeist was the swift and apparently irreversible loss of Victorian imperial confidence, although signs of insecurity were undoubtedly present from the 1880s onwards. Clearly, the death of the long-lived (if not always much-loved) Queen in 1901 gave strong impetus to the sense of change. The British Empire was essentially at its geographical height, but the political dialogue of the times became increasingly and almost morbidly pessimistic regarding what has often been referred to as the 'condition of England' question: 'the imagined threat for people in the 1890s and opening years of the new century was . . . not from violent revolution but from the continual deterioration and eventual degeneration of the imperial race'.[3] Many factors converged to create this perception. From the 1870s onwards, agricultural depression led to a flood of inward migration to the cities, places which, owing to the work of Victorian social reformers and the steady flow of increasingly 'scientific' reports on the living conditions of the lower classes, were already strongly associated with crime and vice.[4] The period also saw a distinct, if paradoxical, convergence of demographic concerns: on one hand, Malthusian fears about the pressures of population expansion on natural resources, and on the other, emerging statistical evidence that fertility and birth rates were falling, particularly amongst the middle classes.[5] When such concerns were coupled with greater understanding of genetics and the (albeit simplistic) insertion of a bastardized form of Darwinism into almost every aspect of social awareness and cultural dialogue, the basis for insecurity amongst both social elites and the newly respectable and expanding middle classes is evident. Fears of literal biological degeneration were pervasive, triggered initially by media reports on the British army's 'failure', despite technical victory, in the Boer War, widely attributed to the declining physical state of the lower class infantry. This perception of physical decline was in turn routinely linked back to the demoralizing and degenerative effects of urban life, although the 1904 Inter-Departmental Committee on Physical Deterioration concluded there was no evidence of long-term physical deterioration.[6]

3 Solway, *Demography and Degeneration*, 40. The territorial apogee of the Empire was not physically reached until after World War One with the signing of the Treaty of Versailles, but by that time mental uncertainty about its future was well-entrenched.

4 See H. Mayhew, *London Labour and the London Poor* (London: Dover, 1861); Parliamentary Papers, *Royal Commission on the Housing of the Working Classes 1884–5*; W. Booth, *In Darkest England and the Way Out* (London: Funk and Wagnalls, 1890).

5 Solway, *Demography and Degeneration*, xxi; National Council of Public Morals, *Commission of Inquiry into the Declining Birthrate* (London: Chapman and Hall, 1917a).

6 *Report of the Inter-Departmental Committee on Physical Deterioration*, 1904, Cd. 2175; *Royal Commission on the Militia and Volunteers*, 1904, Cd. 2064.

The Committee expressed doubts about the sources of degeneration concerns, rejecting the idea of a direct hereditary taint, suggesting (contrary to the populist angst) that environmental conditions (neglect, malnutrition, poor housing, pollution) were not restricted to the cities, and emphasizing the excesses of parental alcohol and tobacco abuse. For some interest groups such as the campaigners for urban renewal and the mainstream medical profession, this provided ammunition for their own reform agendas leading to improvements in education, health care, and housing, including medical examinations and free meals for school children, and the monitoring of newborns by health officers.[7] It also provided impetus for the emerging Mothercraft movement and social hygiene campaigns targeting sexual ignorance and disease. For others, the Committee's caution in concluding there was no need for any 'large measure of legal assistance' but some refinement of the existing law, signified government reluctance to take positive action.[8] A *Times* editorial cynically concluded that the Committee should simply 'recommend "a single Act of Parliament" to prohibit the sale of cigarettes and tobacco to children below a certain age'.[9]

Those who believed in the redemptive powers of a nurturing environment had plenty of targets for action. If the degrading effect of urban life was indeed the result of ignorance and/or the awfulness of living conditions, these could at least be addressed through incremental legal and social reforms. But the paradigm shift of biological understanding that took place in the late nineteenth century raised the possibility of something more frightening: the spectre of an irredeemable nature. New (or at least wider)[10] understandings of genetics, Mendelism, and Darwinism became the springboard for a different, and potentially more sinister, 'scientific' approach to a variety of social problems. Building on Galton's 1860s work ('It becomes a question of great interest how far moral monstrosities admit of being bred') in the 1890s, Karl Pearson and others developed mathematical principles of biometrics which appeared to give empirical support for eugenics-based understandings of how to deal with the rising social tensions surrounding degeneration.[11] Such work would in turn become central to some of the major sources of legislative activism of the early twentieth century. The Eugenics and Moral Education Society, founded in 1907 and swiftly renamed the Eugenics Education Society, later becoming the Eugenics Society in 1926, was, in Solway's view, 'the organized articulation of neo-Darwinian, educated, middle-class anxieties about the future'.[12] Its members were amongst the most passionate advocates of new laws to isolate and control the lives (and fertility) of 'defective' members

---

7 Education Acts 1906, 1907; Notification of Births Acts 1907.
8 *Report of the Inter-Departmental Committee on Physical Deterioration*, 93.
9 *The Times*, 29 July 1904.
10 Agricultural improvers of the late eighteenth and early nineteenth century were arguably a century ahead of the urban intelligentsia of the late nineteenth century with regard to a practical grasp of genetically sound principles of breeding.
11 F. Galton, 'Hereditary talent and character', part two, *Macmillan's Magazine* 12 (1865): 323.
12 Solway, *Demography and Degeneration*, 37.

of society. Their influence is strongly seen, if not fully implemented, in their evidence to the Royal Commission on the Care and Control of the Feeble-minded and resultant Mental Deficiency Act 1913.[13]

Those who contested the dogmatic assertions of degeneration were forced to concede the strength and impact of the perceived crisis; 'even those Edwardian critics who doubted that eugenics was anything more than a pseudoscientific rationalization for middle- and upper-class elitism nevertheless recognized it was also an increasingly important feature of the pessimism infecting their generation.'[14] The *Edinburgh Review* complained in 1911 that the press and public refused to be dissuaded by any evidence disproving the decline of the race and that the country was obsessed with 'the inveterate superstition of degeneration'.[15]

Obviously, there were other factors feeding this sense of social instability (changes in the status of women and the dissemination of knowledge about birth control, and growing fears about 'weak and indolent' habitual offenders, for example) but the sense of crisis did not fade.[16] By the 1930s degeneration – biological and cultural – was a deeply rooted precept of the British (and European) intelligentsia, reframed by writers such as Ortega-y-Gasset and Leavis as the rise of mass civilization whereby the escalation of the newly literate classes threatened to overwhelm 'civilized' culture with (much degraded) popular manifestations.[17] Even as improvers tackled the environmental dangers of the inner cities a new cause for concern developed amongst the previously comfortable classes: suburbanization. The expansion of housing around the cities, driven by demand for better living conditions and facilitated by improvements in public transport, created the 'ecological catastrophe'[18] whereby people commuted to increasingly white-collar employment which itself generated an erosion of deference. Carey, discussing the rise of these young male 'clerks', notes a study of the Manchester suburbs in the early twentieth century which appeared to demonstrate that 'a new culture of socialism, cycling, free-thinking and the flouting of respectable norms was flourishing among clerks, teachers, shop assistants, telegraphists and other white-collar youth.'[19] Social elites and the 'respectable' middle classes now rubbed shoulders with the common mass of humanity on a daily basis, making it difficult to remain insulated or ignore cultural differences. Even if the lower

---

13 *Royal Commission on the Care and Control of the Feeble-Minded*, vols 1–7 (Cd. 4215–21, London 1908), i–vii; *Royal Commission on the Care and Control of the Feeble-Minded*, vol. 8 (Cd. 4202, London 1908), viii.

14 Solway, *Demography and Degeneration*, 47.

15 Ibid, citing *Edinburgh Review*, July 1911, vol. 214, 153–64. Such fears were also clearly related to the increasing awareness of the growth of Germany as a would-be imperial power.

16 W. Tallack, *Penological and Preventive Principles, With Special Reference to Europe and America*, (London: Wertheimer, Lea and Co., 1899).

17 J. Ortega-y-Gasset, *The Revolt of the Masses* (New York: W. W. Norton, 1932); F. Leavis, *Mass Civilisation and Minority Culture* (Cambridge: Minority Press, 1930).

18 J. Carey, *The Intellectuals and the Masses: Pride and Prejudice Among the Literary Intelligentsia 1880–1939* (London: Faber and Faber, 1992), 49.

19 Ibid, 49.

classes were not literally out breeding their 'superiors' to the extent feared, the geographical and economic changes in living and working conditions for all ensured that intrusion of the masses into previously elite spaces and activities would have a significant impact. Politically, Edwardian radicalism and conservatism were no longer distinguished by class but 'heterogeneous elements often distinct and incompatible'.[20]

The battle against demoralization

Against this background, indecency, increasingly framed as the 'demoralization' of behaviour and culture, became a central concept in the promotion of legal activism by moral campaigners. Whether in the behaviour of the masses and their entertainment, or in the 'new highbrow' society that sought to distinguish itself from such 'degraded culture', indecency was perceived as both symptom and cause of a degenerate populace that produced and thrived on indecent activities and images, corrupting the innocent and the young. In the rhetoric of moral campaigners such as the NVA's Samuel Smith MP:

> When they see the purest and holiest things of life turned into derision, and disgusting licentiousness treated as the normal rule of life, is it likely that their own moral standard will remain high? Is it not certain that the same effects will follow in London as in Paris: that a decadent drama, and, what always accompanies it, a decadent literature, will produce a decadent nation?[21]

At the heart of the indecency agenda was, arguably, a single key component in the cultural equation of the early twentieth century: literacy. The beneficiaries of the Education Act 1870 had come of age. Now a newly empowered force in politics with increasing leisure time and adequate living standards, these progressively rapacious consumers of goods, services, and, crucially, entertainment, constituted a lucrative market that producers sought to exploit. As Alfred Harmsworth (Lord Northcliffe) argued, when launching the *Daily Mail* in 1896: 'A newspaper is to be made to pay. Let it deal with what interests the mass of people.'[22] The people wanted books, but not necessarily 'improving' literature. As the sales and expansion of the popular press and New Journalism demonstrated, they wanted newspapers which reported on sordid crimes, sexual matters, and the reality of their own lives.[23] They wanted evenings out in an atmosphere of conviviality and frivolity (first in the music halls and later in the cinemas; see Chapter Five). In short, this

20 S. Hynes, *The Edwardian Turn of Mind* (Princeton: Princeton University Press, 1968), 7.
21 *Hansard* HC Deb, 15 May 1900, vol. 83 cc.276–308, 277. Samuel Smith MP (1836–1906) was an ardent writer of letters on moral topics, enthusiastic supporter of the National Vigilance Association and persistent opponent to female suffrage. He was Member of Parliament for Flintshire 1886–1906, and also co-founded what is now Edge Hill University.
22 Carey, *The Intellectuals and the Masses*, 6.
23 Rowbotham, *et al.*, *Crime News in Modern Britain*, Chapter Four.

educated mass did not want what the moralists thought they should want. The things they demanded and consumed so enthusiastically were, from the more elevated perspective, indecent and demoralizing, generating 'a lot of patronizing and paternalistic comment' about how the 'evil affected those least able to resist'.[24] In 1887, Samuel Smith, effectively the parliamentary mouthpiece of the NVA, drew the attention of the Home Secretary to the sale of 'indecent' books and pictures, quoting from the *British Weekly*:

> One of the worst and most obtrusive evils of the present time is the sale of indecent books and pictures. Zola's novels . . . were sold in London until recently at a somewhat high price. They have now been reduced to 2s, and may be seen in City book-shops side by side with Bibles.[25]

Causal effect was routinely attached to unacceptable literature, supposedly justifying the repression of literary freedom through the continuation of the Victorian respectability agenda, the imposition of 'public morality', and the desire to eradicate 'poison, pollution and infestation'.[26]

Hynes notes that the metaphor of 'poisonous' publications 'became so common in the discussion of indecent literature that in time it almost ceased to be metaphorical and was used, for example, in ways to suggest that Balzac's *Droll* stories might literally cause convulsions'.[27] The anti-feminist Hugh Stutfield described contemporary fiction as 'erotic, neurotic, and Tommyrotic', whereby the 'excitement of modern life . . . found in the debased emotionalism apparent in so many of the leading writers' of the day could affect the mental health of women (who were of course considered by individuals such as Stutfield to be intellectually inferior even before the consumption of such corrupting literature).[28]

In 1888, Mr Louis Jennings MP asked the Home Secretary, Henry Matthews, to consider

> the necessity of adopting more stringent measures for the suppression of the thieves' literature, and other demoralizing and indecent publications, which are now so extensively circulated among the young, and which led to the Tunbridge Wells murder and so many other crimes.[29]

Jennings was referring to the 'sensational' and 'extraordinary' case reported a month earlier of William Gower, 18 years, and Joseph Dobell, 17 years, indicted for the murder of Bensley Lawrence, an engine driver, by shooting him through the head at a sawmill in Tunbridge Wells after first drawing lots. In the shadow of

---

24 Hynes, *The Edwardian Turn of Mind*, 258.
25 *Hansard* HC Deb, 21 July 1887, vol.317 c.1615.
26 See T. Lewis, 'Legislating morality', 145.
27 Hynes, *The Edwardian Turn of Mind*, 255.
28 H. Stutfield, 'Tommyrotics', *Blackwood's Magazine* 157 (1895): 833–34.
29 *Hansard* HC Deb, 12 November 1888, vol.330 cc.892–2, 892.

the Whitechapel murders, the local community and examining magistrates struggled to comprehend the crime and its motives. Dobell brazenly admitted he had
shot someone to a fellow workmate who refused to believe him. During confes-
sions to the police, both Dobell and Gower threatened to 'pop off' two other men.
As Dobell and Gower showed no remorse and there being no apparent motive, the
point was made that 'the prisoners were in the habit of reading literature of the
"penny dreadful" order, and it is to the perusal of this kind of reading that their
ruin is ascribed.' They were later convicted and sentenced to death.[30]

On 13 November 1888, in a Commons' question to the Home Secretary, Liberal barrister and nonconformist Francis Channing MP, speaking on behalf of
Samuel Smith and the NVA, highlighted concerns that Gower and Dobell had
been addicted to books and newspaper serializations such as *Dick Turpin*, *Var-
ney the Vampire*, *Feast of Blood*, *Sweeney Todd*, and numerous newspaper stories
about the lives of notorious criminals such as the Rugeley poisoner and Burke
and Hare: 'these stories, attractively written, are widely circulated, and read by
enormous numbers of children, and instigate many of them to the commission of
crime.'[31] Matthews conceded that Channing may be quite justified in supposing
that 'there is a large circulation of demoralizing literature'.[32] Thus 'poisonous'
publications were invoked as the scapegoat to explain the inexplicable, foreshadowing the comments, a century later, of Justice Morland in 1993 (rejected by the
Home Office) that exposure to violent videos might have encouraged Venables
and Thompson to kill James Bulger.[33]

Meanwhile, Oxford and Cambridge Universities led a 're-education' initiative
promoted in the popular press (and especially targeting women) to establish community Home Reading Circles mentored by lecturers and teachers who would
stipulate 'appropriate' reading 'to encourage and direct home reading in such a
way as to give zest and purpose to what is now to a great extent aimless, vapid or
without adequate results'.[34] Initially an exercise in improving the intellectualism
of the middle class 'desultory reader' as '*Titbits* and *Scraps* can hardly satisfy
his mind', it was also influenced by the 'demoralizing' rhetoric of educational
reformers and religious moralists, including the Society for the Promotion of
Christian Knowledge. The National Home Reading Circles Union was founded in
April 1889 by Dr J. B. Paton, who asserted that the country was being 'inundated

---

30 *Lancashire Gazette*, 20 October 1888; convicted, *Daily News*, 15 December 1888; execution, *Bury
    and Norwich Post*, 8 January 1889. Also see P. Dunae, 'Penny dreadfuls: Late nineteenth-century
    boys' literature and crime', *Victorian Studies* (winter, 1979): 133–50.
31 *Hansard* HC Deb, 13 November 1888, vol. 330 c.1028. Though it is interesting to note that all
    these examples date from the early Victorian period (the latest being Dr William Palmer's exploits
    in the mid-1850s) rather than any of the more contemporary 'penny dreadfuls' of the late-Victorian
    period. This may of course reflect more on Channing and Smith's adolescence than that of Gower
    and Dobell.
32 *Hansard* HC Deb, 13 November 1888, vol.330 c.1028.
33 *The Independent*, 26 November 1993.
34 Following the American Chautauqua Literary Circle model, *Leeds Mercury*, 28 September 1888;
    also *Leeds Mercury*, 14 July and 8 December 1888; *The Standard*, 3 October 1888.

with a vast flood of wicked, malicious and frivolous literature', and that young people needed to be taught not *how* to read, but *what* to read through temperance societies, the workplace, Sunday schools, and elementary schools.[35] The Bishop of London confirmed the need to help those who 'have acquired the gift of reading' but who might be depraved by the evils of 'aimless, ill-regulated reading'.[36] Ultimately, these reading circles remained a middle-class interest and never really engaged the working-class readership, particularly working-class women.[37]

Mobilizing the morality troops

Purity organizations had lobbied hard in the nineteenth century to push their agendas forward but such activism reached new heights during the Edwardian era. The NVA led the mission to secure the moral health of the nation, patrolling the corridors of power and the streets and venues of working-class life in their attempts to hold back the tide of immorality. In April 1900 the NVA held a conference on 'Public Morals' at Birmingham, which was covered by the *Birmingham Daily Post*. Dr Thomas Savage, pleased that the 'craze for a certain class of novel was on the wane', pontificated on the 'debasing tendency' of print imagery and press advertising: 'Some notice ought to be taken of the newspapers whose columns to a great extent were filled with betting news and advertisements of a very questionable character when read between the lines.'[38] Other moralists were less convinced of the waning of the popularity of demoralizing novels, being concerned that such novels written by 'bad characters' poisoned the mind, thereby shifting the rhetoric from demoralization to 'impurity'. Reverend Sherbrooke Walker asserted that moral health was analogous to physical health, requiring 'wholesome' and 'pure' literature to feed the mind. He called on the 'authorities to be empowered to destroy absolutely, literature which was, perhaps, more pernicious to the mind than bad fish or anything else was to the body'.[39]

William Alexander Coote OBE, moral reform campaigner and co-secretary of the NVA, praised the 'splendid' Birmingham police force who 'had long assisted in the social and moral life of the city . . . creating a sweeter and purer Birmingham'.[40] This reference was to the recent police prosecution of Robert Wells, convicted at Birmingham Assizes in March 1900 for 'occupying a room for the purposes of publishing an obscene libel' and 'publishing a book containing indecent matter'.

35 *Pall Mall Gazette*, 11 July 1889.
36 *Daily News*, 15 April 1889.
37 R. Snape, 'The National Home Reading Union 1889–1930', *Journal of Victorian Culture* 7, no. 1 (2002): 86–100.
38 *Birmingham Daily Post*, 27 April 1900.
39 Ibid.
40 Ibid. The Birmingham police force was well known for its involvement in the moral life of the city; through its work with the Birmingham Police Aided Association, created in 1893 in order to help clothe destitute children and 'to foster friendly and humane relations with the poorest classes of the population' (J. W. Reilly, *An Account of 150 Years of Policing Birmingham* [Birmingham: West Midlands Police, 1989], 42). Reilly states that this organization (which operated until 1968) helped almost a quarter-of-a-million poor children.

Wells, a self-proclaimed professor of the pseudo-science of phrenology, delivered two public lectures at the Birmingham Exchange Rooms, including the euphemistically titled, 'How to be Successful' to 700 adults (half aged between 16 and 20 years). He also sold copies of his book *Marriage Physiologically Considered*. Police Superintendent Van Helden had sent an undercover officer, Detective Sergeant Richardson, to take shorthand notes. At the police court committal, the prosecutor, Mr Stubbins, contended that the book and lectures were a 'mass of filth' and Wells (originally a farmer's labourer) was no scientist.[41] Justice Darling, at the Assizes, considered Richardson's notes, which included 'indecent' references to medical texts and Elizabethan plays, wholly unfit for publication, warning both the press and the public. The defence argued, unsuccessfully, that they were of an 'educational and instructive character' likely to 'prove beneficial to the health of those who heard and studied them'. Wells was sentenced to twelve months imprisonment despite pleading that he had delivered lectures all over the country during the previous twenty-five years and that he had sold thousands of copies of his book, which was first published in 1880 and was then in its twentieth edition.[42] A petition to reduce his sentence was later rejected by the Home Secretary.[43]

The case caused further controversy as not all members of the press took kindly to Darling's veiled threat of censure. Howard Gray, editor of the *Birmingham Daily Argus*, wrote an article bylined 'A Defender of Decency' which included 'scurrilous abuse' criticizing Darling's instruction as an insult to the press.[44] Answering an order of contempt of court at the Queen's Bench Division, Gray was suitably grovelling, condemning the words he had used as 'intemperate, improper, ungentlemanly, and void of the respect due to his Lordship's person and office'. But Gray also stood up for his professional integrity, especially as Arthur A'Beckett was in attendance on behalf of the London District of the newly formed Institute of Journalists: Gray defended 'his strong feeling that sufficient trust had not been placed in the judgement, good taste and discretion of the journalists and press'. A fine of £100 and £25 costs were imposed under threat of imprisonment at Holloway.[45] While Gray's personal indictment of Darling and, more importantly, his implicit application of such criticism to the administration of justice were ill-considered, the case heralded the beginnings of greater tensions and conflicts about the control and censure of the press which would not be resolved for another quarter century.

Undoubtedly, the NVA formed a crucial nucleus of activists in the crusades against indecency, having developed into a genuinely grass-roots organization across the

41 *Birmingham Daily Post*, 16 February 1900.
42 *The Times*, 20 March 1900. Other books by Wells include *Vital Force Series* (London, Oldhams, 1878); *Woman: Her Diseases, and How to Cure Them* (London: Burns, 1880); *A New Illustrated Hand-Book of Phrenology, Physiology and Physiognomy*, (London, Vickers, 1885); and *The Best Food, and How to Cook It* (London, Vickers, 1893).
43 *Leicester Chronicle*, 2 June 1900.
44 *R v Gray* [1900] 2 QB 36.
45 Ibid.

country, but it was by no means the only significant organization involved. There were many other foci for those individuals and organizations involved with the indecency agenda, who all had their own priorities and perspectives but moving in similar political spheres, often with overlaps of personnel such as the LCPPM. Founded in 1885, its chairman was the ubiquitous Coote with his ambitious agenda to tackle the 'flaunting of immorality before persons of all ages and positions in life'.[46] Convinced that 'there is a strong consensus of public opinion of which we are in the centre in our work,' the reality was that general public and political opinion was far more disparate and ambivalent.[47] Coote and his organization were renowned for instigating prosecutions against shop owners for selling indecent pictures, books, and certain 'rubber goods'. From the late 1890s he bombarded the Home Office with evidence from the LCPPM's officers of 'indecent' advertisements and publications, numerous notes on a range of 'indecent' activities including 'disorderly houses', prostitution, 'offensive' plays, and more problematically from a feminist perspective, material relating to sexual health and disease. As Walkowitz observes, campaigns of the late nineteenth century against pornography, vivisection, and regulated prostitution had 'facilitated middle-class women's forceful entry into the world of publicity and politics, where they claimed themselves as part of a public which made sense of themselves through public discourse'.[48] It was to be one of the ironies of later moral activism that these representatives of 'first-wave feminism' would devote so much of their energy to ensuring that other women would be kept in a state of sexual ignorance: the label of indecency was relentlessly attached to any attempts to disseminate information about menstruation, conception, and contraception.

In 1889 Lord Meath had secured the enactment of the Indecent Advertisements Act. s.3 made it an offence to affix or inscribe on 'any building, post, tree etc.,' or to exhibit to public view 'any picture or printed or written matter which is of an indecent or obscene nature', punishable with one month imprisonment or a fine of 40 shillings, or three months where anyone gives or delivers such material to another. The s.5 definition of indecency confirmed that any 'advertisement relating to syphilis, gonorrhoea, nervous debility, or other complaint or infirmity arising from or relating to sexual intercourse shall be deemed to be printed or written matter of an indecent character within the meaning of the Act', thereby including 'improper' medical information relating to abortifacients. However, as the LCPPM pointed out to the Home Office, the statute did not apply to the new practices of printed advertisements in newspapers and leaflets posted to houses and shops of rubber goods and other paraphernalia preventing conception or 'remedies' for 'female ailments'.[49] In January 1899 Francis Channing wrote to *The Times* demanding that action be taken forthwith to

---

46 TNA HO 45/10837/331148, collection of notes and letters from the LCPPM.

47 Ibid.

48 J. Walkowitz, *City of Dreadful Delight: Narratives of Sexual Danger in Late-Victorian London* (Chicago: University of Chicago Press, 1992), 7.

49 TNA HO 45/10837/331148, minutes.

effectually stamp out this evil [which] threaten[s] the nation with the lim-
itless extension of one of the gravest of social dangers. It has now been
demonstrated that an infamous class of persons have been and are making
enormous profits by pandering to debasing and odious crimes – absolutely
destructive of society, by trading on credulity, and by cruel extortion from the
panic-stricken victims they have enticed into correspondence.

Channing was, of course, targeting the press, holding newspaper editors and proprietors culpable for 'the insertion of these disgraceful advertisements' published
in 'hundreds of papers' and 'seen by thousands of people'.[50] Such advertisements
had, however, been appearing in the press for the past 150 years; 'Trowbridge
Pills' aka 'Golden Pills of Life and Beauty' (a concoction probably containing
a high percentage of ferrous sulphate) appeared in newspaper advertisements as
early as 1744.[51] Over 100 years later the pills were still being peddled; an advertisement in the *Bristol Mercury*, 12 November 1853, noted that 'married ladies
will find them particularly serviceable.' This perhaps serves as a good illustration of the 'robust vulgarity' of the eighteenth century compared to the 'delicate
sensibilities' of the late Victorian period. The inclusion of such newspaper advertisements from the mid-eighteenth century onward also raises interesting questions about the perceived readership of such publications; it suggests that a literate
female audience was readily assumed by the purveyors of such goods. The other
alternative that such advertisements were brought to the attention of females by
their spouses or partners seems less likely.

Meath immediately responded that he had included a clause in the Bill prohibiting this but it had been rejected.[52] Meanwhile, Home Office papers reveal that
Permanent Undersecretary Sir Kenelm Digby sought advice on the issue from the
Director of Public Prosecutions, Lord Desart, who emphasized the malevolent
rhetoric: 'The evil with which it was desired to deal had assumed formidable
dimensions.'[53] Desart confirmed the weakness of the legislation in proceedings
he instituted in June 1899 against James Armitage Fox and four others (unreported) for the insertion of immoral advertisements for supposed abortifacients
which on initial medical examination were thought to be harmless concoctions.
The Director of Public Prosecutions tested a charge of inciting women to procure
a miscarriage contrary to section 59 Offences Against the Person Act 1861 but
the indictment was dismissed by the magistrate, and due to the initial medical
evidence deeming the ingredients harmless, the full offence (of attempting to procure a miscarriage) could not be committed. Dissatisfied, Desart then preferred
a Bill to the Central Criminal Court before Mr Justice Darling, who was rapidly

50 *The Times*, 11 January 1899.
51 P. S. Brown, 'Female pills and the reputation of iron as an abortifacient', *Medical History* 21 (1977): 294.
52 *The Times*, 12 January 1899.
53 HO 144/192/A466557 Indecent publications, etc: Reports on various publications and questions of prosecutions (1888–1899), letters and minutes.

developing a reputation as *the* judge for cases involving immorality and publication.[54] Darling approved the convictions because during the trial it was shown that the drugs could in fact cause harm therefore incitement could be proved, but he also affirmed that no offence would be committed by advertisers and sellers if the drugs advertised had no harmful effect. The 'evil' therefore 'remained untouched by the proceedings'.[55] Desart recommended legislative reform focussing the minds of the Home Office personnel on the meaning of 'indecent' and whether it should be limited to publications where the content was obscene or should also incorporate publications about sexual matters more generally.

In 1899, frustrated with the Home Office's sluggishness, the NVA's parliamentary supporters (Channing, Sir John Kennaway, and Samuel Smith) brought yet another Bill to reform the Indecent Advertisements Act, which prompted Gibson Bowles MP to complain with some apparent weariness: 'I repeat my protest in this case. I did hope that hon. members would abstain from the practice of bringing in these Bills at the public expense.'[56] In July 1900, Smith delivered a scathing diatribe in the Commons seeking to progress the reform. He was highly critical of the Metropolitan Police and the Home Secretary for not maintaining the 'cleanliness' of the capital's streets and business premises, and not enforcing the OPA 1857: 'London is infested with low illustrated papers full of indecent pictures, these are largely circulated amongst school children.' Smith had shown a magistrate '16 pictures of women in a nude position, calculated to have an injurious effect on the minds of young men in London' but was advised that no law had been broken. Contemptuous of any 'pretence' that such images were artistic he even criticized W.H. Smith for becoming more lax in the literature it sold and advocated the removal of 'penny in the slot' machines that showed females in stages of undress: 'I bring these evils before the House assured of the sympathy of the Home Secretary.'[57] Sir Matthew Ridley (who had replaced Sir Henry Matthews as Home Secretary) did infer some sympathy, but he strongly defended the actions of his office and the Metropolitan Police. Ridley doubted that the law could do more to 'clean' the streets and agreed that a publication sent to him by Smith comprised 'not very beautiful pictures', but neither was it in his view obscene. He criticized Smith's partiality in 'deciding his own standard of what was indecent and obscene'.[58] In support, H. J. Wilson confirmed, 'None of us expect to make people moral by Act of Parliament,' but of course that was exactly what Smith sought.[59] Meanwhile, the Home Office continued to work on its own draft Bill but never got beyond a

---

54 Despite regularly hearing trials on the Midlands Circuit, Central Criminal Court, and later appeals at the Court of Criminal Appeal, and making significant comment about the role of the press in reporting cases of immorality, especially regarding *in camera* cases, there is no such reference in his biography: D. Walker-Smith, *The Life of Lord Darling* (London: Cassell, 1938).

55 TNA HO 144/192/A466557C Indecent publications, etc: Reports on various publications and questions of prosecutions (1888–1899), letters and minutes.

56 *Hansard* HC Deb, 25 July 1899, vol.75 c.253.

57 *Hansard* HC Deb, 13 July 1900, cc.1539–46 passim.

58 Ibid, cc.1555–56.

59 Ibid, c.1564.

single amending clause: 'anyone who writes or publishes, or causes or procures to be written or published [an indecent publication] be punished with a maximum twelve-month sentence of imprisonment.' Concerns about its potential application to the editors and proprietors of the press ensured its failure to progress.[60]

The moralists regrouped, becoming even more politically active. The democratization of politics as a result of the expanding franchise ensured that MPs, and the government which relied upon their support, were increasingly pressured by concerns about 'public opinion', however nebulous and contradictory that opinion may have been, or what exactly constituted 'public'. Politics was no longer the preserve of elite interest groups but an exercise in mass participation, most obviously at election time, but also through legislative activism and local politics. The LCPPM and the NVA now 'served as funnels directing religious, feminist and respectable opinion to the Home Office and local government and their voice was very powerful'.[61] In October 1900, with representatives in twenty-eight London boroughs, Alfred Barry, Vice-Chairman of the LCPPM, wrote to *The Times* canvassing support for those standing in the Borough Council Elections who would use all legal powers available 'for the cause of morality'.[62] Letters to individual MPs, so easy to ignore, were augmented by more intensive forms of mass parliamentary lobbying, although as seen earlier, at times this could prove counterproductive. Mr H.C. Richards MP complained in Parliament to the Attorney General about the 'continued distribution of objectionable papers among Members of the House by the NVA'.[63] Letters to the press, along with the traditional methods of public meetings and rallies, became increasingly important in efforts to widen awareness and attract new members. In this increasingly complex political environment, moral campaigners were making their voices heard and could claim entitlement to access, if not influence, when legal decisions were to be made.

The troops were finally marshalled with the launch, in 1901, of the National Social Purity Crusade under the umbrella of the National Council of Public Morals (hereafter NCPM). This was coordinated through the Conference of Representatives of London Societies Interested in Public Morality, which included the NVA, the LPCCM – which by 1911 was renamed the PMC – the Social Purity Alliance, the Salvation Army, and the Society for the Rescue of Young Women and Children. The PMC was at the vanguard of this campaign. James Marchant (formerly of the NVA) became its secretary, and the Bishop of London, the Victorian moralist James Winnington-Ingram, its president. Opinion is divided on its success. Hynes argues that the consortium achieved little until renamed the PMC, when its *Manifesto on Public Morals* was published, commenting that it

---

60 TNA HO 144/192/A466557C/32.

61 Bristow, *Vice and Vigilance*, 202. However, such power wielded by moral organizations appears to have been something of a metropolitan phenomenon; see Chapters Six and Seven in this book for an examination of actual prosecutions in a provincial town – the figures do not seem to reflect a high level of engagement by such societies in the provinces.

62 *The Times*, 31 October 1900.

63 *Hansard* HC Deb, 24 May 1900, vol.83, c.1111.

was 'loud and long in its failing' albeit securing 'some important battles against pernicious literature'.[64] Bristow is more positive, highlighting the role of the PMC in providing a platform and an 'ambitious public campaign in 1908' to promote its clearly stated aim of 'the regeneration of the race – spiritual, moral and physical'.[65] Hunt distinguishes its 'purity pledge' from the temperance pledge, opining it is 'difficult to get a sense of the impact of the purity rhetoric' despite 'the large numbers of tracts and pamphlets that probably reached millions of adolescents and young adults' identifying 'its mix of moral uplift, incitement of sexual anxieties and warning of national catastrophe that were likely to have compounded feelings of sexual trepidation, especially when linked to the enforced sexual ignorance that afflicted so many'.[66]

The legal arsenal

As identified earlier, while law was the preferred weapon of the moral campaigners, many were frustrated that the OPA 1857 was not effectively enforced and that, technically, words such as 'indecent' and 'immoral' had no relevance under the Act, except in so far as their repetition could substantiate that the tendency of a book or picture was to 'deprave and corrupt'. The NVA's interpretation of the law was not always embraced by the courts, or indeed by the government. Lord Mount-Temple, arguing in 1888 for stronger laws to control indecent publications and photographs, noted that 'stipendiary magistrates in London had been unwilling to give the official meaning to the legal terms "obscene" and "indecent" the meaning that the Vigilance Associations contended for,' highlighting the promotional strategies adopted where the 'NVA often prosecuted a proper case when they did not bring success, for the sake of attracting public attention to these evil practices'.[67] This could result in subtle distinctions as Chief Inspector Drew of Scotland Yard made clear in his evidence to the 1908 Joint Select Committee on Lotteries and Indecent Advertisements: 'What in the opinion of the police is the difference between a photograph of an obscene nude person, and one which might be considered indecent, although not obscene, and that is where the hair is clearly shown on the private parts.'[68] This distinction subtly reflects the view of 'highbrow' art as in classical statuary and 'lowbrow' pornography, and it resonates with the (unproven) allegations of John Ruskin being shocked by the sight of his new wife's public hair on their wedding night. Moral campaigners were understandably reluctant to accept such nuances. If something was, in their eyes, immoral or offensive it was automatically 'demoralizing' and indecent and *should* be illegal. The limits of the 'deprave and corrupt' condition would thus be

---

64 Hynes, *The Edwardian Turn of Mind*, 289.
65 Bristow, *Vice and Vigilance*, 144–5.
66 Hunt, *Governing Morals*, 177.
67 *Hansard* HL Deb, 27 July 1888, vol.329 cc.620–5, 621.
68 *Joint Select Committee on Lotteries and Indecent Advertisements*, 1908, Minutes of Evidence, para. 436.

tested and if possible expanded through precedent to encompass, implicitly if not explicitly, indecency. If (and when) the OPA 1857 failed to deliver the desired results, it merely became confirmation in the eyes of many activists that a new law was needed.

Major prosecutions under the OPA 1857 were comparatively rare but the Act provided a useful tool for the seizure of a huge range of material. When the SSV ceased activity in 1880 it had accumulated more than '385,000 obscene prints and photographs; 80,000 books and pamphlets; five tons of other printed matter; 28,000 sheets of obscene songs and circulars; stereotypes, copper plates and the like', all designated, if not successfully prosecuted, by the Society as 'obscene'.[69] When the NVA took over the task it was intent on stemming the tide of indecent foreign literature, particularly that from France as illustrated in the 1888 prosecution of Henry Vizetelly, the English publisher of Emile Zola's novels (and other translations of French novels). On 10 August 1888 Vizetelly was charged with publishing an obscene libel at Bow Street Magistrates' Court. Citing passages from *Nana* in support, Herbert Asquith, prosecuting counsel, argued that 'no decent-minded person would say that their publication would not be detrimental to public morals.'[70] The case was committed to the Central Criminal Court where the Solicitor-General, Bodkin-Poland, read more than twenty selected passages from *La Terre* to the jury to support his contention that the book was 'filthy from beginning to end'.[71] The Recorder said this case was different to *Hicklin* where 'the object of the publication was no doubt extremely good', here the 'book was published for the sake of gain . . . deliberately done in order to deprave the minds of persons who might read the books'. Vizetelly changed his plea to guilty and was fined £100. In May 1889, he was again prosecuted for publishing Zola's works despite expurgating some of the offending text. The Recorder repeated his warning about 'spreading impure literature' which 'did a great deal of mischief to a large class of persons'. Vizetelly pleaded guilty but had broken his recognizance of £200 from the previous trial not to publish any more books and so was sentenced to three months in prison.[72]

Vizetelly's experience demonstrates both the rising power of the moral campaigners and the dangers of obscenity laws for those who sought to disseminate material that went against conventional morality. However, as seen in *Vizetelly*, it is often difficult to discern from newspaper and the Old Bailey reports the exact legal basis of such prosecutions. Prosecutors were quick to use the terminology of *indecency, filth*, and *immorality*, which was automatically reproduced by the court reporters, even where the true legal standard being applied was that the work must

---

69 Bristow, *Vice and Vigilance*, 49. The Society had obviously been proactive in this area for several decades; *The Era*, 30 July 1843, reported that 'In the five years between 1839–43 the SSV's officers seized 37,186 obscene prints and pictures . . . 4,598 books and pamphlets . . . besides large stocks of letter-press and obscene songs, in sheets, and of snuff-boxes and other articles with infamous devices.'

70 *The Times*, 11 August 1888.

71 *The Times*, 1 November 1888.

72 *The Times*, 31 May 1889.

be obscene within the meaning of the OPA 1957 and *Hicklin*. Evidently in some low-level cases, where legal argument would have been limited, the indecency campaigners had, in fact if not in law, succeeded in rendering indecency itself the offence, merely by repetition of implicit 'indecency/immorality equals obscenity' arguments.

Furthermore, the OPA 1857 was not the only legal weapon against indecency. While in some reports the prosecution was clearly brought under the 1857 Act, others indicate that the common law or other statutory provisions were utilized.[73] For example, from 1901 to 1910 more than a dozen cases were prosecuted at the Old Bailey using a range of charges, including 'unlawfully conspiring with other persons to obtain money by false pretences with intent to defraud';[74] 'publishing, selling and uttering an obscene libel';[75] 'unlawfully conspiring to publish obscene pamphlets, books, and libels';[76] and 'unlawfully publishing and sending obscene libels, to wit, certain obscene photographs, prints and a certain obscene book, and conspiring with others to publish obscene libels'.[77] These demonstrate not only the ingenuity of the prosecutors in identifying other potential offences such as conspiracy, the fraudulent obtaining of money from sales and the use of advertisements to directly assist in the commission of a crime, but also the complexity of drafting an appropriate charge to prevent a successful defence. As Common Serjeant Sir Frederick Bosanquet confirmed, 'Really the common law is (though people will not believe it), as Lord Coleridge said, a very elastic thing in the sense that the old principles cover new modes of committing crime.'[78]

To the extent that prevention was often better than prosecution after the event, the Customs Consolidation Act 1876 remained a useful tool in the moral arsenal. As Lord Chancellor Lord Halsbury pointed out in 1888, prosecutions could result in public attention being drawn to 'that which had been circulated only by the hundred' such that 'its circulation was increased by many thousands.'[79] The Customs Consolidation Act, on the contrary, contained prohibitions and restrictions on imports, with provisions for forfeiture. In addition to the usual customs' targets of coin, spirits, and snuff, the table of prohibitions under s.42 included 'indecent or obscene prints, paintings, photographs, books, cards, lithographic

---

73 For example see *R v Avery, The Times*, 4 October 1900; *R v Bocca, The Times*, 14 April 1904; *R v Wegel, The Times*, 3 August 1905, all County of London Sessions; *R v Marsham et al.*, Bow Street Police Court, *The Times*, 17 February 1902; *R v Jacombe*, West Ham Police Court, *The Times*, 4 October 1906.

74 *OBP* online, 1900, New Court, trial of Ernest Caxton, convicted and sentenced to eighteen months hard labour, and William Brooks, convicted and sentenced to twelve months hard labour (t19000625–423423).

75 *OBP*, Central Criminal Court, trial of Isabel Thomson, found not guilty (t19000625–429429).

76 *OBP*, Central Criminal Court, trial of Ella Rowland, Anna Sinclair, Allan Laidlaw, Charles Coleman, Edward Coleman, all pleaded guilty and sentenced to six months, nine months or to enter into a recognizance (t19020407–326).

77 *OBP*, Central Criminal Court, trial of Edward de Marney, found guilty. Case referred to Crown Cases Reserved, full transcript available (t19061022–58).

78 Ibid.

79 *Hansard* HL Deb, 27 July 1888, vol.329 cc.620–5, 625.

or other engravings, or any other indecent or obscene articles'. This was clearly wide enough to satisfy the most ardent moral campaigner, if the authorities could be persuaded to enforce it to their satisfaction.

Post Office legislation provided an additional line of defence and enforcement. The Post Office Act 1870 authorized the Postmaster General, with the approval of the Treasury, to make regulations:

> preventing the sending or delivery by post of indecent or obscene prints, paintings, photographs, lithographs, engravings, books, or cards, or of other indecent or obscene articles, or of letters, newspapers, supplements, publications, packets, or post cards having thereon, or on the covers thereof, any words, marks, or designs of an indecent, obscene, libellous, or grossly offensive character.

Under s.4 Post Office (Protection) Act 1884 it became an offence to send matter of the same character through the post, or to send a postal packet 'having thereon any words, marks or designs of an indecent, obscene or grossly offensive character'. The powers were later consolidated in the Post Office Act 1908,[80] which further provided in s.17 that if any postal packet posted or sent by post contravened the Act, or any warrant or regulations made thereunder, 'the transmission thereof may be refused, and the formity with packet may, if necessary, be detained and opened in the Post Office'. Section 56 gave power to the Secretary of State to order a warrant for the opening, detaining, and delaying of posted letters if they were grossly indecent. Thus the Indecent Advertisements Act 1889 in conjunction with the Postmaster General's powers provided a useful weapon against another of the 'demoralizing' tendencies of the period, the spread of information relating to sexual health and contraception. As much of this material was imported, it could be intercepted; if displayed, it could be the subject of prosecution. As illustrated by the case of Wells earlier, obscene libel under the common law, older statutory measures such as s.4 Vagrancy Act 1824, and powers under the Town Police Clauses Act 1847 (extended to all urban districts by s.171 of the Public Health Act 1875) continued to be used in the pursuit of indecency well into the twentieth century. The use of such measures was confirmed by Sir Robert Hunter, Solicitor to the Post Office, in evidence to the 1908 Joint Select Committee.[81]

However, the indistinguishable fusion of indecency with obscenity resulting in the suppression and censure of indecent, as opposed to purely obscene, material sent through the post, was causing concern as revealed in correspondence

---

80 Postmaster general's powers, section 16; offences relating to sending through the post, section 63.
81 Confirmed by Sir Robert Hunter, Solicitor to the Post Office, evidence to the Joint Select Committee on Lotteries and Indecent Advertisements, Parliamentary Papers (1908) *Report from the Joint Select Committee on Lotteries and Indecent Advertisements, Together with the Proceedings of the Committee, Minutes of Evidence, and Appendices* (London: HMSO), 1908, Minutes of Evidence, paras. 49–50.

between Kenelm Digby at the Home Office and Sir Spencer Walpole, Secretary of the Post Office.[82] In 1897 Walpole intimated that Her Majesty's Government should make up its mind on what matter should be intercepted, requesting that the meaning of 'indecent' at least be partially defined in statute and the Postmaster General's warrant be extended to stop postal packets sent by and to dealers in 'indecent wares', who should be punished with twelve months' maximum imprisonment or a £10 fine. Walpole drafted an amendment to the Post Office Act defining 'obscene matter' as including 'any indecent or obscene print, painting, picture, photograph, book pamphlet, paper or written or printed matter'; but because of the proposed penalty suggested that the power to stop such obscene post be transferred to the Home Secretary. Digby agreed that while the Postmaster General 'would hold public opinion on his side', the proposed transfer of power would cause legal arguments about its exercise, especially 'at times of political excitement'. He recommended that either the Postmaster General retain the enhanced power, or, as it would be 'unwise' to raise the issue in Parliament, 'let sleeping dogs lie'. Walpole suggested a compromise that the Home Secretary could direct the Postmaster General to open and stop mail where 'satisfied' that it was of an obscene matter. Typically, the Home Secretary's power was triggered at the request of the Commissioner of the Metropolitan Police. In a folder marked 'Confidential No.16' there is a summary of the number of warrants issued 1891–1898. While these are generally in single figures, the number of cases and amount of materials stopped for each year increases, from one case in 1892 to twenty-four cases listed together as one warrant in 1898. In 1896 two warrants were listed, but one related to the seizure of 12,630 open packets sent by Charles Carrington from a bookshop in Paris and, ironically, whose other publications are listed in the 'Publications Today' section of *The Times* – though there is no public report of the seizure.[83] In 1895 one warrant relates to more than 4,000 closed letters stopped or intercepted from the addresses of a known gang of dealers in Amsterdam. It is clear that the extent and questionable nature of the Home Secretary's existing discretion was not well known, even in Westminster, as the law officers advised 'it is undesirable to discuss,' this power and it should not be raised in the public domain. They also advised that no further delegated power should be given to the Post Office. In 1898 the Home Secretary concurred, 'I am not prepared to introduce legislation'.[84]

The futility of stopping the flood of indecent literature is apparent in a letter sent in 1899 by Walpole's replacement, Sir George Murray, regarding the large numbers of indecent catalogues addressed to undergraduates at Oxford University stopped by the Postmaster General at Oxford post office. Murray was of the

82 TNA HO 45/9752/A59329 Indecent Publications etc.: Sending obscene matter through the post. Suggested legislation (1897–1898).
83 *The Times*, 25 March 1897, 27 April 1898, and 13 May 1898. Douglas argues that he should be as well known for his publication of classical literature as for erotica; P. Douglas, 'Charles Carrington and the Commerce of Risque', *International Journal of the Book*, 4 (2004): 63–76.
84 TNA HO 45/9752/A59329.

opinion that 'if full grown men (and women for that matter) choose to indulge in unwholesome tastes of this kind' they should be allowed to do so, though school-boys and undergraduates needed to be protected by the law from the temptations of 'gratifying the testes to which Bourier [distributor of the indecent material] and his class pander so successfully'.[85] A successful attempt to protect enterprising young schoolboys was the Treasury prosecution of William Reid in February 1902 'for unlawfully and knowingly sending through the Post Office certain obscene prints, books and advertisements and for unlawfully and scandalously publishing and uttering certain lewd, wicked and obscene prints at Eastbourne on October 19 1901'. Reid was found to have nearly 250 orders and quantities of advertisements on his premises. He had also been acquitted in 1900 for selling certain books of an 'improper kind'. A small boy at a prep school in Eastbourne had seen an advertisement in a comic for a 'Magic revealer' (a small magnifying glass), price 6d, and, unfortunately for Reid, ordered one on school notepaper. The boy was seen opening the package on his desk, revealing 'a small charm containing an indecent photograph and a bundle of most indecent and suggestive advertisements and catalogues' referring to obscene book photographs and extracts from unexpurgated editions of Boccaccio's *Decameron* and *The Heptameron*.[86] Mr Kemp, for the defence, submitted that 'mere vulgarity and bad taste did not constitute a criminal offence' and that Reid had no knowledge that he was sending his material to a schoolboy. Mr Justice Grantham confirmed that this was exactly the kind of situation that Cockburn alluded to in *Hicklin* as it would 'deprave and corrupt those who minds are open to such immoral influence and into whose hands a publication of this sort may fall'. As Reid had received repeated warnings he was sent to prison with hard labour for six months.[87]

Nevertheless, by the early twentieth century, the indecency campaigners were coming to the conclusion that the available laws were substantively inadequate and lacked appropriate enforcement. Frustration with the limitations of the OPA 1857 was apparent, even after the 'success' of *Vizetelly*. The NVA's interpretation of the law was not always embraced by the courts, or indeed, by the government.[88] Samuel Smith openly complained in Parliament that:

> the Home Office and the Home Secretary do not enforce Lord Campbell's Act as it ought to be enforced . . . London is infested with low illustrated papers full of indecent pictures. . . . The law is strong enough, but I contend it is not put into force. It surprises me that London magistrates refuse to convict in such cases. The Home Secretary has seen some pictures which were brought before the Lord Mayor, and which he refused to proceed against. The silly argument is used that they are works of art.[89]

85 Ibid., letter, 8 December 1899.
86 The 'small charm' may have concealed a Stanhope microview – see Chapter Five.
87 *The Times*, 21 February 1902.
88 *Hansard* HL Deb, 27 July 1888, vol.329 cc.620–5, 621.
89 *Hansard* HC Deb, 13 July 1900, vol.85 cc.1.475–572, 1546–7.

In 1901, asked whether he would instruct the police to prosecute 'obscene muto-scopic pictures', the Home Secretary, Charles Ritchie, replied:

> There are many pictures which may be suggestive and objectionable, but which are not so indecent or obscene as to afford grounds for a success-ful prosecution, and as a result of inquiries I understand that the exhibitions referred to are of this nature.[90]

A few years later, asked about the 'open sale of immoral literature', Mr Akers-Douglas' assurance that the matter was 'under the constant supervision of the police, and they inform me that they believe that at no time has there ever been less trafficking in immoral literature in London than there is at present' serves to underline just how much the indecency problem lay in conflicting perceptions rather than substantive law.[91]

Conclusion

Moralists were beset on all sides: by mass popular culture aimed at the new, con-sumerist, participatory lower classes, and by the failure of elite culture to 'hold the line' for civilized values. The intellectuals, writers, and artists of the early twentieth century, far from joining the cause against the 'demoralization' of the arts, took what must have been, to those seeking reassurance by clinging to the comfortable artistic life of polite Victorian society, the most unhelpful and dis-turbing option, a step into 'modernist' forms of expression which deliberately sought to exclude the masses by becoming unconventional, intellectually inac-cessible, even outrageous.[92] Thus, moral campaigners found themselves battling not only the popular press and the new realms of common entertainment, but also the intellectual elites represented by the likes of D. H. Lawrence and James Joyce. In terms of 'contested ground', this was difficult and complex terrain to negotiate, and the choices open to moral activists not always obvious. Countering genetic degeneration by means of eugenics was controversial, difficult in practice, and not entirely morally unambiguous. Dealing with degeneration by tackling socio-environmental factors required extensive State or philanthropic funding and, ideally and probably crucially, governmental participation – and besides, it tended to be the established domain of experts and professions. Some morality campaigners sought to be active citizens and professional experts, but more often, indecency campaigning provided a route of participation for those – particularly women, but also lower-middle-class men – who were not necessarily welcomed into other, more specialized, areas of activism. Although little was accomplished by way of new laws at the turn of the twentieth century, the indecency campaign-ers had achieved a lot in a few years by establishing in the public consciousness

90 *Hansard* HC Deb, 6 May 1901, vol.93 cc.756–7, 757.
91 *Hansard* HC Deb, 1 June 1905, vol.147 cc.434–5, 434.
92 See Carey, *The Intellectuals and the Masses.*

art, literature, and a whole range of public entertainment as a 'serious and growing evil', meeting relatively little opposition in the political and legal establishment. On the ground they had some success in convincing local magistrates and police who were morally and politically empowered to use the very wide-ranging laws that had already been at their disposal, and with the help of the vigilance groups, would become increasingly robust in their use. But despite some strong evidence that existing laws could be effective in supressing objectionable material and behaviour, the moralists wanted more, and as highlighted in the next chapter, it was the Joint Select Committee on Lotteries and Indecent Advertisements in 1908 that was their next target.

4 A real or imagined enigma? 'Stemming the tide of corruption'

Indecency 1908–1960

Introduction

As evidenced in the previous chapter, the efforts of the moral crusaders in the early years of the twentieth century show how existing legal provisions could be effectively utilized to suppress objectionable material and behaviour. Despite such relative success, NVA sympathizers and others continued to make further demands in Parliament for stricter statutory measures to control indecency, as well as stronger enforcement action. Proposals to amend the Indecent Advertisements Act 1889 had failed, but given that on average Parliament administered some 300 Bills each year[1] the chances of securing an enactment without significant Home Office sponsorship were slim. In the overheated climate of early twentieth-century politics, calls on the government to 'do something' about a vast array of social issues and problems were numerous and the most effective response from the perspective of besieged ministers was often to resort to Royal Commissions and Select Committee inquiries. These provided a valuable opportunity for campaigners to make their concerns heard and could be usefully exploited to press for additions to the statute book. In the context of indecency, almost as soon as the Indecent Advertisements Act 1889 was enacted, campaigners, in particular the NVA, sought to extend its provisions to control the newspaper and magazine press.

After almost two decades of continued pressure from the vociferous 'moral minority', the Government finally relented and commissioned a Joint Select Committee on Lotteries and Indecent Advertisements in 1908. This was a watershed moment as far as the moral campaigners were concerned, and it therefore marks the starting point of this chapter. Despite recommendations made to assuage their concerns, ultimately the tangible consequences, in terms of legislative outcome of the Committee's review, was relatively small, even negligible. However, the evidence presented and subsequent report provide a snapshot of both the state

---

1 For example in 1901, 294 bills; 1904, 302 bills; 1911, 373 bills, see PP Arrangements of the Papers of the House of Commons and of the Papers Presented by Command (1901: 373); (1904: 365), (1911: 348).

of the law and the perspectives of significant actors in the increasingly heated public debates over indecency and 'demoralization', whilst also showing, through absence, some serious limits to that debate. The inquiry exposes the dogmatic efforts of the moral campaigners to prosecute and stamp out expression of indecent ideas, revealing the continuing contestation about the meaning of indecency and what should properly constitute indecent material. The boundaries between the more narrow legal classification of indecency and indecent publications became progressively blurred, subsumed into the campaigners' generalizations of immorality. The moralists were of course intransigently convinced of the actuality and reality of an increasingly immoral world, but the law often proved intractable and lawmakers were (along with much of the police) reluctant to step into what they perceived to be a more imagined than practised 'immoral' world.

More than any other statute of the time, the Indecent Advertisements Act 1889 epitomizes such tensions. From the point of view of the moral campaigners there were numerous problems with the Act in terms of instigating prosecutions. 'Indecent advertisements' were very narrowly defined in the Act, which specifically referred to any advertisement 'relating to syphilis, gonorrhoea, nervous debility, or any complaint or infirmity arising from or relating to sexual intercourse' as of an indecent or obscene nature. The statute also made the affixer of offensive material a less important figure in the immorality haze with a fine of up to £2 or one month in gaol with or without hard labour; the supplier of the indecent material could be fined up to £5 or three months with or without hard labour. To the moralists' frustration, finding the name and location of the supplier could often prove extremely difficult. The main problem, however, was that the Act did not apply to advertisements in newspapers or magazines. Sir Edward Troup (Permanent Under-Secretary of State) reiterated this in a note dated 11 November 1916 to Sir H. C. Monro, Secretary of the Local Government Board, about the report of the Royal Commission on Venereal Diseases, stating that 'the Indecent Advertisements Act 1889 applies to adverts of this class in leaflets and posters, but not in newspapers'.[2]

Metropolitan Police records make it clear that the 1889 Act quickly proved relatively ineffectual and difficult to prosecute. A summary produced on 14 February 1890 of Metropolitan Superintendents' divisional reports on the working of the Act stated that 'quack doctors and others affected by the operation of the Act, are evidently aware of its provisions, and have so modified the wording of their advertisements as to avoid infringing it'. The report does state some positive aspects, in that 'the posting of bills in urinals has also greatly fallen off' and 'the act has practically abated the annoyance formerly caused to foot passengers by the distribution of indecent pamphlets within the streets' – the latter phenomenon noted especially in C (St James), D (Marylebone), E (Holborn), J (Bethnal Green), and N (Islington) divisions.[3]

---

2 TNA MH 55/530 Venereal Disease Act, 1917: prohibition of treatment of venereal diseases by unqualified persons, and the advertising of remedies (1917).
3 TNA MEPO 2/237 Indecent publications: Suppression of (1889–1890).

There were also problems with the interpretation of the law, with several examples of leaflets advertising a cure for 'nervous debility' being found by magistrates not to be indecent advertisements. On 14 November 1890 a letter to the Commissioner of the Metropolitan Police from Dr Leslie Phillips, Hon. Secretary of the Medical Defence Union (based in Birmingham), claimed that the Act was 'in this city a dead letter, there not having been a single case of proceedings in the Birmingham police court under it since 1st January last when the Act came into operation'.[4] Similarly, the British Medical Association (BMA) reported in the *British Medical Journal* (hereafter, *BMJ*) of 3 December 1892 that 'it is found in practice that so serious are the defects of that Act that it may be much doubted whether it has in any degree effected the objects for which it was passed.'[5]

Similar problems persisted with regard to the illicit sale of abortifacients. The *BMJ* of 7 February 1920 reported on a criminal case that had recently concluded at the Old Bailey where two men had stood accused of procuring abortions, commenting that 'the need for strengthening the law as to the advertisement and sale of abortifacient drugs has long been urged by the British Medical Association.'[6] Abortion was an offence under the Offences Against the Person Act 1861 (sections 58 and 59). Both the act of performing an abortion and the supply of drugs or instruments to procure the same were illegal, but the sale of often medically dangerous remedies to procure a miscarriage was not dealt with specifically either in this Act or the Indecent Advertisements Act 1889. With regard to the latter Act, advertisers easily evaded prosecution by offering preparations for vague and unspecified 'female irregularities'.[7]

The PMC had tried repeatedly to get the Indecent Advertisements Act 1889 amended to include the advertising of illegal abortifacients, but despite several attempts hampered by the outbreak of war, no significant amendments were passed. The British Medical Association managed to get one treatment placed on the Poisons Schedule in April 1917: diachylon, which caused lead poisoning leading to miscarriage of a foetus, but which could also cause permanent blindness. Following this limited victory, the British Medical Association campaigned with renewed vigour to ban the advertisement of abortifacients, but without much success. It is also interesting to note that in 1929 the Association refused an offer to cooperate with the PMC and send a joint deputation to the Home Secretary to campaign against the continuation of advertisements for both abortifacients and 'appliances for preventing conception'.[8] In an editorial entitled 'The Association and Public Morals', the British Medical Association argued that whilst abortion was a criminal offence and therefore a matter for the police, contraception was 'an open question' and 'a practice which had some association with medicine, but it had association also with eugenics, morality,

---

4 Ibid.
5 'Objectionable advertisements', *BMJ* 2, no. 1,666 (3 December 1892), 1,248.
6 'The sale and advertisement of abortifacients', *BMJ* 1, no. 3,084 (7 February 1920), 192.
7 'Abortion, therapeutic and criminal', *BMJ* 2, no. 3,756 (31 December 1932), 1,190–91, 1,191.
8 'The Association and public morals', *BMJ* 2, no. 3,599 (28 December 1929), 270–6.

and even religion'.[9] Mr Turner, a supporter of the PMC, replied in its defence
that the PMC 'had expressed no opinion on the practice of contraception. What it
was out against was the public exhibition of pamphlets and appliances to all and
sundry' – yet another example of the private/public dichotomy often exhibited by
such moralists, especially with regard to issues of class.[10]

Similar problems arose with regard to advertisements offering cures for venereal disease. Since the Boer War, many companies had seen an opportunity to
profit from the proffering of 'cures' for gonorrhoea, syphilis, and other sexually
related diseases. As a result there was a proliferation of advertisements in newspapers (not necessarily always those in the lower ranks of respectability – William
Shadforth, proprietor of Shadforth's Prescription Services, advertised in *The
Times* during January 1915). However, reticence to discuss this subject publi-
cally led to considerable problems with the rapid increase of sexually transmitted
diseases resulting from the non-combative activities of numerous British soldiers
whilst on the Western Front. A Royal Commission on Venereal Diseases was commissioned between 1913 and 1916; it reported some of its preliminary findings in
June 1914.[11] A document detailing the debate following these preliminary findings
is held in TNA and it throws an interesting light on the response of the government and civil service.[12]

Sir Almeric Fitzroy (Chief Clerk to the Privy Council, 1898–1923) remarked
that the Commission wanted to make the treatment of venereal disease by the
medically unqualified a penal offence, but recognized that this would cause dif-
ficulties in 'the effective operation of such a law' – so instead recommended opt-
ing for the banning of any advertisement offering a cure for venereal disease. The
Commission and the government were particularly incensed by carefully worded
advertisements such as that published in the *Daily News and Leader* on 25 October 1916 by William Shadforth:

RASH, PUSTULAR ERUPTIONS, HARD OR SOFT SORES, SWOLLEN
GLANDS (Formula 606.) (Deeper Seated Blood Impurities) *Potas. Soda,
Iron, Quinine, Mercury, Iodide, Mercuric Chloride, Nux Vomica, Stillingia,
Jacoranda, Sarsaparilla.* In tablets, 1s 1½d (36), 2s 8d (144). With directions.

Such preparations, whilst undoubtedly containing ingredients used by the medical profession to treat and cure venereal disease – such as mercuric chloride, nux
vomica (strychnine) and stillingia (for syphilis) – were obviously dangerous if
taken incorrectly or to excess. The main argument against the existence of such
advertisements was medical, although there were also large doses of both moral

9   Ibid., 274.
10 Ibid.
11 For further details of this commission and its aftermath, see D. Evans, 'Tackling the 'hideous
    scourge': The creation of the venereal disease treatment centres in early twentieth-century Britain',
    Social History of Medicine 5, no. 3 (1992): 413–3.
12 TNA MH 55/530.

opprobrium and professional self-preservation present in the discussions. The main result of the long-standing Commission was the passing of the Venereal Diseases Act 1917, which imposed a maximum fine of £100 or a prison sentence of up to six months (with or without hard labour) on those found guilty of advertising remedies for sexually transmitted diseases or of medically unqualified persons claiming to treat such problems.

'As indecent as one could imagine'?

As highlighted in Chapter Three, the clamour for legal reform and a more robust intervention in terms of enforcement had been growing for some time. However, the question of whether the 'problem' of indecent material was a genuinely significant and real one on the ground, or one perceived to be more in the minds and hype of the purists, is difficult to assess, not least because of the contemporary ambiguity and uncertainty over whether such matters could be publicly discussed and debated without breaking the law. Senior police officers often acted automatically on complaints received, initiating summons and applications to the magistrates for the 'offending' literature to be destroyed but imagining its content rather than actually looking at the material subject to the complaint. Official police statistics shed some light on the matter but can only be referenced speculatively because of the broad range of legal provisions available and generic cataloguing. For example, the Report of the Commissioner of the Metropolis for the Year 1906 (also published in 1908) provides a comprehensive statistical analysis of the incidence of crime, offences, and outcomes in the Greater London area. Just three prosecutions were brought that year for publishing indecent advertisements under the 1889 Act, and all resulted in convictions with a fine and/or one month imprisonment imposed.[13] Additionally, thirty-eight summonses were issued on the application of the police (typically in response to complaints) for 'exhibiting, publishing or selling obscene printed matter' together with an equivalent number of applications for destruction orders under the OPA 1857. All were secured, resulting in thirty-eight convictions out of a total of 18,458 summons' applications for all offences that year.[14] A further 680 individuals were summonsed under by-laws (normally exercised at the discretion of a police constable) for the ambiguously phrased 'committing an act of indecency': this was the third highest group in terms of violations after 'driving a vehicle without a lamp' (1,528) and 'animal diseases' (1,618).[15] These figures suggest that there was a concerted effort, at least in London, to tackle perceived indecent acts in public. Without more detail of such prosecutions it is difficult to identify the true nature of the conduct that was appearing to cause offence. Nationally, the actual number

---

13 *Report of the Commissioner of the Metropolis for the Year 1906*, 1908, Cd. 3771, 55, 69.
14 Ibid., 47. Offences of indecent exposure are counted separately at 150; fifty offences under the Vagrancy Act 1824 are recorded which could also include this offence.
15 Ibid., 45. By-laws were also used to convict two persons for indecent bathing in Essex, twenty in Middlesex, and four in Surrey.

of summary prosecutions for indecent advertisements as reproduced in the annual *Judicial Statistics* (hereafter *JS*) for England and Wales was small, typically averaging circa 100 a year.[16] This suggests two probabilities: the difficulty of defining indecency and the willingness of the police to initiate such prosecutions. Interestingly, the Postmaster General's annual report for 1906 (again published in 1908) makes no mention of any interventions or seizures of indecent publications, perhaps because there was a reluctance to draw public attention to a discretionary power that might raise objections, as identified in Chapter Three.[17]

Within the context of these official reports the lobbyists were no doubt delighted when the Government finally announced that a Select Committee on Lotteries and Indecent Advertisements would be appointed to join with a Committee of the House of Commons to review the law. By modern standards, this Joint Committee worked with remarkable speed.

The originating motion was passed by the House of Commons on 25 March 1908. The membership, established by 2 April under the chairmanship of Lord Beauchamp, was skewed towards a more broad-minded liberal perspective; the other Lords were Earl Donoughmore, Earl Dalhousie, Lord Herschell, and the founder of the Catholic Union, Viscount Landaff. Recruited from the House of Commons were Liberal MPs Hastings Duncan, Herbert Craig, and H.J. Wilson, Gervase Beckett, the Conservative, and William O'Malley, an Irish Nationalist. The first meeting took place on 7 April, six days of witness evidence followed, a draft report was drawn up and presented on 20 June, and the final report published on 23 July 1908. Twenty-six witnesses were heard. The report was short, running to seven pages with just forty-six paragraphs. Its conclusions regarding the need for amendments to the law were somewhat limited, with no major legal impact proposed. It would appear that, apart from those with a significant vested interest, the Committee's work barely touched the public consciousness. *The Times* simply reproduced some of the testimony and the final report; it (unusually) fails to offer any editorial opinion or commentary on the inquiry.[18] *The Spectator*, reflecting a more traditionalist stance, expressed some disappointment with the membership: 'It is impossible to stifle a wish that the personnel . . . had been stronger' but was largely satisfied with the conclusions drawn. Ironically, the report and minutes of the Committee have been more widely cited since, testimony perhaps to the fact that in retrospect it represents and captures a particular mood and moment in the history of British law.[19]

The two-pronged remit of the Committee was to:

> consider and inquire into the law (1) as to lotteries, including the sale of lottery bonds, competitions for prizes which involve an element of chance, and

16 For example, in 1906 117 persons were proceeded against, *JS, England and Wales 1906 Part 1. CS*, 1908, Cd. 3929, 72.

17 *Post Office Fifty-fourth Report of the Postmaster General*, 1908, Cd. 4240.

18 See *The Times*, 23 June, 11 September 1908.

19 Bristow, *Vice and Vigilance*; Heath, *Purifying Empire*; Hunt, *Governing Morals*.

advertisements relating thereto; (2) as to indecent literature and pictures and advertisements relating to things indecent or immoral; and to report what Amendments, if any, in the law are necessary or desirable.[20]

This dual agenda reflects some success by the moral campaigners in ensuring that the issue of indecent literature was part of the brief, but it also created an awkward dichotomy since the relationship between the problem of lotteries and competitions on one hand, and indecent material on the other, appears somewhat tenuous. On the face of it, the only connecting factor was that the new popular newspapers were implicated as offenders in relation to both, displaying advertisements for lottery prizes and 'indecent' paraphernalia in their publications. The Committee sensibly avoided overcomplication by treating the lotteries aspect as distinctly separate from the wider issue of indecency.

Lotteries had been illegal since the Lottery Act 1823, but a number of Irish lotteries carried on throughout the nineteenth and early twentieth centuries in defiance of the law. Many of these were in aid of religious and other charitable foundations, and it has been argued that the Irish authorities were loath to crack down on them for fear of stirring up a religious hornets' nest. Several of the lotteries received implicit and occasionally explicit support from both senior Home Rule advocates and the Catholic Church hierarchy. Coleman states that this problem reached its peak in 1930, following the legalization in Ireland of charitable 'Hospital Sweepstakes'. She remarks that 'almost 57 per cent of prize-winners' in the 1930 Manchester November Handicap race were British.[21] A Royal Commission on Lotteries and Betting was established in April 1932 in order to deal with the problem of the huge amounts flowing out from a Britain (several millions of pounds) in the midst of an industrial and financial depression. Its findings resulted in the Betting and Lotteries Act 1934, which introduced numerous restrictions on large-scale lotteries, including the banning of the importation of lottery tickets or associated advertising material (including lists of sweepstake winners), whilst relaxing the rules for small charitable lotteries with prizes under £10 in value.

However, in a contemporaneous example of what might be perceived as almost too perfect timing – that, arguably, appears more likely than not to have been deliberately orchestrated by the moral campaigners – the Committee's inquiry needs to be considered in the context of the legal actions mounted against Robert

---

20 *Hansard* HC Deb, 1 April 1908, vol.187 cc.627–9. The question of lotteries is largely beyond the scope of this book. Lotteries had been illegal since the 1823 Lotteries Act, but a number of Irish lotteries carried on throughout the nineteenth and early twentieth centuries in defiance of the law. A Royal Commission on Lotteries and Betting was established in April 1932 in order to deal with the problem of the huge amounts flowing out from Britain in the midst of an industrial and financial depression. Its findings resulted in the Betting and Lotteries Act 1934, which introduced numerous restrictions on large-scale lotteries, whilst relaxing the rules for small charitable lotteries with prizes under £10 in value.

21 M. Coleman, 'A terrible danger to the morals of the country: the Irish hospitals' sweepstake in Great Britain 1930–87', *Proceedings of the Royal Irish Academy. Section C: Archaeology, Celtic Studies, History, Linguistics, Literature* 105C, no. 5 (2005): 197–220.

Standish Sievier during the spring and summer months of 1908. Sievier was the editor and publisher of the *Winning Post*, a horse-racing magazine. He was also a gambler, bookmaker, and racehorse owner who fell under the wrath of the moral campaigners' radar. The *Post* was held up as an indecent publication for its promotion of gambling, and one that illustrated the increasingly ambiguous and nebulous nature of what constituted 'indecency' according to certain prevailing individual standards and perspectives. Even the Church of England appeared somewhat ambivalent with regard to the immorality or otherwise of gambling: the Bishop of Winchester stated in a House of Lords debate upon the problem of betting on 1 May 1934 that the State should 'only [be] called upon so to interfere when organized betting has reached the pitch that it leads to grave social consequences', but went on to state 'that through this increase of betting crime has often been caused, poverty has been intensified, and character has frequently deteriorated'.[22]

On 17 March, Sievier was charged at Bow Street Police Court with 'sending through the post a packet enclosing certain indecent articles, to wit – five numbers of a newspaper called the *Winning Post*' contrary to section 4 Post Office (Protection) Act 1884. The prosecution was instigated by Mr Herbert Muskett, a solicitor whose firm acted as official legal advisors for the Commissioner of the Metropolis, who had been informed that the paper had regularly published material that 'exceeded the bounds of public decency and proprietary'. Detective Inspector Lawrence wrote to the publisher and was sent copies of the *Winning Post*. Lawrence concluded that a number of paragraphs came within the definition of indecent, others were 'suggestive', 'ambiguous', and some 'perilously near obscene'. According to Muskett, the 29 February issue in particular was apparently 'so crude and indecent' that it 'could no longer be tolerated'.[23] The prosecution acknowledged that all such paragraphs appeared on the front page only and that the content of each issue was solely devoted to 'legitimate sporting matters'. Sievier pleaded guilty on the advice of his counsel (Mr Bodkin) after Muskett hinted that a more serious charge on indictment might be forthcoming, but claimed that such 'witticisms' were no different to similar ones published in London from when he was a small boy. He added that they were not likely to corrupt anyone and as a successful racing paper it was read by all, including the great and the good. The magistrate, Mr Marsham, agreed that of the paragraphs he was shown one was perhaps indecent, but cast doubt on the others, commenting only that these tended to 'spoil the tone and deteriorated the value' of the paper suggesting that the prosecution was repressive. However, he commended the prosecutors for raising the case as these matters can go from 'bad to worse', and he imposed the maximum £10 fine for Sievier's single violation and £5 costs. Sievier had of course pleaded guilty, but his culpability lay more in the fact that he had not appeared to heed previous warnings from the magistracy made in other similar cases.

The moral campaigners were determined not to let the *Winning Post* off the hook. In July 1908, Mr Robert Corfe of the Royal Societies Club summonsed Charles Awdry, a partner in W.H. Smith and Sons, for selling a certain indecent

22 *Hansard* HL Deb, 1 May 1934, vol.91 cc.924–72.
23 *The Times*, 18 March 1908.

publication, namely the *Winning Post Summer Annual 1908* edited by Sievier. This time the summons was brought under the Metropolitan Police Act: Corfe claimed that 'nearly the whole of the book in question was obscene' with some passages and pictures worse than others, and a story that was as 'indecent as one could imagine'.[24] In an admission that the campaigners had been monitoring the publication for some time, Corfe confirmed he had bought the last three issues but sent the 1908 edition immediately to the Home Office demanding its seizure, and sent a further copy to the Select Committee – he received no response from the Home Office. W. H. Smith and Sons originally received 40,000 copies of the book for sale but once the summons was issued recalled all remaining copies. The defence counsel pleaded that Awdry was not legally liable as an offence under the Act and could be committed only if gross carelessness or an intention to act illegally could be shown. The prosecution conceded there was a 'legal difficulty'. Corfe tried again, saying he could not be satisfied that W. H. Smith and Sons would stop selling the book, but the magistrate had already decided the summons would fail.

Meanwhile, Sievier needed his lawyers again. This time his former barrister, Mr Bodkin, represented the Crown, with Sievier well served by Rufus Isaacs KC, in a headline-grabbing case at the Central Criminal Court where another racehorse owner, Solomon Joel, alleged he had been blackmailed by Sievier. *The Winning Post* was again at the centre of the charge and Sievier accused of threatening to publish certain libellous and defamatory matter extorting Joel to pay £5,000. The jury acquitted Sievier as it transpired that he had been entrapped by the Metropolitan Police.[25] Curiously, Detective Chief Inspector Drew was found hidden behind a curtain at Joel's residence, revealing himself to arrest Sievier – thus providing more rich material for the growing genre of detective fiction. More intriguingly, Sievier, Lawrence, Drew, Corfe, and Muskett were all called as witnesses by the Committee together with Coote: no affiliation details are provided for Robert Corfe, but he is described as someone who has been 'interested in the question of indecent literature and publications for a number of years'.[26] The concerns of the moral campaigners, led by the Bishop of Manchester, about the impact of betting and gambling on the unemployed in particular, continued well into the 1920s and 1930s with the 'proliferation of the 'increasing evil' of tote clubs in towns and cities'.[27]

'I did not even see the literature'

The evidence presented to the Committee is notable for the unanimity with which witnesses asserted the problem. Seven police witnesses were called who outlined in some detail the range of offences available but nevertheless complained about

24 *The Times*, 10 July 1908.
25 *The Times*, 30 June; 8, 14, 24, 28, 31 July 1908. Some 500 people sought entrance to the court to watch the case, 200 of whom were turned away.
26 Parliamentary Papers, 1908, *Report from the Joint Select Committee on Lotteries and Indecent Advertisements, Together with the Proceedings of the Committee, Minutes of Evidence, and Appendices* (London: HMSO), para. 512.
27 M. Clapson, *A Bit of a Flutter: Popular Gambling and English Society c.1823–1961* (Manchester: Manchester University Press, 1992), 125.

the process and limitations of the law. A recurrent theme was the uncertainty, previously identified by the Home Office, that lay in the words 'indecent' and 'obscene' and, further, whether either of these terms adequately covered the problem. In relation to the issue of trafficking in immoral literature, Leonard Dunning, Head Constable of the City of Liverpool, stated:

> It seems to me that the amendment should be by way of broadening the definition; a strict interpretation of the words indecent or obscene does not cover all that may be reasonably looked upon as objectionable, and I think that the test of the offence should be whether the production, publication, sale or advertisement of the articles complained of is in the opinion of the Court . . . likely to be injurious to public morals.[28]

Detective Superintendent John Stark agreed that there was a difficulty in dealing with 'matters which are vulgar and on the borderline between [indecent and obscene]'.[29] W.P. Byrne, Under-Secretary of State for the Home Department, suggested that 'when a suitable form of words is found descriptive of the things that ought to be punishable for indecency, Magistrates ought to have summary power to deal with them,'[30] while Herbert Muskett argued that

> In any new legislation upon this subject the word 'indecent' might be very conveniently used in conjunction with the word 'obscene' [on the grounds that magistrates] are sometimes inclined to give effect to the objection which is raised on behalf of this class of offender, that there is some distinction between the meaning of the word 'indecent' and the meaning of the word 'obscene'.[31]

It appears that lay magistrates could be considered more 'reliable' than professional stipendiaries. Dunning noted that

> we take these cases before the Magistrates sooner than before the Stipendiary or Deputy Stipendiary, because the latter take what seems, perhaps, a narrow view of the words 'indecent or obscene' whereas the Magistrates are really more apt to look on the broad principle of whether it is an undesirable publication.[32]

Coote reiterated the importance of magistrates' attitudes in the successful pursuit of the NVA cause: 'Their sympathies are entirely against this sort of thing [i.e. indecent material], but they hold different opinions as to whether public action should be taken against certain things.'[33] *The Spectator* agreed: 'Widely different

28 *Joint Select Committee on Lotteries and Indecent Advertisements*, para. 650.
29 Ibid., para. 1,055.
30 Ibid., para. 267.
31 Ibid., para. 314.
32 Ibid., para. 654.
33 Ibid., para. 755.

views may be held even among men of education and culture as to what is indecent and what is not.'[34] Coote also complained about legal process and the incon-
venient need for evidence, referring to an exhibition in London of art illustrating
the works of Rabelais:

> There were a number of these pictures which were absolutely indecent, as
> will be readily understood, because Rabelais could hardly be illustrated with-
> out producing something like indecency. Our difficulty in that matter was
> that although we had complaints and we had seen it, we could not get process
> except under this Act [the OPA 1857], unless we produced something to show
> that these things were on exhibition.[35]

On the subject of indecent postcards, Major Pulteney Malcolm, Chief Constable
for Kingston-Upon-Hull, expressed frustration at the unwillingness of his witnesses to come forward: 'The difficulty comes in all these cases that the persons
who give the information have generally a great dislike of being brought into
Court in any way.'[36] He conceded: 'I did not even see the literature. It was only
reported to me.'[37] Despite such inconveniences, to the question of whether he
had secured convictions in the case of all these postcards, the reply is swift:
'We did'.[38]

Such contradictions abound: evidence was given of the use of wide-ranging
laws securing successful convictions as also underlined in the Metropolitan Police
Commissioner's Report, whilst complaints were made about the limitations of such
provisions and urging amendment. In retrospect this points to concern about the possible safety of some of these convictions. The moral campaigners had no doubt that
public opinion was on their side: 'We assume that there is no controversy among the
public now as to the need of putting down such things as these.'[39] Paradoxically, at
the same time they made it clear that the public's demand for the offending material
was a major factor: 'It has become such a paying concern that it has developed into
a vast industry.'[40] Only four representatives of the press were called to give evidence. Of these, three were only questioned on the issue of lotteries with regard to
prize competitions in their publications. The fourth, Nelson Faviell Henderson, one
of the proprietors of *Scraps* newspaper, was present, not to defend the newspaper
industry, but to rebut previous evidence regarding his own publication, which was,
he insisted, 'of an absolutely clean and wholesome character'.[41]

In short, no dissenting voices were heard – no literary authors or publishers, no
defenders of a free press or a different moral perspective gave evidence. Perhaps

34 *The Spectator*, 19 September 1908.
35 *Select Committee on Lotteries and Indecent Advertisements*, para. 726.
36 Ibid., para. 710.
37 Ibid., para. 711.
38 Ibid., para. 713.
39 Ibid., para. 732.
40 Ibid., para. 515.
41 Ibid., para. 624.

the only voice of moderation could be heard on the second day of evidence: Byrne, from the Home Office, stated, somewhat surprisingly, 'We have had very little complaint about indecency in current literature in England addressed specially to the Secretary of State' which, given the amount of correspondence received by the Home Office from the NVA, could presumably be interpreted as referring to a lack of complaints from ordinary members of the public and professional bodies. He further mused that the Home Secretary, Gladstone, heard 'very little about them, I suppose, because it is admitted that practically books are not published which could give rise to a successful prosecution'. He conceded that there had been 'several instances' where the Home Secretary had received complaints against picture galleries but that the offending material did not usually go beyond 'the bounds of legitimate art'. One exception was the Rabelais exhibition, cited as an example of a 'scandal of the public' which was 'discontinued under the threat of prosecution,' prompting Byrne to conclude that, 'such things are not common'.[42] Regardless, the Committee appeared to have already come to its conclusion by 21 May. The chairman reassured Corfe that 'I think the Committee have practically agreed that they are quite satisfied in their minds as to the existence of the evil.'[43] It is hardly surprising, therefore, to find the final report so unequivocal:

> Although the definition of obscenity which was laid down by Lord Chief Justice Cockburn in the case of *Reg. v. Hicklin,* and which the Committee are informed has been accepted as accurate, is wide and far-reaching, it is apparently not always easy to make it apply in many cases where it would be desirable to take proceedings, but in which the matter complained of although objectionable and indecent, cannot with any accuracy be described as obscene. Magistrates who would themselves be willing to convict, if the cases were left in their hands, often do not feel justified in sending them on for trial.[44]

On this point, the Committee concluded, 'not only would the cost of prosecutions be greatly reduced, but also that a more speedy and effectual remedy would be found for that which they believe to be *a serious and growing evil,* if cases of this description were left to the decision of the Magistrates' [emphasis added].[45] However, the Committee was unwilling to endorse the suggestion that the Postmaster General be granted powers to intercept and stop the transmission of obscene material and also recommended that any amending Act should include an exemption to cover genuine works of art and books of literary merit.

If nothing else, the Committee and its report provide an intriguing insight into the creation of the indecency agenda and the importance of mobilizing local activism and enforcement in the form of the police and lay magistrates. In the end, although

---

42 Ibid., para. 221.
43 Ibid., para. 516.
44 Ibid., para. 39.
45 Ibid., para. 40.

the legal impact was minimal, the Committee served to consolidate the view that indecency was, indeed, 'a serious and growing evil'. As Coote said in his evidence:

> When there is strong public opinion, which, by the bye, is growing in strength through the formation and action of your Committee, even at the present time, it strengthens the magistrates. No law can be carried in front of public opinion, as you know, but when a public opinion has been expressed on the matter it is easy to get convictions, it is easy to extend the definition of 'obscenity' or 'indecency,' but without that public opinion there is always a reason why they should not do it.[46]

The aftermath: Here comes the flood (of Bills)

While campaigners were no doubt disappointed that there was no immediate legislative response, the inquiry stimulated a number of outcomes. One was the Committee's recognition of the need to develop an 'international arrangement' to regulate international trade in obscene publications and its recommendation that the Foreign Office liaise with their overseas counterparts such as the French Chamber of Deputies, who had recently announced plans in March 1908 to suppress the publication of obscene literature.[47] The Home Office had already surveyed eight other countries in 1903, including France, Germany, Holland, and the United States, about their laws regarding public advertisements and produced a comparative summary.[48] Although ultimately the Committee's recommendation was not taken up by the government, it highlighted the growing realization that there was a need to consider and negotiate the adoption of international treaties to address interstate problems, something already picked up in relation to the white slave trade and human trafficking (another of Coote's campaigns), thereby marking the early twentieth-century origins of modern international law.[49]

Another issue that the inquiry emphasized was that of press responsibility: the desire to control and suppress media advertising started to become confused with a wider debate about the need to curtail press reporting, particularly in relation to 'moral' matters which increasingly focussed on divorce proceedings. Six months after the Committee's report was published, the Lord Chief Justice, Viscount Alverstone, speaking on the theme of the 'Evils of Publicity' confirmed that, 'There was a very useful law in this country against the publication of indecent advertisements.' In the next breath he berated the press: 'But, somehow or

---

46 Ibid., para.753.
47 *Joint Select Committee on Lotteries and Indecent Advertisements Report*, para. 35; Heath, *Purifying Empire*, 89. Regarding the French censure see *The Times*, 21 March 1908.
48 House of Commons Accounts and Papers, *Return of the laws for regulating or restricting the exhibition of posters, bills and advertisements*, 1903 (no. 323).
49 One of the first international treaties of the International Convention for the Suppression of the White Slave Traffic, 14 May 1910.

another, when the too faithful pen of a newspaper reporter insisted on putting in his journal every detail of some unsavoury evidence in the Divorce Court nobody seemed to object.'[50] In *Scott v Scott* the House of Lords overruled a Divorce Court judge who had ordered the hearing to be held in camera. Lord Shaw acknowledged that there was no legal authority permitting a judge to close the court, confirming that press freedom is 'one of the surest guarantees of our liberties'.[51] Thus the overlying moral confusion about the nature of public indecency infiltrated the courtroom, with some judges unwilling to allow intimate matrimonial matters to be aired in open proceedings or be reported in the press. At the national Institute of Journalists' conference in 1913, J. S. R. Phillips, author of *The Growth of Journalism*, highlighted the irony that if Divorce Court reports were to be censured because they ' "debauched the public mind". . .it would be entirely ridiculous to allow the publication of novels such as in the last few years had been issued from the press by hundreds' and that if the press were singled out for publishing divorce cases then newspaper reports of plays and novels should also be 'subject to the same degree of censorship'.[52] Eventually the Judicial Proceedings Act 1926 clarified the position in respect of divorce proceedings, limiting publication to the judicial summary of the case and identification of the parties concerned.

Over a year after the report's publication and with no immediate legislative response, Gladstone was still being asked in Parliament to take steps to prevent breaches of the law, particularly in relation to the sale of picture postcards and mutoscopes at railway stations and other public places (see Chapter Five). He confirmed that the Postmaster General had issued a public notification that the sending of such postcards was a serious criminal offence, and that the police utilized the criminal law as best they could in all cases that came to their notice 'with the result that exhibitions of the grosser sorts have been largely stamped out'. He also acknowledged that a Bill had been drafted in response to the recommendations that could target those 'exhibitions which are of a demoralising and disgusting character, though not coming within the law relating to obscene exhibitions'.[53] Here, at least, was some cause for satisfaction on the part of the moral campaigners, but their hopes for far-reaching change were not realized.

The publication of advertisements for abortifacients continued. A couple of examples from *The Penny Illustrated Paper and Illustrated Times*, 21 May 1910, will suffice to indicate the carefully worded nature of such advertisements:

1. Ladies: My Improved Remedies act in a few hours when all else fails. Surprisingly effective. Success Guaranteed. Send stamped envelope for Free Sample. Nurse F. Hammond, 24 Boscombe Road, Southend, Essex.

---

50 *The Times*, 4 February 1909.
51 *Scott v Scott* [1913] AC 417 at 476.
52 *The Times*, 21 August 1913; J. S. R. Phillips, *The Growth of Journalism*, Cambridge History of English Literature (Cambridge: Cambridge University Press, 1916).
53 *Hansard* HC Deb, 9 September 1909, vol.10, cc.1,632–3W, 1,633W.

2. Book For Ladies. Contains Everything Important. Very Interesting. 200,000
    copies already sold. Post free 1s 2d. Doctor Allinson, 169 Room 4, Spanish
    Place, London W.

No Nurse F. Hammond was listed as living at 24 Boscombe Road, Southend in
the 1911 census; the property is recorded as being inhabited by a William Frederic
Stafford (insurance inspector) and his wife Kate, together with George Nicholls
(a Post Office pensioner) and his wife Susannah. It is entirely possible that both
families may have moved there between May 1910 and April 1911. It is of course
also possible that the name was a pseudonym of one of the members of either family. By contrast, Doctor Allinson was indeed a genuine medical man – Dr Richard
Allison, a physician and surgeon – who is listed as living at 4 Spanish Place in the
1911 census. It is interesting to note that he was confident enough of not being
prosecuted to put his real name to an advert that appears to contravene the spirit
of the 1889 Act, strengthening the suggestion that it was regarded as something
of a 'lame duck'.

In 1909 and 1910 Private Members' Bills to amend the Indecent Advertisements Act 1889 were presented, but without success.[54] Simultaneously, others
were trying a different tack by incorporating restrictions on indecent publications
into more generic but highly ambitious Bills designed to consolidate the criminal
law to cover all aspects of immorality and indecency. The Jewish Association for
the Protection of Girls and Women and the NVA sponsored one such Criminal
Law Amendment Bill in 1909 to amend the Criminal Law Amendment Act 1885,
Vagrancy Act 1898, and fatally, permit the police to detain young women and
girls involved in prostitution. This last proposal caused deep divisions between
the Home Office and the Metropolitan Police Commissioner, Sir Charles Warren, who had issued a laissez-faire policy to his officers as they were unwilling to
make such arrests, thereby ensuring the Bill's failure. In June 1910, the Liberal
MP Joseph King presented the Morality Bill, but as this short title infers, it was
evident from the beginning that its enactment would also be an impossibility.[55]
Originally tabled as the Criminal Law Amendment, &c., Bill in March 1910 it was
a facsimile of the 1909 Bill. However, when re-presented in June its stated aim
had changed to one of *substituting* rather than amending not only the 1885 Act and
Vagrancy Act, but additionally the Incest Act 1908, the OPA 1857, and Indecent
Advertisements Act 1889. These were to be replaced with a single statute to create
a 'comprehensive measure which shall materially strengthen the Law relating to
offences against morality and indecency'.[56]

The idea to draft a new Act that would codify and punish all variants of immoral
and indecent behaviour was an enterprise doomed to failure because of its breadth,
controversial nature, and the unlikelihood of reconciling all interested parties.

54 *Hansard* HL Deb, 26 October 1909, vol.4 c.417; *Hansard* HL Deb, 16 June 1910, vol.5 c.900.
55 *Hansard* HC Deb, 14 June 1910, vol.17 c.1,202.
56 Morality Bill 1910 (179).

Stand-alone, subject-specific clauses, such as Clause 11, which sought to increase the penalty for indecent publication to £50 and/or six months' imprisonment where a misdemeanour, £100 and/or twelve months on indictment, and extend the powers of the Postmaster General were less problematic.[57] But Clause 17 exemplifies the implausibility of the Bill: enabling a person (including someone without any previous convictions) to be placed under police supervision for keeping premises for immoral purposes, living on immoral earnings, soliciting for prostitution (males), and selling indecent publications. While literature promoting the sale and use of contraceptive aids can be reconciled with the desire to regulate prostitution, such an association was ill-conceived: in demonizing all 'indecent' publications it failed to acknowledge any wider educational value or distinguish them from the more serious immoral practices. The Bill was lost only to be replaced by two further Bills couched in similar vague and generic terms: the Prevention of Immorality Bill 1911 to make 'further provision for the protection of women and girls, for the suppression of immoral and indecent literature, etc., and otherwise for the prevention of immorality and indecency', and in 1912, another Prevention of Immorality Bill to 'consolidate and amend enactments relating to offences against morality and decency, to offences against the person, to certain premises, literature etc'.[58] A key sponsor was the Bishop of London, Sir Arthur Winnington-Ingram, chairman of the PMC, who would become a significant figurehead in the morality campaign over the next two decades.[59] Unsurprisingly, this confusing proliferation of legislative excess ultimately proved counterproductive. The Bills spawned the Criminal Law Amendment Act 1912, not a consolidating statute but a short Act that mainly enhanced the powers of the police to detain anyone involved in facilitating prostitution and harmonized Scottish law, and one that did not include any provisions regarding the control of indecent literature.

Déjà vu: 'Improper' literature

The printed word had caused problems for moral censors since the introduction of movable type in the mid-fifteenth century. For many moralists, it was not only the inherently indecent or improper nature that they perceived to be contained within certain publications, it was that such indecency was becoming increasingly available to all sectors of society. As Sigel has pointed out, 'before the 1880s, the majority of pornography consisted of expensive, hard-to-find literary texts.' Much of the available obscene literature was written by and for 'discerning gentlemen' of the same class as 'Walter', the author of the 1888 'autobiography' entitled *My Secret Life*, which cost up to £100 for the complete eleven-volume work, or Stanislaus de Rhodes, a London-based lawyer widely acknowledged to be the author

---

57 Today £50 would be approximately £3,000 and £100 nearer £6,000 (see http://apps.nationalar chives.gov.uk/currency/results.asp#mid).
58 *Hansard* HC Deb, 15 February 1911, vol.21 c.1,064.
59 *The Times*, 19 July 1910.

of another well-known work of Victorian erotic fiction, *The Autobiography of a Flea* (1887).[60]

Whilst such works of 'literature' were clearly objectionable to the moral campaigners as a result of their often pornographic content, they were available only to a relatively small sector of society due to their typically prohibitive cost. A short book (more properly a pamphlet) entitled *Philosophy of Marriage*, 'a treatise on the obstacles to a happy union' which was widely available, highlights the concerns about an increasingly literate working class. The publication was the subject of a prosecution brought by the SSV and heard at the Central Criminal Court on 4 February 1873. The book was described as being 'not only calculated to effect the destruction of public morality, but was an absolute injury to society . . . passages were calculated and intended to excite immoral passions, irrespective of the position or age of the persons reading them'.[61] However, the most telling passage in *The Times*' report was its recounting of the Deputy Recorder's summing-up. He stated that books from the time of Chaucer could be found 'containing expressions more or less obscene. It did not follow that an obscene book was properly the subject of an indictment', and then went on to ask:

> What was it that made the distinction? If topics were treated, not in a scientific, but in a popular and pamphlet form, in order to be disseminated generally and indiscriminately, *among all classes*, and at a very low price, then the whole effect of the alteration of the form in which they were being disseminated was such as to render the book a subject for indictment. [Italics added for emphasis.][62]

The offending books were destroyed, and two of the three defendants, John Dennison and John Davidson, each had to enter into recognizances of £500, whilst the third, Henry Romilly, had to enter into a recognizance of £100. Clearly, to the judiciary in this case it was not only the subject material but its availability to the lower classes of society that was a major cause for concern. The book in question appears to have been on open sale for several decades; the *Morning Post* of 5 February 1873 stated that the book had sold more than 30,000 copies. The title is the same as a 364-page medical treatise published in 1837 by Dr Michael Ryan, a member of the Royal College of Physicians and Surgeons. The book's catchy full title was *The Philosophy of Marriage in its Social, Moral and Physical Relations; with an Account of the Diseases of the Genito-Urinary Organs which impair or*

---

60 Lisa Z. Sigel, 'Filth in the wrong people's hands: Postcards and the expansion of pornography in Britain and the Atlantic World 1880–1914', *Journal of Social History* Autumn (2000): 860. The author of *My Secret Life* remains a mystery, but the book remains a shocking portrayal of late Victorian attitudes to child rape and sadism. It is however interesting to note that it is now regarded as a 'classic' of its type and is widely available.

61 *The Times*, 13 December 1872. This trial was connected to the prosecution of Dr Kahn's exhibition of anatomical models (see Chapter Five).

62 *The Times*, 5 February 1873.

destroy the reproductive functions; and induce a variety of complaints; with the physiology of Generation in the Vegetable and Animal Kingdoms, and was based around a series of lectures given at the North London School of Medicine.[63] The book was republished in London in 1839 and 1843, and an advertisement in the Bradford Observer on 21 April 1842 reproduces a review in the Quarterly Journal that states:

> We have seen the manuscript of this work; and have no hesitation in strongly recommending it for the perusal not only of all married women, but also single females. It is evidently the work of a scientific man, and may be read by the most fastidious female.

The book (now freely available on Google) was a serious, sober, and detailed account of the reproductive function and venereal diseases. It serves as an exemplar of how the moral climate changed throughout the Victorian period: in 1837 it was being advertised as a book for public consumption, yet a generation later it was being castigated as an indecent publication, not fit for public or private perusal. This concern over what exactly constituted 'indecent' literature continued into the early decades of the twentieth century and served to hamper the publication of several works of what are now regarded as classic literature.

James Joyce's struggles to have his collection of short stories, The Dubliners, published in England are well documented.[64] His eventual publisher, Grant Richards (who was himself no stranger to controversy), had originally agreed to publish The Dubliners in 1906, but on receipt of Joyce's manuscript found himself objecting to some of the language and content of the stories contained within. Joyce was frustrated by this turn of events; in a letter dated 20 May 1906, he wrote to Richards:

> If I eliminate them what becomes of the chapter of the moral history of my country? I fight to retain them because I believe that in composing my chapter of moral history in exactly the way I have composed it I have taken the first step towards the spiritual liberation of my country.[65]

It appears that several of the problems regarding the moral tone of the publication lay not with the publisher but with the contracted printer, who refused to typeset certain of the stories. Joyce was clearly exasperated with this turn of events, stating in a letter to Richards dated 5 May 1906 that 'His marking of the first passage makes me think that there is priestly blood in him: the scent for immoral allusions

63 Ryan, M., The Philosophy of Marriage (London: John Churchill, 1837).
64 See for example, R. Scholes, 'Grant Richards to James Joyce', Studies in Bibliography, vol. 16 (1963): 139–60.
65 Letter from Joyce to Richards, 20 May 1906 – reproduced at http://theamericanreader.com/20-may-1906-james-joyce-to-grant-richards/.

is certainly very keen here.'[66] Two of the passages that the printer refused to compose were 'a man with two establishments to keep up, of course he couldn't', and 'She continued to cast bold glances at him and changed the position of her legs often; and when she was going out she brushed against his chair and said "Pardon!" in a cockney accent.' The printer's objections to these and other passages seem to us today almost laughable: the young lady was not only forward, but working class to boot, doubly deviant, indeed. However, this incident throws an interesting light on the moral code of the day. Apart from any moral considerations that the printer may have had regarding Joyce's work, he was almost undoubtedly also thinking of any future damage to his business and reputation in agreeing to print such controversial literature.[67]

During the first decades of the twentieth century there was something of a resurgent flourish in the moral minority's campaign to suppress 'improper' literature and its availability to the masses. The *San Francisco Call*, in an article dated 14 August 1910 and headed 'Crusade for "Pure Literature" Launched' reported on a campaign by the Royal Society of Literature 'to Wage War on Bad Books'. The newspaper went on to state that 'a joint committee appointed by the Royal Society of Literature and the Society of Authors has been considering the best mode of creating a permanent body to represent the interests of 'pure literature.' Consequently, an academy, on similar lines to the Académie Française, had been created. The *San Francisco Call* reporter was clearly enjoying himself at the expense of the 'Old Country' when he wrote that 'apropos of the alleged designs of the new academy on the immorals of the English public, authors, journalists and publishers recently conferred with the Purity Crusaders.' Once again, fear of the foreign (specifically Continental) reared its head: John Murray, publisher, 'after his invariable discussion of the difficulty of fixing the border-line between the goody-goody and baddy-baddy book', was reported as stating that 'Karl Marx, Nietzche and other "foreigners" to be the producers of noxious literature'. The paper then went on to report that in the opinion of the president of the Associated Booksellers of Great Britain and Ireland, Henry Keary, 'books written by women were by far the worst, and that ladies were more eager to obtain these books than men.'

While campaigners, especially the London PMC, spearheaded by the Bishop of London, Arthur Winnington-Ingram, were trying to secure legal reform in Parliament, they also uncompromisingly persevered with their agenda of prosecution, which some (Sievier for example) might call *persecution*. In 1909, six partners in W.H. Smith and sons were prosecuted for selling *Sievier's Monthly*, and Siever himself was convicted for sending an indecent publication through the post.[68] On 28 March 1911 Sievier was to meet his nemesis yet again. Recalled to Bow Street Magistrates' Court before Marsham, with Muskett representing

---

66 http://everything2.com/title/A+Letter+to+Grant+Richards%252C+May+5%252C+1906.

67 *The Dubliners* was eventually published (with minor amendments and emendations) by Richards in 1914.

68 *The Times*, 7 September, 3 December 1909.

the Commissioner of the Metropolis, he was fined another £10 for sending a copy of the *Winning Post* through the mail. Muskett confirmed that 'there could be no two opinions about the bad taste or vulgarity' of the single offending paragraph.[69] Concerns about the problem of demoralizing literature were beginning to reappear in public forums but with a slightly different label and new rhetoric of 'improper' books. The distinction between 'indecent' and 'improper' books was debated in the letters page of *The Times*, opening with a letter under the byline 'Improper Books' defending the right of authors to write for adults and challenging parents, guardians, and teachers to regulate 'what young folks should read'.[70]

Sir Robert Anderson, former Assistant Commissioner at Scotland Yard, confirmed that if a book were in the 'legal sense obscene' it was indecent and a matter for the police, but if 'improper' in terms of 'intention and effect, corrupt and corrupting' it could 'escape the meshes of the criminal law'. An alternative was recommended that the libraries take responsibility 'to cope with the evil' amid concerns that such matters of public censure should not be left in private hands.[71]

A few days later Muskett was back at Bow Street with a summons from the Police Commissioner against Harry Sutton, the director of Hygienic Stores at Charing Cross, and an order for the destruction of 272 obscene books. Detective Sergeant Curry had purchased three copies of the French author Honore Balzac's *Droll Stories*, described as 'indecent from beginning to end'. Despite his anathema to the 'indecent' nature of his work, Muskett did acknowledge that Balzac was 'one of the literary giants of the world',[72] Balzac's vignettes of sixteenth-century life in Touraine with illustrations by Gustave Doré published in 1832, were applauded as a work of art by his English translator in 1874 and Balzac since recognized as the creator of realism in literature.[73] The magistrate, Sir Arthur Rutzen, in ordering the destruction, is reported as asserting that 'to his mind a more foul or filthy black spot had not been found in London for a long time, and the police had done uncommonly well in bringing these proceedings.' In November 1911, John Reuter, who had been a bookseller for twenty-one years, was sentenced to nine months imprisonment at the London Sessions and ordered to pay the costs of the prosecution after having been found guilty of unlawfully

---

69 *The Times*, 29 March 1911.
70 *The Times*, 11 September 1909. For a discussion of the perceived corruptive effects and subsequent condemnation of penny dreadfuls and other forms of late nineteenth and early twentieth century literature for children, see Dunae, 'Penny dreadfuls'. Dunae argues that the perceived threat from such literature was great, as it was specifically targeted at lower-class youths who, as a result of the Education Act 1870 and subsequent iterations, were now able to read and write. He further argues that this type of literature was eventually subsumed into a more 'respectable' guise with the growth of empirical (i.e. anti-Germanic) sentiments, child burglars, and ne'er-do-wells being transformed into militaristic and heroic figures.
71 *The Times*, 15 December 1909, 6 January 1910.
72 *The Times*, 29 December 1909.
73 Ironically, Balzac first trained as a lawyer: H. de Balzac, *Droll Stories* (London, William Mitchell, 1874).

selling an improper book to Detective Sergeant Bishop and of procuring other similar books.[74]

Infuriated, Clement Shorter, a journalist and literary critic, wrote to *The Times* castigating the 1908 Committee for not hearing any representatives of writers or publishers and criticizing a recent deputation to the Home Secretary that lacked the 'presence of any men of letters' including the publishers of 'Hardy, Swinburne, Bernard Shaw, H.G. Wells and Maerterlinck'.[75] The Royal Society of Literature hosted a debate on censorship where the leading literary critic and author Edmund Gosse's commented 'these days people like opinions to be either snow white or jet black,' *The Times'* reporter confirmed that Gosse was 'anxious that the decency of language should be preserved but he was also very solicitous to defend the liberties of the press'.[76] This reflects the mounting concern about State censorship but as Hynes confirms, 'neither official censors nor moral crusaders could stop the Edwardian revolution, . . . they could only temporarily separate artists from their natural audiences.'[77]

But still the moral campaigners, and the PMC in particular, were intent on doing more than merely separate literature from its readers. At Bow Street in 1920 Sir Charles Biron disagreed with Muskett that the translation of Guy de Maupassant's *Une Vie* published in English as *A Woman's Life* was intrinsically indecent, acknowledging that there were now many books regarded as classics which contained passages offensive to modern taste but it would be absurd to censure them all on the grounds of indecency. He fined the manager of the Anglo-Eastern Publishing Co., who had pleaded guilty, £10 with £10 costs, but not because of any indecent content but because his translation was 'not honest' and was 'an outrage' from any artistic point of view, undermining the author's true purpose.

The literary revolution had therefore come and gone, leaving the moral campaigners and the NVA and PMC in its wake. There was another short-lived spat in the late 1920s when the PMC challenged the Home Secretary, Sir William Joynson-Hicks, to revisit the legal position in light of the debates leading to the Judicial Proceedings (Regulation of Reports) Act 1926.[78] Section 1 of the Act simply provided, in relation to any judicial proceedings, that 'It shall not be lawful to print or publish, or cause or procure to be printed or published – (a) in relation to any judicial proceedings any indecent matter or indecent medical, surgical or physiological details being matters or details the publication of which would be calculated to injure public morals.' There was to be no censure of any indecent or improper literature. Joseph Kenworthy (somewhat surprisingly a Liberal MP who later resigned from the party and joined the Labour Party), asked Joynson-Hicks

---

74 *The Times*, 25 November 1911.
75 *The Times*, 29 December 1909.
76 *The Times*, 23 October 1913.
77 Hynes, *The Edwardian Turn of Mind*, 306.
78 For a detailed account of the passage of this bill and the discussions that it engendered, see TNA HO 45 12288 Publications (including Indecent Publications): Unsavoury details of divorce cases, etc: restriction on publication (1924–1926).

to reconsider whether his powers to prevent the publication and sale of indecent books were sufficient. The Home Secretary replied:

> I am advised that, speaking generally, the law is reasonably adequate, and the difficulties which arise in enforcing it are due not so much to any defect in the law itself as to differences of opinion in the minds of magistrates as to what in any particular case constitutes punishable indecency within the law.[79]

In 1928 State responsibility for matters indecent compared to matters immoral was finally clarified officially. Joynson-Hicks made his position, and the distinction between them, very clear at the Author's Club Christmas dinner in 1928, asserting that his role was in 'no sense of the term a censor of morals'. The police role was to deal with crime and not 'immorality in a private house,' but they did have a duty to prosecute anyone committing an indecent act, including the publication of genuinely indecent literature. Similarly, the Home Office was responsible for dealing with the importation of indecent literature but not any public immorality unless so legislated by Parliament. To the relief of the authors present, Joynson-Hicks said he was 'prepared to leave himself in their hands . . . for the overwhelming majority of them desired to publish books which were uplifting and made for the welfare of the country'.[80]

In March 1929 the PMC tried once more sending a deputation to the Home Office, which included representatives from the Salvation Army, the Christian Association, and the National Union of Teachers, with the aim of 'stemming the tide of corruption pouring out of the publishing houses', specifically relating to the translation of classic texts, publications on birth control, and 'the little nasty shilling books with flaming pictures outside and full of naughtiness within'.[81] Tides of course cannot be tamed, and (ironically) at Folkestone and Dover an oncoming tide was causing Mr Cazalet MP a different concern. He pointed out that 'Customs officials at English ports . . ., demand now to examine every book and pamphlet that visitors may possess', and asked the Financial secretary of the Treasury whether he could 'induce his officials to use a little more discretion and tact in carrying out these duties'.[82] Sir Oswald Mosley MP also asked the Home Secretary about a parcel of books 'held up for nearly two months in the Customs on account of the presence of a book by Monsieur Jules Romain, which had previously been imported freely to this country'.[83] In 1937, Home Secretary Sir Samuel Hoare, replying to a question about interception warrants issued to the Postmaster General, stated: 'The present system of preventing the transmission of indecent matter through the post is, I believe, working effectively and I have no reason to consider the taking of any further action.'[84] He declined to reveal the number of warrants issued.

79 *Hansard* HC Deb, 18 February 1926, vol.191 cc.2096–7, 2096.
80 *The Times*, 11 December 1928.
81 *The Times*, 6 March 1929.
82 *Hansard* HC Deb, 29 April 1929, vol.227 cc.1294–5.
83 *Hansard* HC Deb, 14 March 1929, vol.226 cc.1235–7, 1236.
84 *Hansard* HC Deb, 29 July 1937, vol.326 c.3286.

From high art to indecent images – democratizing indecency

As previously mentioned, concern over the decency or otherwise of visual imagery had been voiced in the Western world virtually from the moment Gutenberg developed movable type in the mid-fifteenth century. As printing technology advanced rapidly in the late eighteenth and early nineteenth century, more opportunities for visual public indecency in the form of images blossomed, as alluded to by Philip Whitehead MP, who remarked in a 1973 Commons debate on the Cinematograph and Indecent Displays Bill (then awaiting its second reading before Parliament) that:

> Something which I received through the mails only the other day is a scatological cartoon of the reigning monarch seated upon the lavatory with the consort. It is a cartoon by Gillray [1756–1815] and the reigning monarch is George III. Most of us would not now consider that material to be grossly offensive.[85]

But at the time it certainly was considered as such by many: Gillray took full advantage of the new opportunities in printmaking to promote his satirical and often extremely frank drawings to a wide audience. As the introduction to the 2001 Tate exhibition, *James Gillray: The Art of Caricature*, stated, 'Gillray's prints, from the time they were first produced, belonged both to the street and to the connoisseur's study.'

By the late nineteenth century, many popular attractions took similar advantage of technological developments in printing to publicize their delights to a wide audience by means of the advertising hoarding or billboard. In 1890 Captain Molesworth, managing director of the Royal Aquarium, Westminster (somewhat ironically now the site of Methodist Central Hall), engaged the energetic services of a young female aerialist, Adelaide Wieland, who performed under the stage name 'Zaeo'.[86] Despite its name, the Royal Aquarium served as a variety hall between 1876 and 1903, offering a panoply of visual and aural 'delights'. George Robey gave his first professional performance there in 1891, whilst other acts included a 'human cannonball'.[87] In order to publicize Zaeo's act, Molesworth commissioned a number of large posters in full colour depicting the rather statuesque young woman in what amounted to a kind of flouncy leotard and flesh-coloured tights. This poster (which today appears quaintly evocative of the 'Naughty Nineties') immediately aroused the wrath and ire of the NVA, which complained to Bow Street Magistrates' Court. The complaint may have implicitly been more about the type of 'lowbrow' entertainment that the venue was increasingly making available to the lower classes in order to bolster its box-office takings, together

85 *Hansard* HC Deb, 13 November 1973, vol.864 cc.377–437.

86 For further details of Zaeo's long career, together with the moral opprobrium that such circus performers often attracted, see P. Tait, *Circus Bodies: Cultural Identity in Aerial Performance* (London: Routledge, 2005).

87 Music Hall and Theatre History website: www.arthurlloyd.co.uk/RoyalAquarium.htm.

with the general appearance of female artistes in skimpy costumes rather than the particular depiction of Miss Zaeo's personal décolletage and bare(ish) legs; the venue had been the subject of much moral opprobrium since it first opened.

Yet another series of heated correspondence appeared in the metropolitan newspapers both criticising and defending the poster, but by far the most entertaining was the one that appeared to have silenced the moralists. On 28 May 1890 the *Daily News* published a rebuttal of the indecency exhibited in the poster from an obviously exasperated Captain Molesworth. He wrote a letter to Sir John Bridge, Chief Magistrate at Bow Street Magistrates' Court, stating that 'members of the Vigilance Society [the NVA], who appear to be strangely susceptible to temptations disregarded by pure-minded persons' were incorrect in their assertions as to the immodesty and indecency of the poster. He went on to say (tongue planted firmly in cheek) that he would be 'willing to have the lower limbs of Zaeo's picture enveloped in artistically designed unmentionables provided the Vigilance Society will pay the cost of printing and posting the same'.[88] It appears that the offer was not taken up by the NVA.

Traditional art exhibitions caused similar concern. On 23 June 1929 a letter from Dr L. J. R. Knutshen, who began his missive with the phrase 'I do not in any way pretend to be a prude', and then immediately went on to suggest otherwise, was received by the Commissioner of the Metropolitan Police.[89] In his letter, Dr Knutshen stated that a number of pictures by D. H. Lawrence currently being exhibited at the Warren Gallery in Maddox Street, London, 'even in Paris, Vienna, or Berlin, in my opinion should not be exhibited except in private'.[90] The gallery, run by Phillip and Dorothy Trotter (née Warren) was a respected venue and had been in existence for a number of years. Other letters of complaint were received by the Commissioner (rather intriguingly including one from the publisher Grant Richards, whom one would have assumed would have steered away from such matters after his tribulations with Joyce), but the Metropolitan Police files make it quite clear that the Home Office (specifically in the form of Sir John Anderson, Permanent Under-Secretary of State) did not want to be involved in a prosecution under the OPA 1857. On 27 June a note stated that 'it is not the wish of the Government to interfere', and this was reiterated on 3 July with another note stating 'it is not the wish of the Home Office that any steps should be taken.' The Commissioner subsequently decided that it would be enough to ask Miss Warren (aka Dorothy Trotter) to close the exhibition and that if she demurred, then the police would obtain a warrant from Marlborough Magistrates' Court under the OPA 1857.

The Home Office were clearly unwilling for either the Metropolitan Police or the government to be deeply involved in what promised to be yet another brief

---

88 For a detailed account of the Zaeo scandal, see T. Davis, 'Sex in public places: The Zaeo Aquarium scandal and the Victorian moral majority', *Theatre History Studies* 10 (1990): 1–13.

89 TNA MEPO 2/9428 Indecent exhibition of pictures by D.H. Lawrence at The Warren Gallery, 39A Maddox Street, W1 (1929).

90 Ibid.

outburst of moral outrage, but the situation changed following the publication of an article condemning the exhibition in the *Evening Standard* of 3 July 1929; quoting an anonymous art critic, the paper stated that 'this author-artist, weary perhaps of the easier task of being subtly misbehaved in print, has elected to come straight to the point, and is frankly disgusting in paint'. Sir Ernley Blackwell, Legal Assistant Under-Secretary of State, wrote to the Commissioner that 'action would probably have to be taken in view of this'.[91] A warrant was accordingly granted from Marlborough Street magistrates and thirteen paintings were seized on 5 July. Phillip and Dorothy Trotter were summonsed on 11 July, but their court appearance was immediately adjourned until 8 August. At the trial the Trotters were fined £5 5s costs and the paintings were ordered to be returned to the artist. Three books (basically expensively produced exhibition catalogues) had also been seized by the police, and these (in a somewhat chilling presage of the subsequent events of the night of 10 May 1933 in Berlin) were subsequently burned in the police station furnace on 3 September 1929. One of the paintings, 'A Boccaccio Story', was allegedly damaged whilst in police custody and was the subject of protracted correspondence from Lawrence's solicitors, but the others were all returned to him.[92] This episode demonstrates the problems faced by the moralists with regard to art and indecency; the courts were content to return the paintings to the artist, but refused to order their destruction (as demanded by several of the complainants), instead merely choosing in effect to implicitly state that there was a clear boundary between what constituted 'public' and 'private' indecency.

By 1857 the panoply of visual imagery available to the public had also expanded to include the new medium of photography. First regarded as something of a novelty at the time of its invention by Niépce in 1826/7, the medium had developed rapidly and some thirty years later it was growing exponentially in popularity (although the first camera affordable to the masses, the Kodak Brownie, was not sold until 1900). In 1859 developments in micro-photography allowed the patenting of the Stanhope Lens in France. This led to a craze in the production of small handheld items that could readily be concealed in a waistcoat pocket, containing Stanhope viewers. Although the most popular micro-images were topographic, there was also a thriving market in risqué Stanhope viewers produced in various forms, including small pocket knives, cigar cutters, signet rings, etc. Now often highly prized by collectors, these usually contained an image of a full-frontal nude or otherwise scantily clad young woman, and were popular with 'gentlemen around town'.

Many of the erotically posed photographs contained within the hidden confines of the Stanhope were loosely based on statues from classical antiquity, and such public exhibition of the female (and less occasionally, but as shown later, often equally controversially, male) nude caused numerous problems for Victorian and

91 Ibid.
92 Lawrence was incensed by the decision of the court, but died on 2 March 1930 before he could mount an appeal. For an account of the paintings (several of which are now in collections in Mexico), see K. M. Sagar, *D. H. Lawrence's Paintings* (London: Chaucer Press, 2003).

Edwardian moral guardians, both in the form of statuary and two-dimensional art. One of the most interesting examples of the dichotomy between 'high' art (i.e. designed for viewing by the educated elite) and 'low' nudity (i.e. easily accessible to the majority) can be seen by examining the controversy surrounding the erection of eighteen large statues sculpted by Jacob Epstein high up on the frontage of the new British Medical Association fronting Agar Street in the Strand in 1908. The statues were a depiction of the 'Ages of Man' and the concomitant development of science, and were one of Epstein's first major commissions. They were around eight feet in height, and many depicted the human form in a naturalistic and unconfined state. The statues were almost immediately condemned by the irrepressible Coote, Secretary of the NVA, along with Nonconformist and Jesuit leaders.

One of the campaigners is reported to have given the dire warning that 'if left in their present condition [the statues] will most assuredly become a splendid draw to all the unchaste and libidinous curiosity seekers in London'.[93] An anonymous letter (from 'an indignant and pained citizen' dated 6 June 1908) asked 'if the public thoroughfares of London are gradually to be made copies of the streets of Naples?' by the inclusion of such statues, again an intertwining of moral turpitude with Continental depravity.[94] On 17 June 1908, Mr Hyslop, the organizing secretary of the Protestant Alliance (founded 1845 by the seventh Earl of Shaftesbury), commented that the statues 'are certain to form the subject of adverse comment by a very large section of the public'.[95]

The moralists' campaign to have the statues either altered or various prominences covered was taken up by the *Evening Standard & St James' Gazette*, which published numerous letters from opponents of the statues. This in turn garnered severe criticism by the BMA, which mounted a spirited defence of the statuary in the *BMJ*. The *BMJ* of 27 June 1908 stated that

> The attitude of the *Evening Standard* and *St. James's Gazette* reminds us of an old picture in *Punch* of an elderly virgin in seaside lodgings complaining of men bathing in front of her window. When it is pointed out to her that they are a mile or more off, she says, 'Yes, but then one can see with a spyglass!'[96]

The *BMJ* was particularly scathing about the claimed detrimental effects that seeing depictions of the human form would have on an excitable and libidinous public, stating that

> If this sort of prudery is carried to its logical conclusion any one visiting a gallery of pictures or sculpture will have to get a certificate of virtue from his pastor.[97]

---

93 *BMJ* 2, no. 2,479 (4 July 1908), 46–7, 46.
94 TNA MEPO 3/385 So-called indecent statue in Carlos Place W.1 (1908–1930).
95 Ibid.
96 *BMJ* 1, no. 2,478 (27 June 1908), 1,593–4, 1,594.
97 Ibid., 1,593.

The journal kept up such satirical commentary, remarking in its next edition that the *Evening Standard & St James' Gazette*

> might, of course, go further in its educational enterprise and point out that Cleopatra's Needle is a phallic emblem, and explain to young men and maidens the symbolism which has been attributed to the 'vesica' window. Indecency can be found in almost everything if one knows where to look for it.[98]

Despite the barrage of criticism, both the police and the London authorities declined to take any action against the statues: 'The matter is not one in which Police can take action . . . sleeping dogs should be permitted to lie.'[99] The statues remained in their original and unaltered state until the mid-1930s, when *The Times* reported that following the sale of the building to the Rhodesian High Commission (it was rechristened Rhodesia House and later renamed Zimbabwe House), the statues were due to be removed, ostensibly because they were deemed to be situated too high up on the building, not suited to the austerity befitting governmental edifices, and were becoming increasingly susceptible to the effects of the British climate.[100]

In 1930 in a Metropolitan Police file which concerned another 'indecent' statue, an anonymous individual stated that 'somewhat similar statuary was placed outside the new offices of the BMA, Agar Street, in 1908 and gave rise to some complaint and a good deal of unfavourable comment. The statuary is still there but nobody now notices it.'[101] This file resulted from an anonymous letter to the Commissioner of Police concerning a slightly larger than life-size bronze statue by the noted sculptor A. F. Hardiman, which had been erected in a niche in the wall of a private residence owned by Major Stephen Courtauld in Carlos Place, London W1 in early 1930.[102] It was a heavily stylized and rather Brutalist representative of St George in the form of a completely naked man wielding a curved sword. The police officer despatched to make a report of the statue stated that 'the figure is certainly the subject of many lewd jokes from certain passers-by', but once again, it was decided that the police should take no further action.[103]

While much activist energy was devoted to suppression of traditional forms of artistic expression, another graphical manifestation of emerging popular culture had emerged to challenge propriety. The first picture postcards (in the form of souvenir advertisements) appeared in Britain in 1872, but it was not until 1886 that they began to gain popularity, after the Universal Postal Union allowed

---

98 *BMJ* 2, no. 2,479, 46. A vesica is the elliptic shape formed by two overlapping circles and is reminiscent of the birth canal.
99 TNA MEPO 3/385.
100 *The Times*, 24 April 1935.
101 TNA MEPO 3/385.
102 Ibid. Major Stephen Courtauld was a prominent member of the famous textile family, and redesigned Eltham Palace into one of the triumphs of the Art Deco age in Britain.
103 The statue was removed from Carlos Place and now stands proudly in a similar niche at Eltham Palace without engendering any negative comments.

international traffic in such items. In September 1894 the Royal Mail allowed private individuals to post picture postcards stamped with a halfpenny postage. It has been claimed that between 1894 and 1919 more than 140 billion postcards were posted throughout the world, and that in 1909 alone, some 800,000 million postcards were sold in England.[104] Although these claims seem somewhat inflated (the latter being sourced from *The Vigilance Record*, 'The Organ of the NVA'), the trade in such items was undoubtedly huge. Among the picturesque views of the Great Orme or the Isle of Wight, a number of less edifying postcards were also produced – though not sent uncovered through the post, as this would have been an offence in itself. These postcards, usually featuring nubile young women in various stages of undress, albeit often with a nod to classical statuary, became widely known as 'French postcards'. Whilst numerous such images *were* produced in Paris, the main publishers tended to be based in Germany (albeit obviously still dangerously Continental).

A Home Office investigation into the receipt of allegedly unsolicited pornographic material (unspecified but most likely to be photographic postcards) from abroad in the autumn of 1894 exemplified the increasing problem of such material originating abroad and being imported or posted into England. The investigation was instigated by a letter dated 2 October 1894 from the enraged Mayor of Bedford, whose office had received 'an indecent catalogue' from a 'Hungarian Jew' named Bellak, who was operating a mail-order business from Belgrade in Servia (now Serbia). The Mayor stated that he was 'horrified and disgusted beyond measure' by the contents of the catalogue, for which he insisted none of his staff had sent. The Home Office official stated in his reply that the problem of 'cautiously worded advertisements placed . . . in newspapers of a low order' was an ever-increasing one. The outcome of the investigation resulted in letters being sent to the Servian Ambassador and Bellak finally being fined 60 francs and expelled from Servia.[105] By the end of the first decade of the twentieth century, the importation of such 'indecent' material was causing considerable concern; these 'awful effusions of an effete civilisation' were feared to be corrupting the morals of English men and youths.[106] *The Times* of 11 February 1914 commented on this increasing and 'vulgarising traffic' under the strapline 'Offensive Picture Postcards'. It reported that the Retail Tradesmen's Association of Southport had formed a censorship committee in order to stem the sale of such offensive items from their town. Similar self-appointed moral guardianships were created in Douglas, Blackpool, Lowestoft, Great Yarmouth, and Ramsgate, all significantly popular tourist destinations with both the working classes and lower-middle classes.

However, despite such actions, indefatigable campaigner Canon Hardwick Drummond Rawnsley, co-founder of the National Trust and author of 'The child and the cinematograph show and the Picture Postcard Evil', claimed that 'the

104 Sigel, 'Filth in the wrong people's hands', 861.
105 TNA HO 144/192/A466557D.
106 'Picture postcard fiend', *Penny Illustrated Paper*, 15 June 1912.

output of these demoralising picture postcards still goes forward . . . Great Britain is being flooded with picture postcards that are just beyond the border line'.[107] Although they needed little if any cultural or artistic knowledge to be 'appreciated', indecent picture postcards did often pay passing acknowledgement to 'high' art; many of the poses were pale reflections of statuary from classical antiquity or of well-known stories such as Salome. As Sigel comments, 'High art unproblematically became low art because the central icon – female nakedness – eclipsed the distinction between the two worlds.'[108] More than any previous technological development, postcards brought about a 'democratization' of pornography: they 'required little financial sacrifice, even for the poor' and, as importantly, they could be understood 'without the skills of literacy [or] the cultural referents of art and literature'.[109] They were therefore seen by campaigners such as Rawnsley as especially challenging to the maintenance of morals among the poorer, less educated classes.

'A matter of legitimate controversy': Continuing campaigns

Throughout the 1930s, successive Home Secretaries faced questions in the House of Commons about indecent material. MPs asked repeatedly about the availability of indecent postcards,[110] and attention was drawn to indecent cinema posters.[111] Despite the fact that the OPA 1857 ensured literature and art would continue to be forcefully suppressed by magistrates throughout the period, campaigners were rarely satisfied. In 1937, the Bishop of London complained: 'I took in twenty-one filthy books to one Home Secretary and told him to read them and see what he could do about them. To the last Home Secretary-but-one I took in about a dozen filthy periodicals. Are we to wait for Mussolini or Hitler to come and put these down?'[112] The cause of such complaints seems clear: even though Home Secretaries would often seem sympathetic to the moral cause (for example, Sir Herbert Samuel stated in 1932, 'We are all aware that there are in our midst certain tendencies towards indecency and degradation'[113]), in practice, the response of government was rarely anything more than politely negative when pressed to do more.

Nevertheless, campaigners and their parliamentary spokesmen continued to spread their concerns widely at the expense of more focussed forms of moral attrition and often with what can only be viewed as a strange sense of timing and priorities. In 1938, Robin Turton MP sought to introduce the Public Places

---

107 *Hibbert Journal* xi. (1913), 3–11.
108 Sigel, 'Filth in the wrong people's hands', 865.
109 Ibid., 865.
110 *Hansard* HC Deb, 8 May 1930, vol.238 cc.1112–3, 1112; *Hansard* HC Deb, 02 July 1931, vol. 254 cc.1440–1, 1440.
111 *Hansard* HC Deb, 29 March 1938, vol.333 cc.1831–2, 1831.
112 Bishop of London, 'London as it should be', in Bristow, *Vice and Vigilance*, 224. This was obviously an implicit reference to the previously mentioned burning of the books by the Nazis some years earlier.
113 *Hansard* HC Deb, 15 April 1932, vol.264 cc.1135–99, 1155.

(Order and Decency) Bill, which aimed to amend the Vagrancy Act 1824, the Universities Act 1825, the Metropolitan Police Act 1839, and the Town Police Clauses Act 1847 in order to 'reform the law of the streets'.[114] In 1939, Day, the MP who had worried so much about postcards, asked about the number of charges of indecency brought by the police under the Hyde Park regulations.[115] In 1940, the Postmaster General was asked whether he was aware 'that booklets advocating birth control, and giving many details of sex problems unsuitable for children to read about, are being sent through the post in open envelopes . . .?'[116] In 1941, Reginald Sorensen MP complained that the PMC had 'made certain sweeping statements which are very much resented by those who use these shelters' that air raid shelters had 'been used for immoral purposes during "all-clear" periods' (the Under-Secretary of State for the Home Office agreed that 'this matter has been greatly exaggerated').[117] In 1943, Commander Robert Bower MP challenged the Secretary of State for Air over the vexed question of the editorship of the *Royal Air Force Journal*, the chosen candidate having been previously convicted of publishing indecent matter.[118] There was legitimate health-related concern about the spread of venereal disease amongst both the military and civilian population, cited as 'one instance of the demoralization and disease that follow war. We have taken young people from their homes and herded them together, and immorality and disease have spread'.[119]

After the war, Muskett and the Police Commissioner resumed their efforts to seek more orders of destruction, but the war had liberalized public attitudes. They now found it harder to convince the magistracy of the need for censure. Enforcement activity relating to sexual offences, principally prostitution and homosexuality, continued as matters which fell squarely within the parameters of the criminal law. But the moral campaigners wanted suppression of indecent *ideas* and, particularly the PMC, continued their pursuit of indecent literature and other printed material throughout the war and well into the 1950s.

Bishop Winningham-Ingram retired in 1939 but the chairmanship of the PMC devolved to the next Bishop of London, aided from 1940 by the next zealous PMC secretary, George Tomlinson. With the end of the war, social and cultural change was moving the tide of attitudes against the moral campaigners and the new Labour government was less easily persuaded of the moral case for intervention. The newspaper serialization in 1947 of *Forever Amber*, a romance novel by Kathleen Winsor which was banned in the United States and condemned by the Catholic Church for indecency, led to a refusal to prosecute by the DPP on the

114 *Hansard* HC Deb, 20 July 1938, vol.338 cc.2209–12, 2209.
115 *Hansard* HC Deb, 26 July 1939, vol.230 cc.1629–30W, 1629W. The answer was five in April, three in May, and eight in June.
116 *Hansard* HC Deb, 19 June 1940, vol.362 cc.144–5.
117 *Hansard* HC Deb, 23 April 1941, vol.371 cc.170–1.
118 *Hansard* HC Deb, 14 July 1943, vol.391 c.173 in response, Sir Arthur Sinclair was satisfied that 'since his appointment the paper has prospered and given satisfaction'.
119 Mrs Hardie MP, *Hansard* HC Deb, 15 December 1942, vol.385 cc.1807–87, 1814.

grounds that it did not warrant proceedings under the criminal law relating to indecent and obscene publications. When William Gallacher MP (described ironically by Quintin Hogg MP in the same debate as a 'champion of Christian morals'[120]) suggested that it was 'time that the law was altered so that there could be prosecutions in cases of this kind, which involve an appalling waste of newsprint for such a filthy publication' he was met by an uncompromising reply from the Home Secretary Chuter Ede:

> I am reluctant to do anything that restricts the right of publication. I am constantly being urged to restrict publication of documents in which, I understand, the hon. Gentleman himself is interested, and I have consistently declined to yield to such overtures.[121]

In 1959, when challenged by Eric Fletcher MP about government inaction in the face of imports of 'millions of cheap, American, pornographic publications,' Home Office spokesman Frederick Erroll MP retorted: 'I have described the adequate powers which the Government possess to prevent it coming into the country. While, according to the hon. Member, I may have merely described the law, the fact is that the law is effective.'[122]

Campaigners still had a few successes: in 1949 the president of the Board of Trade was asked in Parliament what steps he had taken 'to prevent the import of sadistic literature directed to the young from the United States of America and Canada'.[123] This referred to American graphic novels and horror comics such as *Tales from the Crypt* and *The Vault of Horror* which, echoing early twentieth-century campaigns against demoralizing literature, were believed to be a cause of juvenile delinquency and encourage illiteracy because of the visual content. Moral campaigners, educationalists, and the clergy demanded the censure of these 'harmful comics' while their US publishers protested against attempts to impose a ban. The Archbishop of York issued a warning about their damaging effect which was supported by the Company of New Elizabethans (a moral campaign group) and a number of Yorkshire schools.[124] The issue came to a head in 1954 following a 'moral furore' and media frenzy when hundreds of armed children were apparently found patrolling a Glasgow graveyard in search of vampires.[125] In October, Glasgow Corporation sent a deputation to the Secretary of State for Scotland demanding a ban supported by the Educational Institute of Scotland. One of its representatives asked, 'Where is the line to be drawn between harmless blood-and-thunder comics of the old-fashioned kind and the

---

120 *Hansard* HC Deb, 31 July 1947, vol.441, cc.613–4.
121 Ibid.
122 *Hansard* HC Deb, 10 December 1959, vol.615 cc.715–6.
123 *Hansard* HC Deb, 12 April 1949, vol.463 cc.2634–5.
124 *Yorkshire Post and Leeds Intelligencer*, 11 March, 1 September 1952, 29 April 1953.
125 See e.g. HC Deb, 31 January 1952, vol.495 c339; *Hansard* HC Deb, 21 October 1954, vol.531 cc.1376–8.

horrific kind which might corrupt?'[126] Edinburgh Library even announced that it would house a collection of the comics for 'reference purposes' and as a 'museum piece'.[127] Simultaneously, the Comics Campaign Council (created in 1953) visited the Home Secretary asking him to review the current law.[128]

Legislative action in the form of the Children and Young Persons (Harmful Publications) Act 1955 was secured which made it an offence to print, publish, or sell any literature likely to fall into the hands of, and corrupt, a child or a young person through any portrayal of the commission of crime, acts of cruelty or violence, or incidents of a repulsive or horrible nature.

The advent of a Conservative government more sympathetic to the cause of moral reform in 1951 led to a final flurry of activism against literature and art, culminating in the 'puzzling 1954 "purge"' when Home Secretary Sir David Maxwell Fyfe 'sanctioned . . . the last blanket onslaught on serious literature'.[129] The targets of this 'purge' were varied as was the practical enforcement. On 30 July 1954, Swindon magistrates ordered the destruction of a number of copies of Boccaccio's classic text *Decameron*,[130] and a few months later the stipendiary magistrate at Leeds declared it was no longer considered to be obscene – while confirming the destruction of 108,000 copies of *A Basinful of Fun* and its 'revolting picture of the winner of a bikini girl competition'.[131] Moving from the sublime to the ridiculous, in an interesting example of history almost repeating itself with an echo of the 1890s' furore concerning 'indecent' postcards, the focus moved on to the saucy seaside postcards filled with innuendo and buxom ladies in bathing suits created by Donald and Constance McGill which sold by the millions.[132] In 1950, 297 'obscene' postcards were ordered to be destroyed, by 1953 this had increased to 32,603.[133] The Blackpool police had been particularly diligent, prosecuting fourteen traders in 1950 and another seventeen in 1951. Some 10 million postcards were sold each summer in the town but the impact of such prosecutions on local businesses led to the creation of the Blackpool Censorship Committee in October 1951 to mitigate the situation.[134] The Committee took a relatively liberal approach, but other seaside towns which followed suit adopted a more stringent

---

126 *Aberdeen Evening Express*, 15 October 1954.

127 *The Times*, 29 October 1954.

128 *The Times*, 19 October 1954; for an in-depth analysis of the Council's role see M. Barker, *A Haunt of Fears: The Strange History of the British Horror Comics Campaign* (Mississippi: University Press of Mississippi, 1984).

129 Bristow, *Vice and Vigilance*, 226.

130 M. Barker, 'Getting a conviction' in J. Lent (ed.) *Pulp Demons: International Dimensions of the Post-war Anti-comics Campaign* (Madison NJ: Fairleigh Dickinson University Press, 1999), 79. Swindon magistrates had also ordered the destruction of a number of postcards and books in January 1954, which led to an unsuccessful appeal to the High Court by Chain Libraries to have the decision overturned; see *Thomson v Chain Libraries* (1954) 1 WLR 999.

131 *The Times*, 12 October 1954.

132 Between 1904 and 1962 an estimated 200 million McGill cards were sold; see U. Smartt, *Media and Entertainment Law* (London: Routledge, 2011), 347.

133 British Cartoon Archive: www.cartoons.ac.uk/dpps-obscene-postcard-index.

134 See M. Hearn, *Saucy Postcards: The Bamforth Collection* (London: Constable, 2013).

approach which caused problems for manufacturers and traders. All prosecutions were notified to the Director of Public Prosecutions, Sir Theobald Mathew, with the aim of creating a reference list of prohibited postcards to encourage greater consistency in prosecutorial decisions. This proved impossible as the verdicts on the list of 1,300 postcards proved too random.[135] McGill himself was eventually charged under the 1857 Act and convicted in a so-called show trial at Lincoln magistrates in July 1954 where he was fined £50 with £25 costs.[136] The futility of such prosecutions was highlighted by Sir Leslie Plummer MP to the 1957 Select Committee on the Obscene Publications Bill, who asked, somewhat rhetorically, 'Is there any common approach amongst Chief Constables to the Donald McGill kind of postcards – No, there is not. Each Chief Constable is a law unto himself . . . It is beyond the wit of the Home office to secure co-ordination amongst a hundred Chief Constables.'[137]

Reputable book publishers were also being hauled in front of the courts. Walter Baxter, author of *The Image and The Search*, which dealt with a woman who took many lovers after the loss of her husband in the war, was prosecuted twice alongside his publisher Alexander Stewart Frere, chairman of Heinemann, for publishing an obscene libel. The first trial in October 1954 resulted in a hung jury.[138] During the second prosecution at the Central Criminal Court, Mr Justice Lynskey gave the jury, comprising ten men and two women, a week to take the book home to read. Gerald Gardiner QC for the defence acknowledged that 'there might be something in the book that might shock people or possibly disgust some' but there was nothing that would deprave or corrupt. Lynskey, in his summing up, reassured the jury that the 'law was very clear' but invoked the rhetoric of 'evil' implicitly asking them to consider whether there was any link between such publications and the numerous immoral cases on his list of 'indecency, incest and abortion'. Continuing his summing up the following day, he backtracked significantly: 'I do not want you to think, nor suggest to you, nor even hint, that this book had anything to do with those cases', reminding them what he had meant was that such crimes were committed by people with corrupt and deprived minds.[139] With the second jury unable to agree the prosecution withdrew their case.

In the same year, *The Philanderer*, written by Stanley Kauffmann and published by the impeccably reputable Secker and Warburg, was also prosecuted for obscene libel.[140] Mr Justice Stable's direction to the jury that the book should be taken as a whole, foreshadowing the changes which would take place in 1959 rather than adopting the traditional 'purple passages' approach, is generally credited for

---

135 British Cartoon Archive.
136 For an essay written in defence of such postcards, see G. Orwell, 'The art of Donald McGill', *Horizon Literary Journal* 4, no. 21(1941): 153–63.
137 Minutes of evidence taken before the Select Committee on the Obscene Publications Bill 1956–1957 (122) (London: HMSO 1958) 16.
138 *The Times*, 19 October 1954.
139 *The Times*, 30 November, 1 December 1954.
140 *Reg. v. Martin Secker & Warburg Ltd.* [1954] 1 WLR 1138; [1954] 2 All ER. 683.

the resultant acquittal (although Kauffmann's wife had predicted that a successful prosecution was unlikely because the book was 'so dull that no jury, enlightened or otherwise, would be able to finish reading it'[141]). *The Spectator* said that the judge's summing up 'represents the liberal and humane view of the standards of taste of the mid-twentieth century'.[142] A few months later, however, *September in Quinze* by Vivian Connell (first published in 1952) did not fare so well. A different judge, Sir Gerald Dodson, directed that 'a book which would not be expected to influence an archbishop might influence a callow youth or young girl budding into womanhood'[143] and the jury duly convicted.[144] This legal onslaught and public expression of judicial opinion had a particular impact on publishers: 'It is the directors of old-established firms of unimpeachable reputation who are anxiously thumbing through the manuscripts of established writers in the fear that some delineation of lust (described perhaps, only to illustrate its evil consequences), some unguarded reference to the facts of life, some touches of Rabelaisian humour, will involve a prosecution.'[145]

Conclusion

This was a short-lived victory for moral conservatism. If anything, the 1954 cases were a final retrenchment of activism around the OPA 1857. The prosecutions changed the dynamic: where previously 'indecent literature' could be portrayed as the work of a few 'decadent' minds (such as D. H. Lawrence) assisted by fringe publishers of pornography, now mainstream, reputable publishing houses were in the line of fire. Although this produced a brief chilling effect, it also fuelled opposition. Claims of indecency in printed material were now being interpreted as matters of taste. There was even a very obvious linguistic shift in the meaning of the word *demoralization* (first evident in the parliamentary debates of World War Two), to its modern sense of weakening morale rather than morals. Crucially, the core meaning of the OPA 1857, the concept of 'to deprave and corrupt', began to be questioned. In the debate on the report from the Select Committee on Obscene Publications of Session 1957–1958, Robin Bell MP stated, 'What tends to corrupt is itself a matter of legitimate controversy, and opinions on it change from time to time.'[146] Where once indecency campaigners sought to extend the law beyond obscenity, now they were on the defensive, trying to ensure the continuance and enforcement of a discredited piece of legislation. For more than half a century, they had sought to expand the boundaries of the law relating to publications beyond the

141 A. Cummings, 'Why Stanley Kauffmann's *Philanderer* still rings a bell', *The Guardian*, 12 March 2010, www.theguardian.com/books/booksblog/2010/mar/11/stanley-kauffmann-law-philanderer: accessed 27 September 2014
142 *The Spectator*, 22 October 1954, 4.
143 As described by Viscount Lambton when moving the second reading of the Obscene Publications Bill 1957, *Hansard* HC Deb, 29 March 1957, vol. 567 cc.1491, 1494.
144 *Hutchinson* (1954) unreported.
145 *The Spectator*, 22 October 1954, 4.
146 *Hansard* HC Deb, 16 December 1958, vol.597 cc.992–1051, 1037.

terms of the OPA 1857 to cover their own perceptions of indecency. But now the wheel turned full circle, and obscenity law itself came under sustained attack. The 1954 'purge' turned out to be a watershed, the start of the end for the OPA 1857.

The Society of Authors, founded in 1884 to protect the rights of writers, formed a committee under the chairmanship of Sir Alan Herbert to examine the issues raised by the recent prosecutions. Concluding that the problem lay with the uncertainty of interpretation of the law surrounding the *Hicklin* test, in 1955 they submitted a Bill to Parliament intended to completely reform obscenity law. The Bill inevitably underwent revisions, and several different versions were introduced unsuccessfully into Parliament, but the momentum was unstoppable and the influence of the indecency campaigners clearly on the wane. Viscount Lambton, moving the second reading of one of the reform attempts in 1957, makes a revealingly dismissive comment:

> Every now and again there have been most glaring exceptions to the rule of tolerance which has prevailed. The last of these came in 1954. The pattern is always the same. The country has what one might describe as a fit of morality. The pattern of this fit is nearly always the same. One of our great national newspapers, somewhat ungrateful for that which is, in fact, the basis of its circulation, will decide that London is the modern Babylon, and that morals in this country are the talk of the world. What follows after that is automatic. Constituents write to and question their Members. Members write to and question the Home Secretary. Home Secretaries, in the past, have always considered that they should act. So certain streets or districts in London are 'cleaned up', certain pederasts are imprisoned, certain publishers are prosecuted. The fit subsides, and England is safe again.[147]

Within two years, the OPA 1857 was repealed and replaced by the Obscene Publications Act 1959. Although the new legislation still contained the *Hicklin* terminology of 'to deprave and corrupt' it also included a statutory requirement to take account of the likely audience and to take the work as a whole,[148] and a defence that 'publication of the article in question is justified as being for the public good on the ground that it is in the interests of science, literature, art or learning, or of other objects of general concern'.[149] This made all the difference. The Act continued to be a major restraint on explicit sexual material intended as pornography, and import controls remained to regulate indecent material in the post, but as illustrated by the 'Not Guilty' verdict in the trial of Penguin Books in November 1960 regarding the posthumous publication of D. H. Lawrence's *Lady*

---

147 *Hansard* HC Deb, 29 March 1957, vol. 567 cc.1491–581, 1493.
148 S.1 (1): an article shall be deemed to be obscene if its effect or (where the article comprises two or more distinct items) the effect of any one of its items is, if taken as a whole, such as to tend to deprave and corrupt persons who are likely, having regard to all relevant circumstances, to read, see or hear the matter contained or embodied in it.
149 S.4(1).

Chatterley's Lover, the indecency campaigners would never again be able to bully and prosecute the writers, publishers, and distributors of serious literature with the ease that had prevailed for so long. Instead, they would be faced with a barrage of experts giving evidence of 'literary merit', exposing the claims of indecency and depravity as narrow, provincial, and petty-minded.[150]

The essential problem for those who sought to enforce morality through the law and to suppress the expression of indecent ideas in the world of art and literature was that to them, the equation of indecency with immorality and the legal unacceptability of both was self-evident; to others, tasked with drafting or interpreting statutory provisions, the concept of indecency and obscenity was much narrower but still far from simple. From the nineteenth century to the present day it would appear that few if any Home Secretaries have been immune to the often continual cajoling and persuasion of those seeking to impose their own moral standards on the law. As Kenneth Robinson MP suggested in 1957: 'It requires a measure of courage to suggest reform in the law upon these matters. It inevitably opens the hon. Member to attacks from the stage army of the pure, not only in this House, not only amongst his constituents, but also from farther afield.'[151]

Throughout the first half of the twentieth century, moral campaigners placed indecency in the spotlight and pursued writers, artists, publishers, and printers through the courts, even as their values and moral sensibilities became increasingly divorced from mainstream popular culture. The indecency campaigners never gave up against literature and other individualistic expressions of ideas, but as is demonstrated in Chapter Five, their focus increasingly turned towards the sphere of public entertainment, where in addition to old forms (theatre and music hall), they faced the unprecedented problem of the new, in the form of cinematography and broadcasting.

150 For an interesting article on the post-1960 effectiveness (or otherwise) of the Obscene Publications Act 1959, see D. Watkins, 'The protection of literature under English law in a post-modern age', *Mountbatten Journal of Legal Studies* 12, no. 2 (2008): 3–22.
151 *Hansard* HC Deb, 29 March 1957, vol. 567 cc.1491–581, 1498.

5 'Indecorous and inexpedient'

Visual and aural indecency in the
dramatic arts 1857–1960

Introduction

This chapter examines the conflict over indecency that permeated the world of organized and institutionalized public entertainment during the period 1857–1960, notably with respect to the legal regulation of the visual and aural arts: predominantly theatre, cinema, television, and radio. Subsequent chapters will survey less-organized spheres of leisure activities, in particular the indecency debate in relation to drinking and intoxication.

Searle documents some of the crucial changes in twentieth-century life which were to cause the indecency campaigners so much trouble in this world of public entertainment:

> The rise of real wages by one-third in the final two decades of the nineteenth century allowed all but the very poor to do more with their lives than struggle for bare survival. But this increase in disposable income would have been of limited benefit had it not been accompanied by an expansion of the time available for what contemporaries often referred to, rather disparagingly, as 'play'.[1]

The increasingly beleaguered moral activists, for whom 'decent' behaviour was a touchstone for everything they valued, were witnessing the passing of power to the newly educated and democratically empowered lower classes, and with it the growing dominance of new moral sensibilities which were particularly evident in the development of new drama and cinema. The campaigners were no longer fighting to preserve or reinstate Victorian values: they were fighting to protect and hold their own diminishing moral space in the face of a new popular culture infused with both the highbrow values of modernism and radicalism, and the considerably lower-brow but equally problematic influences of commercialism, both home-grown and, with the advent of cinema, from Hollywood.

Although often examined as discrete aspects of censorship activity, the law relating to the moving arts of theatre, film, and broadcasting needs to be contextualized as part of the wider indecency agenda. The actual nature and content of

---

1 G.R. Searle, *A New England? Peace and War 1886–1918* (Oxford: Oxford University Press, 2004), 529.

censorship has been more than adequately explored elsewhere.[2] The focus of this chapter will therefore be to consider the relevant law in a wider context and with reference to the extent to which moral campaigners sought to influence the regulatory environment of theatre, film, and broadcasting between 1857 and 1960. In the case of theatre, there were unique opportunities to gain influence by the insertion of particular conceptions of 'decency' into the established regime of censorship, while the fledging cinema and broadcasting industries of the early twentieth century offered entirely new territory for the moral and legal contest in a debate that would be conducted in the light of experience gained in relation to theatre.

Theatre censorship: A legal straitjacket

Theatre was, for many centuries, the most regulated and censored form of activity in Britain. Mainstream dramatic theatre had been subject to censorship since the Elizabethan age under the oversight of the Lord Chamberlain's Office. The original motive for this was largely political (theatres, particularly in London, being potential hotbeds for creating unrest and even sedition amongst the notoriously volatile 'mob'). For example, in 1773 Sir John Fielding (Chief Magistrate of Bow Street Magistrates Court, and half-brother of magistrate and novelist Henry Fielding) tried unsuccessfully to prevent a performance by David Garrick at the Drury Lane Theatre of John Gay's *Beggar's Opera* on the grounds that previous productions of the scandalous play had always resulted in an increase of immoral and criminal behaviour within the city. As a backlash against Sir John Fielding's campaign, in the same year a deeply satirical anonymously penned play was staged in the capital. Entitled *The Bow Street Opera in Three Acts. Written on the plan of the Beggar's Opera*, the work was a scathing attack on both contemporary politics and justice. The play featured a very lightly disguised caricature of Fielding as 'Justice Blindman' (Fielding had been blind since an accident at the age of 19), and also featured a thinly disguised portrayal of John Wilkes, a Radical. The following air, sung by Bess Bunter (a prostitute) to Justice Blindman, captures the irreverent tone of the play:

> *In the days of your youth you could bill like a dove*
> *And your surgeon can witness how fervent our love*

---

2 Steve Nicholson, in particular, has had unprecedented access to the Royal Archives, including much of the correspondence with the Lord Chamberlain's Office relating to individual plays, and has explored in detail the thought processes and behind-the-scenes arguments involved in twentieth-century censorship. See S. Nicholson, *The Censorship of British Drama 1900–1968: Volume 1, 1900–1932*, Exeter Performance Studies (Exeter: University of Exeter Press, 2003); *The Censorship of British Drama 1900–1968: Volume 2, 1933–1952*, Exeter Performance Studies (Exeter: University of Exeter Press, 2005a); *The Censorship of British Drama 1900–1968, Volume 3, The Fifties*, Exeter Performance Studies (Exeter: University of Exeter Press, 2005b). For a shorter overview of the history of censorship see D. Shellard, S. Nicholson, and M. Handley, *The Lord Chamberlain Regrets . . . A History of British Theatre Censorship* (London: The British Library, 2011). For both historical background and an entertaining insider's view of life as an Assistant Comptroller in the Lord Chamberlain's Office, see J. Johnson, *The Lord Chamberlain's Blue Pencil* (London: Hodder and Stoughton, 1990).

The life of a justice in kissing should pass
You have oft kissed my face – you may now kiss my arse![3]

The focus on sedition and political unrest gradually shifted and by the mid-nineteenth century the function of theatre censorship was widely associated 'with the policing of public morality'.[4] The Theatrical Licensing Act 1737 ('Walpole's Act') put the Lord Chamberlain's role on a statutory footing by requiring plays to be submitted for approval before performance, and established a near monopoly over serious drama for the Patent Theatres (Theatre Royal Drury Lane and Theatre Royal Covent Garden). The Theatres Act 1843 (also known as the Theatre Regulation Act) was a near repetition of many provisions of the 1737 Act, but with wider geographical effect.[5] It abolished the distinction between patent and non-patent theatres, enabling local authorities to license theatres and music halls throughout the country. Under section 2 no person was to 'have or keep any house or other place of public resort in Great Britain for the public performance of stage plays without authority of Letters Patent or of licence from the Lord Chamberlain or justices of the peace' (in districts outside the jurisdiction of the Lord Chamberlain's Office). Under section 8 the Lord Chamberlain could 'in case of riot or misbehaviour in the theatre, close any patent theatre or theatre licensed by him; also he may close it on any public occasion as shall seem fit to him'. This did not include the closure of a theatre on any other grounds, thus sanctions for breach of the Lord Chamberlain's licence were restricted to fines.[6] Section 9 gave similar powers to local licensing Justices of the Peace in relation to riot or misbehaviour, but extended this to include the power to 'make and alter rules for ensuring order and decency in the theatres, and for regulating the times during which they may be open'[7] thus, somewhat paradoxically, placing the provincial theatres under a tougher regime with the sanction of closure for breach of a licence.

In 1909, Byrne, Assistant Under-Secretary of State for the Home Department, explained that this was probably a 'drafting omission' and that

> the law officers have advised that it is a practice well founded and based on law that the Lord Chamberlain should make rules and regulations and attach them to the licences that he grants, and that that power to make these rules

---

3 *The Bow Street Opera*, 13th Air, Act II. The reference to a surgeon suggests that their 'fervent love' had resulted in a bout of syphilis. For further details of Bow Street Police Office and its various police forces, see D.J. Cox, *A Certain Share of Low Cunning*, and J.M. Beattie, *The First English Detectives*.

4 Shellard *et al.*, *The Lord Chamberlain Regrets*, 10.

5 The 1737 Act had not permitted theatres to be licensed at all in the provinces, although a limited power to grant such licences was given to Justices of the Peace in 1788.

6 Under section 11: every person who for hire shall act or present or cause, permit, or suffer to be acted or presented any part in any stage play in any place not patented or licensed, shall forfeit on conviction not exceeding £10 per diem.

7 The Secretary of State could rescind or alter any such rules.

and regulations is inherent in his jurisdiction, and so far as I know that position has never been disputed.[8]

For provincial theatres, County Councils replaced magistrates as the Licensing Authority by virtue of section 7(a) of the Local Government Act 1888, but section 28(2) permitted the local authorities to delegate these powers, with the result that many simply delegated them back to the Justices in the petty sessions of the district where the application was made.[9]

Section 12 of the Theatres Act 1843 required that one copy of every new stage play and of every new act, scene, or other part intended to be produced and acted for hire in any theatre in Great Britain, must be sent to the Lord Chamberlain at least seven days before the first performance. This provided the definitive copy which – assuming it was not refused, and after any textual changes were made – became the subject of the terms of the stage play licence. Under section 14 the Lord Chamberlain had power to prohibit the performance of stage plays where he was of the opinion that 'it is fitting for the preservation of good manners, decorum or of the public peace so to do.'

The power of licensing stage plays was, in law, very much a personal fiefdom of the Lord Chamberlain, in a similar way to which the British Board of Film Censors (created in 1912) would later be with regard to film. 'The whole responsibility rests, not with the reader or the examiner,[10] but with the man who for the time being is Lord Chamberlain.'[11] The Lord Chamberlain's Office, as a department of the Royal Household, was overseen by the Comptroller, while practical day-to-day exercise of the stage licensing responsibility lay with the Examiner of Plays and his assistants, who alerted the Lord Chamberlain to problems. From 1909 there was also an Advisory Committee to provide guidance.[12] Successive governments preferred to remain neutral. In 1900, the Home Secretary (Sir M. White Ridley), when challenged about 'decadent drama' by the ever-vigilant Samuel Smith MP,[13] was insistent on keeping his department at arm's length from the Lord Chamberlain's Office, stating, 'there is no censorship of the drama in the hands of any Government department, and I hope the day may be long distant when there will be any attempt on the part of the Government to do anything of the kind.'[14]

8 Parliamentary Papers, *Report from the Joint Select Committee of the House of Lords and the House of Commons on the Stage Plays (Censorship) together with the proceedings of the Committee, Minutes and Appendices*, session paper no. 303, vol. 8, 1909, 9.

9 Ibid.

10 The formal title was Examiner (or Assistant Examiner) of Plays but this seems to have been generally interchangeable with 'reader of plays' for most of the period.

11 *Hansard* HL Deb, 19 March 1912, vol.11, cc.506–40, 535–6.

12 The members of the first advisory committee were revealed by the Lord Chamberlain in 1912 to be 'Sir Edward Carson, Mr Buckmaster, Sir Walter Raleigh, Sir Squire Bancroft and Sir Douglas Dawson'. Carson and Buckmaster were prominent lawyers; Raleigh an Oxford professor of literature, Bancroft a well-known actor-manager, and Dawson, at the time Comptroller of the Lord Chamberlain's Office, had extensive experience as a foreign diplomat. See *Hansard* HL Deb, 19 March 1912, vol.11 cc.506–40, at 536.

13 *Hansard* HC Deb, 15 May 1900, cc.276–308, 276.

14 *Hansard* HC Deb, 15 May 1900, cc.276–308, 296.

In 1909, questioned about the continued refusal of a licence for George Bernard Shaw's play *Mrs Warren's Profession*, the Home Secretary stated: 'The Lord Chamberlain acted entirely on his own responsibility in this matter. The responsibility of allowing or disallowing plays or parts of plays submitted to him is placed exclusively upon him.'[15] In 1912 Lord Sandhurst, as Lord Chamberlain, explained the licensing process in detail if not complete clarity in a rare parliamentary appearance:

> The play is received by the Lord Chamberlain. It is referred to a reader, and comes back to the Lord Chamberlain with a synopsis attached, and I beg to point this out to your Lordships that it is the play and not the synopsis which is the predominant partner of those two things. A play may appear objectionable as a whole, or certain phrases or passages in it may appear objectionable to the reader. Then the play comes to me, and after I have seen it and been through these objections – that is, the play, not the synopsis – the play is then circulated to the various members of the Advisory Committee, who furnish me with their views upon the objections . . . The play may possibly be so objectionable as a whole that on the advice of the Advisory Committee I should hardly feel justified in giving the licence to it; or the objections to certain phrases or passages may be upheld by the Advisory Committee. Then the usual course would be that I should be advised by them that the play may be licensed subject to the deletion or the alteration of these phrases, and it frequently happens, after correspondence or an interview with the author or with the manager of the theatre, that these objectionable phrases are deleted or changed, and the licence is granted. But supposing that we cannot come to terms, further communications and further interviews take place so as to see if matters can be arranged. If, however, the objectionable phrases are adhered to, the licence can be given subject to the deletion of those phrases, and the licence is so endorsed.[16]

This process was thoroughly recorded in Readers' reports and correspondence, the archives of which throw remarkable light on the inner workings of censorship.[17] In practice, however, the Lord Chamberlain was a somewhat distant figure. By the end of the nineteenth century, 'successive Lord Chamberlains were content to let their examiners follow their own inclinations, restrained only by the occasional interference of the Comptroller or by the press.'[18] The Lord Chamberlain did not give evidence to the Joint Committee on Stage Plays in 1909, instead he was represented by Sir Douglas Dawson as Comptroller, and the unfortunate Examiner George Redford, who faced hostile questioning from Robert Harcourt MP about not only his decision making but also his qualifications for the job[19] and became a much-derided figure in both the press and the literature of theatre censorship for

---

15 *Hansard* HC Deb, 27 May 1909, vol.5, c.1477W.
16 *Hansard* HL Deb, 19 March 1912, vol.11 cc.506–40, 536–7.
17 See, in particular, Nicholson, *The Censorship of British Drama 1900–1968* (all three volumes).
18 J.R. Stephens, *The Censorship of English Drama 1824–1901* (Cambridge: Cambridge University Press, 1980), 22.
19 *Report from the Joint Select Committee on the Stage Plays (Censorship)*, paras. 376–434.

his somewhat muddled replies. The Lord Chamberlain rarely spoke in Parliament, and generally acceded to the advice of the Examiner. It was thus the latter who most frequently became the target of complaint in the early years of the century.

The early decades of the new century are notable for the profusion of parliamentary committees set up to investigate the 'state of the nation' with the purpose of revising legislation, and the theatre was not exempt. The Joint Committee on Stage Plays in 1909 was a response to the growing calls from writers and critics for the removal of censorship rather than a concession to the indecency activists.[20] A letter to *The Times* signed by more than 70 prominent authors – including Shaw, J. M. Barrie, Joseph Conrad, John Galsworthy, and W.S. Gilbert – is often credited with persuading the Prime Minister to set up the Committee.[21] Its remit was to investigate whether continuation of the licensing regime was desirable and if so, decide whether changes in the law should be made to deal with concerns about the functioning of the Lord Chamberlain's Office.[22]

The 1843 legislative criteria for a stage play licence as 'fitting for the preservation of good manners, decorum or of the public peace'[23] was both all-encompassing and vague, often the ideal criteria for legal meddling in moral issues, but in the case of theatre, something that would ultimately cause great frustration not only to the writers who fell victim to censorship, but also to indecency campaigners. Prior to 1912, the licence itself confirmed that the play in question did not 'in its general tendency contain anything immoral or otherwise improper for the stage'.[24] As Redford was forced to concede to the Committee, this terminology had no support in statute, and the words were removed in 1912 to reflect a more neutral legal tone.[25] Apart from section 14, the legislation provided little guidance on what was permitted. As Shaw asserted to the Committee: 'Not only is there no law for me to find out, but I cannot find out even what the usage of the censorship is.'[26] It was not until the Committee's report in 1909 that the remit of licensing and censorship was in any sense defined. The Committee concluded that it should be the duty of the Lord Chamberlain

> to license any play submitted to him unless he considers that it may reasonably be held:
>
> (a) To be indecent;
> (b) To contain offensive personalities;
> (c) To represent on the stage in an invidious manner a living person, or any person recently dead;

20 The Committee's remit also covered the relationship between the licensing of stage plays and the unlicensed music halls.
21 *The Times*, 29 October 1907.
22 *Report from the Joint Select Committee on the Stage Plays (Censorship)*, v.
23 Theatres Act 1843, section 14.
24 A facsimile illustration can be found in Johnson, *The Lord Chamberlain's Blue Pencil*, 51.
25 *Report from the Joint Select Committee on the Stage Plays (Censorship)*, 577.
26 Ibid., 931.

(d) To do violence to the sentiment of religious reverence;

(e) To be calculated to conduce to crime or vice;

(f) To be calculated to impair friendly relations with any Foreign Power; or

(g) To be calculated to cause a breach of the peace.[27]

The Committee further concluded that submission of plays to the Lord Chamberlain's Office should be optional, but no legislation followed. Instead, the Lord Chamberlain (Earl Spencer) adopted the Committee's approach as the basis of his decision making, a policy confirmed by later holders of the office.[28] In 1926, the Earl of Cromer stated that:

> I personally, to the best of my ability, have been following these particular points in considering the licensing of plays. I would, however, strongly deprecate in the public interests putting down in tabulated form exactly what should be the absolute conditions for passing a play. That does not imply that anything indecent or improper will be passed, but if there is a scheduled list of conditions it is always quite possible for the ingenuity of the modern playwright just to evade that list.[29]

Application of the 1909 criteria was in some respects firm and fairly predictable, despite frequent accusations that the censorship was arbitrary. Open depictions of homosexuality, for example, invariably resulted in censorship: 'until 1958, the Lord Chamberlain officially maintained a total ban on the discussion of homosexuality or the depiction of a homosexual on the British stage. It was a ban that could be artfully circumvented but any recognised allusions to homosexuality were excised.'[30] Political censorship, the original raison d'être of the entire legal edifice, remained in place throughout the nineteenth century and well into the twentieth.[31] The injunction against depiction of living persons, combined with interpretation of 'offensive personalities' and the requirement to consider the sensitivities of foreign powers, ensured that both the Royal Family and the political class (domestic and foreign) were protected from ridicule or dramatized critique. In 1935 even an innocuous chronicle about the childhood of Queen Victoria was refused a licence.[32] Religion was also categorically off limits, with a complete ban on depictions of the Deity or Jesus Christ, regardless of how respectful or insipid the work might be (see also the furore surrounding

---

27 Ibid., xi.

28 Johnson, *The Lord Chamberlain's Blue Pencil*, 66.

29 *Hansard* HL Deb, 10 June 1926, vol.64, cc.365–92, 384.

30 N. de Jongh, *Politics, Prudery and Perversions: The Censoring of the English Stage 1901–1968* (London: Methuen, 2000), 82 and *passim* 82–132; see also Johnson, *The Lord Chamberlain's Blue Pencil*, Chapter Thirteen, especially 171–8.

31 Stephens, *The Censorship of English Drama 1824–1901, passim* 37–60.

32 Johnson, *The Lord Chamberlain's Blue Pencil*, 104. The offending play was *Vickie: A Play of the Girlhood of Queen Victoria* by Consuelo de Reyes.

D. L. Sayers' series of mystery plays broadcast in 1940–1941 discussed later in this chapter).

Escaping the straitjacket

There were exceptions: 'classic' plays which predated the legislation had always been considered exempt from censorship, so Shakespeare and his contemporaries were safe, and the York Mystery plays continued unhindered while newer (and more pious) works were banned, but new translations of foreign classics still required a licence.[33] However, these taboo subjects were just the tip of the censorship iceberg. The statutory criteria of 'preservation of manners', which translated explicitly into 'indecency' in 1909, undoubtedly became a legal straightjacket around stage plays which was hard to escape. The records of the Lord Chamberlain's Office are replete with references to an 'atmosphere of offensiveness' and objections to tone as well as to more explicit material.[34] In 1918, Comptroller Douglas Dawson (responding to the submission of a translation of Brieux's *Maternity*) wrote: 'In a civilised world we do not discuss openly the details of sexual intercourse, or visits to the W.C. and . . . subjects such as venereal disease and procuring abortion.'[35]

The framework of censorship was widely supported by theatre producers, both in London and the provinces.[36] The licensing of a play offered a degree of commercial as well as legal protection. Once granted, a play that opened successfully in London could safely be transferred elsewhere, since local authorities were unlikely to interfere. As Lord Newton explained in 1912:

> Although technically a licence of this character does not secure absolute immunity from prosecution, in practice it does secure that immunity, and it is rare that any attempt is ever made to interfere with a play that has once been licensed. As a matter of fact, the Lord Chamberlain's licence acts as a sort of passport which enables the play to travel throughout the country as a rule immune from interference.[37]

A licence would not necessarily silence the critics of indecency, but it certainly limited both their legal power and their moral weight. In this respect, the majority of commercial producers did not want to escape the law and were the principal

---

33 Shellard *et al., The Lord Chamberlain Regrets*, 152–3. A play entitled *The Life of Christ* by J. W. Brannigan was banned in 1956 despite being described in the Reader's Report as 'reverent, dignified and accurate'.

34 See the comments of Lord Cromer regarding *Fallen Angels*, letter of 5 April 1925, in Shellard *et al., The Lord Chamberlain Regrets*, 102.

35 Ibid., Plate 2.

36 For example, the evidence of William Redfern of the Council of Theatrical Managers, *Report from the Joint Select Committee of the House of Lords and the House of Commons on the Stage Plays (Censorship)*, 2,874–87.

37 *Hansard* HL Deb, 19 March 1912, vol.11 cc.506–40, 508.

advocates for retention of censorship to the Select Committee and for decades thereafter.

Writers of modern plays were thus caught between the law and the reluctance of commercial managers to risk offense. There was, usefully a loophole in the law which allowed the entire regime of theatre licensing to be evaded. This was the use of the increasingly contrived if not utterly fictional status of the 'theatre club'. Quite simply, the 1843 Act stipulated that a licence was required for *public* performance of any play. The solution, therefore, was to present it as a private performance to an audience of 'members' who would pay a small sum to join the club, either in advance of performance or at the door. This stratagem provided a useful outlet for radical and experimental tendencies in serious or highbrow drama, whilst, at least in its early form, keeping such dangerous ideas out of the practical orbit of the masses. The Lord Chamberlain's Office and successive governments seemed happy with this compromise solution, but the contesting parties were not. Radical dramatists, and the occasional producer of similar mind, railed against the boundaries and sought a mainstream airing of their work.

'It is certainly not an indecent act'

A further limitation of the 1843 Act (which essentially drove a coach and horses through the censorship) was that it only applied to 'stage plays', which were widely defined to include 'tragedy, comedy, farce, opera, burletta, interlude, melodrama, pantomime or other entertainment of the stage', but even this had its limits: music alone was not a stage play, for example. The Act banned consumption of alcohol in the auditorium where a stage play was presented, forcing entertainment venues to apply either for a magistrates' music and dancing licence (which permitted drinking but not dramatic entertainment) or a Lord Chamberlain's licence. Theatres and music halls thus developed as distinct and separate realms of activity. Music halls were regulated as buildings under the Disorderly Houses Act 1751, whereby places of public entertainment and houses used for music and dancing in London and Westminster, and within twenty miles from there, were required to obtain a licence from the Justices of the Peace. This left them, and their twentieth-century equivalent variety halls and revues, apparently outside the scope of the Lord Chamberlain's Office, a matter which would be a serious bone of contention for indecency campaigners throughout the twentieth century. There was some modification following the 1909 report, but this hardly clarified the legal position. In 1912, the Liberal Home Secretary, Reginald McKenna, challenged to explain the Lord Chamberlain's intervention prior to the performance of a 'wordless play' at the Palace Theatre, explained:

> Music halls were not, at the time the evidence was given [to the Joint Committee], licensed by the Lord Chamberlain, and were consequently outside his jurisdiction; but an arrangement has recently been made by which the managers of music halls obtain from the Lord Chamberlain or the London County Council, as the case may be, licences as theatres under the Theatres

Act 1843. In the case of the play now in question, I am informed that the Lord Chamberlain judged of its character from the synopsis submitted to him and from the report of his representative who witnessed the full dress rehearsal. A wordless play clearly comes within the definition of 'stage play'.[38]

Davis has shown how several moral campaigning groups bought music hall venues in the late Victorian period order to close them down, often converting them into temperance halls.[39] Despite these drastic and expensive measures, she goes on to state that 'however persistently the Victorian moral majority campaigned against West End music halls, it was never more than marginally and temporarily successful in expunging vulgar or indecent costumes, gestures, words and behaviours.'[40]

It was not only music halls that caused the moralists nightmares: 'tableaux-vivant' in which apparently nude women (who were usually in fact wearing a flesh or marble-coloured body stocking known as a *maillot*) rendered still-life depictions of classical poses from antiquity or otherwise 'respectable' high art. The Windmill Theatre (discussed later) was by no means the first venue to exhibit such depictions, but it undoubtedly became the most (in)famous.

The Edwardian period also saw a vogue for 'exotic' dancing (usually a variation of the Biblical theme of Salomé and the seven veils). This was once again seen as foreign and therefore particularly dangerous to sensitive and susceptible English public morals; as Walkowitz remarks of Maud Allan (one of the most famous exotic dancers), 'Allan introduced a set of codes for female bodily expression that disrupted the Victorian conventional dichotomies of female virtue and female vice and pushed beyond such.'[41]

By the 1930s such exotic dancing had become largely confined to the less salubrious and ostensibly 'private' gentlemen's clubs of Soho and surrounding districts. The Paradise Club situated at 189 Regent Street was one of the better-known such clubs, describing itself in its advertisements as 'London's latest and most exclusive niterie'. The club (which operated from at least 1935 until 1940) was described somewhat less flatteringly (though probably somewhat more accurately) in an anonymous letter sent to the Commissioner of the Metropolitan Police on 14 April 1937: 'It is nothing but a hotbed of "gentlemen" crooks, and prostitutes, the whole place savours of evil and immorality.'[42] The letter goes on to make several disparaging references to the owner's religion (Jewish) and accuses

---

38 *Hansard* HC Deb, 8 November 1912, vol.43, cc.1611–2W, 1612W.

39 T. Davis, 'The moral sense of the majorities: Indecency and vigilance in late-Victorian music halls', *Popular Music* 10, no. 1, 'The 1890s' (January 1991): 40.

40 Ibid., 51.

41 J. Walkowitz, 'The "Vision of Salome": Cosmopolitanism and erotic dancing in Central London, 1908–1918', *The American Historical Review* 108, no. 2 (April 2003): 345; also see J. Walkowitz, *Nights Out: Life in Cosmopolitan London*, (New Haven, CT: Yale University Press, 2012), especially Chapter Three, 'The Vision of Salome'.

42 TNA MEPO 3/941 Alleged indecent dance act and Bottle Parties at "Paradise" 189, Regent Street (1937).

him of being a crook, swindler, and of bribing the police. The author of the letter accused the proprietor of allowing an indecent act to take place there in the form of a 'fan dance' striptease, in which the performer was completely naked.

The Commissioner remarked in a note that 'it is . . . highly improbable that the show is as bad as the anonymous writer alleges,' but still saw fit to authorize a visit to the club by his subordinates. There was probably no shortage of police officers to undertake the onerous duty assigned to them by the Commissioner of gaining admittance to the club and witnessing the performance of the artiste, and on 10 July 1937 two PCs gained admission to what was described as a 'private bottle party' by the simple expedient of claiming they knew one of the guests and paying an admission fee of 7s6d. The police officers ascertained that the 'private' parties were undoubtedly lucrative; they estimated that around £30 per night must have been taken by Reginald John Barton, the receptionist, and Philip Garcia, the proprietor. In his report, Chief Inspector Martin stated that his officers witnessed a 19-year-old girl perform a fan dance in which she briefly exposed her breasts but appeared to cover her 'private parts' at all times. The police officers, who probably had literally seen it all before, stated that in their opinion, 'these acts could not be described as indecent, but very suggestive songs, bordering on obscenity, were rendered during the observation by a man called Eddie Brandt.'

An officer thought that during her dance, the young woman may have on one occasion disclosed 'part of the vaginal aperture', but 'the lady herself subsequently explained to the Police Officer that the illusion of nudity was produced by the skilful use of short trunks and adhesive tape'. Despite such protestations, at their subsequent court appearance, Garcia was fined £40 and £20 costs, and Barton was fined £5. Significantly, the Commissioner of the Metropolitan Police made it clear that in his opinion such acts at bottle parties were increasing due to them being 'openly permitted at the Windmill Theatre', and sought to bring the matter to the attention of the Lord Chamberlain. Interestingly, this viewpoint was shared by Garcia, who commented in an interview with the police that 'It is certainly not an indecent act. They go a lot further at the Windmill Theatre where some are completely naked.'

This would remain an area of ambiguity and contention. In 1940 the Conservative Home Secretary, Sir John Anderson, was asked by Reverend Dr James Little MP to ban nude and semi-nude shows and to ensure that 'no indecency of dress or anything that is in any shape offensive to public decency shall be permitted'. He conceded that the 'control of living performers who can by slight changes of behaviour alter the character of a scene' was difficult.[43]

The 'growing evil' on stage

This then was the legal framework within which stage entertainment operated. But despite, or perhaps because of, the censorship theatre remained a crucial battleground for moral activists. There were many reasons for this. The complexity

43 *Hansard* HC Deb, 4 April 1940 vol.359 cc.308–9, 308.

of legal oversight, divided as it was between licensing of buildings and censorship of text, left a great deal of room for interpretation and uncertainty, while the possibility of evading the censor by means of a private performance ensured that many of the technically 'banned' works of social (and sexual) commentary found an audience. The profitable nature of more lowbrow entertainment also ensured its continued existence, as well as a motive for pushing the boundaries of taste. The Windmill Theatre, which famously 'never closed' during the Blitz, was a prime example, switching in 1932 from unprofitable stage plays to its 'Revudeville' non-stop variety shows, which involved static tableaux of naked or semi-clothed females with considerable commercial success.[44]

Furthermore, the landscape of moral activism never remained static. Throughout the period in question, moral campaigners and their organizations reorganized, refocused, merged, divorced, renamed, and reinvented themselves with bewildering fluidity, united only by their pervasive sense of the rising tide of indecency. Campaigns against white slavery may have been cognitively empathic with temperance movements, and specific social purity efforts and campaigns against pornography certainly had strong links to national organizations such as the NVA and LCPPM, later the PMC. But even though membership of groups may have overlapped quite significantly (records are patchy and more research is need on these commonalities), the organizational structure of indecency campaigning was fragmented, and their targets and concerns were dependent on localized articulations of themes and problems rather than a unified national perspective. The PMC's primary focus throughout their existence was to oppose sexual immorality: as described by Patrick Hannon, their Honorary Treasurer in 1952, their concern was to exercise a 'clean and wholesome directive influence in the public life of the nation'.[45] Undoubtedly one of the most significant ways of achieving 'directive influence' was to exert pressure on those responsible for licensing or producing public entertainment. The PMC 'could draw on a multitude of sympathisers' to both pursue indecency in public places and 'to provide financial backing for their intense lobbying activities',[46] and could call on 'an auxiliary of stage and screen spotters, a full-time film critic, [and] a stern film committee always chaired by a leading Methodist'[47] in their pursuit of immorality on stage or screen.

In British theatre there were numerous troubling influences at work, notably amongst a rebellious intelligentsia which, although its members were often of socially privileged status, encompassed radical and 'deviant' moral attitudes compared to the decency campaigners. Theatre in the twentieth century was a broad-ranging activity from the most basic attraction of nudity (or more often quasi-nudity) in the variety revues, to the intellectual elitism and serious social

44 Music Hall and Theatre History website: www.arthurlloyd.co.uk/Archive/Feb2003/Page2.htm.

45 Sir Patrick Hannon, letter to the *Catholic Herald*, 7 November 1952, http://archive.catholicherald. co.uk/article/7th-november-1952/2/the-public-morality-council.

46 J. Weeks, *Sex, Politics and Society: The Regulation of Sexuality Since 1800*, third edition (Abingdon: Routledge, 2014), 216.

47 Bristow, *Vice and Vigilance*, 222.

purpose of British and Continental drama, from the common and crude, through the safe and conventional, to the experimental and culturally rebellious. The play-wrights were absorbing new ideas, both from abroad (especially Europe) and from new domestic cultures, as the spread of educational opportunity brought different social perspectives into the creative arts.[48] Thus, the 'insiders' of popular culture – the creators, writers, and artists – began challenging moral boundaries in every area, whether in reinterpretations of old art forms such as theatre and painting, or in embracing the new manifestations of the visual and performing arts such as film.

Crucially, in theatre there was often a coming together of artistic talent, politi-cal commitment, and infrastructure. Shaw, for example, brought his Fabian per-spective to contemporary social and moral issues in plays such as *Mrs Warren's Profession* (1894), *Man and Superman* (1903), and *Major Barbara* (1905). Harley Granville-Barker, already a successful (and controversial) playwright himself,[49] became manager of the Royal Court Theatre and thus provided an artistic home. Eleven of Shaw's plays were staged there 1904–1907[50] alongside the equally 'immoral' works of Ibsen, Galsworthy, and Schnitzler. The Royal Court Theatre closed temporarily in 1932 (it was a cinema 1933–1940) but its re-emergence in 1952 as the home of the English Stage Company was to cause further problems, continuing the Granville-Barker tradition of staging provocative new writing by premiering the work of John Osborne, amongst others.

Although throughout the first half of the twentieth century the majority of West End theatres (and provincial repertory theatres) remained essentially conserva-tive, by the 1920s the plays of Ivor Novello and Noel Coward were becoming both immensely popular and hugely successful, with glamorous and expensive productions in major West End venues such as Drury Lane. Coward was a par-ticularly prolific writer of comedies, revues, and serious drama, and his satirical approach to contemporary sexual matters inevitably attracted accusations of inde-cency and worse: *The Vortex* (1924) portrayed a nymphomaniac socialite and her son, a cocaine addict; *Fallen Angels* (1925) centred on two middle-aged women getting inebriated while waiting for their former lover; just the title of *Easy Virtue* (1926) was probably enough to cause apoplexy amongst the indecency campaign-ers; and *Private Lives* (1930) and *Design for Living* (1932) were comedies revolv-ing around extramarital relationships.

These themes were central to conceptions of indecency. At the same time, numerous theatre clubs exploited their legal loophole to provide outlets for the

---

48 This is particularly evident in the 1950s with the emergence of working-class 'Angry Young Men' writers such as John Osborne.

49 *The Voysey Inheritance* (1905) is probably his best known play. *Waste* (1907) contained themes of extramarital relationships, abortion, and suicide as well as politically controversial views about the Church of England, and thus was refused a licence by the Lord Chamberlain: it was performed pri-vately by The Stage Society in 1907 but received a licence only after extensive revisions in 1926.

50 Victoria and Albert Museum, New Drama in the Early 20th Century: www.vam.ac.uk/content/articles/n/new-drama-in-the-early20th-century/.

small-scale experimentalism of new drama, and politics and drama often merged. The Actresses Franchise Pageants League was set up in 1908 to write and produce plays in support of women's suffrage: its members included Ellen Terry and Sybil Thorndike, and by 1914 there were groups throughout the United Kingdom.[51] The Workers' Theatre Movement (which was an affiliate of the Communist Party 1926–1935) began staging what became known as *agitprop* theatre, launching a trend of radical left-wing theatre which continued throughout the century. Even the presentation of theatre was becoming unsettling, with the sumptuous realism of conventional drawing-room sets giving way to more adventurous and stylized set design, and mannered delivery being replaced with more naturalistic vocal readings (as in Granville-Barker's production of *A Midsummer Night's Dream* at the Savoy Theatre in 1913, for example). 'Indecent' writers could perhaps safely be ignored as long as their work was performed only as a marginalized form of 'fringe' theatre. The majority of theatre managers were generally content to offer bland, 'decent' material as long as it was good for business. But the persistence and eventual commercial success of intellectual rebels such as Coward took the new wave of twentieth-century drama firmly into mainstream theatres and popular consciousness, allowing some of the most 'indecent' voices to become celebrities of British theatre. At the same time, lowbrow entertainment continued to be profitable, not least because the censorship of serious drama contributed to the inevitable appeal of the titillating and taboo. The music halls of the nineteenth century became the variety halls and cabarets of the twentieth, continuing the traditions of irreverent songs and stand-up comedy, and often combining these with increasingly titillating revues and tableaux, the main purpose of which was to push the boundaries of sexual display and nudity as far as possible in the cause of light entertainment and profit. Not surprisingly then, moral campaigners found much to complain about.

The records of the Lord Chamberlain's Office, coupled with parliamentary sources and evidence of newspaper correspondence, reveal the weight of pressure placed on the censors by indecency campaigners, and particularly the PMC, in the twentieth century. It was not enough that censorship was in place; there was an urgency in the demands that it should be rigorously enforced in order to stamp out indecency. In 1900, Samuel Smith MP, stalwart of the NVA, had fired the opening salvo of the new era by presenting the motion that 'this House regrets the growing tendency to put upon the stage plays of a demoralising character, and considers that a stricter supervision of theatrical performances is needed alike in the interests of the public and the theatrical profession.'[52] The refrain was a familiar one, as Sir Mark Stewart in the same debate asserted: 'We do not want to pander to an evil which is growing in this country. There is a growing tendency to put on the stage plays of an immoral character.'[53] In 1913, when Sir Robert

---

51 Victoria and Albert Museum, Political Theatre in the Early 20th Century: www.vam.ac.uk/content/articles/p/political-theatre-in-the-early-20th-century/.
52 *Hansard* HC Deb, 15 May 1900, vol.83 cc.276–308, 276.
53 *Hansard* HC Deb, 15 May 1900, vol 83 cc.276–308, 301.

Harcourt MP (a member of the Joint Select Committee) brought a motion for abolition of the licensing system in favour of 'subsequent effective control', Sir John Spear MP countered: 'I firmly believe that the abolition of the censorship would be offensive to the taste of many people and would be a menace to the morality of a large number.'[54] As with demoralizing literature, plays were also regarded by some as causing the deterioration of physical health, especially amongst the military. In a speech at the Aldwych Club in 1916, General Smith-Dorrien claimed 'that on a certain few stages there were allowed indecent performances that directly produced immorality' referring to the numbers of soldiers prevented from frontline duty through contracting a 'preventable disease' and asserting that 'Immorality is a weed impossible to stamp out.'[55] He appears to be alluding to aspects of dramatic narrative or content that might have encouraged such men to seek out sexual gratification, for example with local prostitutes (particularly in London) known to frequent certain theatres. This supports Rapp's discussion of the 'khaki fever' of 1914 where sexual excitement amongst courting couples in London's parks

> reportedly motivated teenage working-class girls to chase aggressively after soldiers [followed by the] 'war babies' scare of 1915 which claimed that soldiers in Britain were fathering large numbers of illegitimate babies, and the apprehension that 'amateur prostitution' was increasing among working-class females who were presumed to be sexually promiscuous.[56]

In 1926, Lord Morris, citing evidence gathered by the PMC, drew the attention of the Lord Chamberlain to 'immoral,' 'degrading,' and 'demoralising' plays in London, and asked whether he would 'take appropriate action to suppress what is deemed indecent and objectionable' before presenting a litany of supportive quotations from newspapers.[57]

---

54 *Hansard* HC Deb, 16 April 1913, vol.51 cc.2036–81, 2036 and 2068.

55 'Morals and the stage', *The Times*, 25 October 1916. The General and the Bishop of London were known as the 'Heavenly Twins'.

56 D. Rapp, 'Sex in the cinema: War, moral panic, and the British film industry, 1906–1918', *Albion* 34, no. 3 (2002): 435; see also L. Bland, 'In the name of protection: The policing of women in the First World War', in J. Brophy and C. Smart (eds.), *Women-in-Law: Explorations in Law, Family and Sexuality* (London: Routledge, 1985), 23–49. These fears were rekindled during World War Two – for example Lord Elton stated in a late-1943 House of Lords debate that 'The family was the first and foremost casualty of the war. Families had been broken up, divorce flourished, and bigamy was almost a national industry. There had been a spread of venereal disease among girls under 16. Juvenile delinquency had risen. Was it not mere wishful self-deception to talk about a better Britain on that basis?' (*The Times*, 10 December 1943).

57 *Hansard* HL Deb, 10 June 1926, vol. 64 cc.365–92, 365–8. Lord Morris refused to identify the names of the plays or performances (though he was possibly referring to Noel Coward's plays *The Vortex* 1923, *Fallen Angels* 1925, and *Easy Virtue* 1926) criticised by a range of correspondents and interviews in the national and local press on the grounds that would provide unwarranted publicity and advertisement.

In 1900 Smith concluded that 'by far the ablest of these corrupting plays' was *The Gay Lord Quex* by Arthur Wing Pinero.[58] Although, according to his parliamentary colleagues in the same debate, Smith was not a theatregoer and it is unlikely he had ever seen *The Gay Lord Quex*, the play had become something of a moral cause célèbre. Several letters had been received by the Lord Chamberlain's Office complaining that the play was 'prejudicial to morals'[59] and the Examiner, George Redford, was attacked in the press when he granted the licence.[60] But often the moral critics were frustratingly coy when it came to naming the subjects of their outrage in public, ostensibly to avoid advertising the objectionable plays. On occasions when plays were actually named, the resultant backlash from supporters of the play, including the author, could be detrimental to the campaigners' argument. Following publicly aired criticism by Sir Edward Russell at the 1902 annual conference of the Institute of Journalists of his play *The Gay Lord Quex*, Pinero penned a robust defence of his work, together with a devastating critique of Sir Edward's critical ability: 'It must be a sad matter for so earnest and industrious a critic as he has proved himself to be to find in the autumn of his critical life his gods displaced.'[61] Pinero went on to state '*Lord Quex* will not, I am convinced, be condemned utterly by intelligent and liberal-minded people because of his lapses – any more than Sir Edward Russell is to be so condemned on account of his present variation from truth, good feeling, and good taste.'

The tactic of citing newspaper criticisms was therefore a useful one. The PMC and similar groups could generate much of the critical momentum themselves through assiduous correspondence to newspaper editors. Lord Morris himself admitted that some of the articles he cited 'were not criticisms by the paper but by correspondents and by persons who were interviewed'.[62] The PMC 'bombarded St James's Palace with complaints and deputations on a regular basis'[63] and with the Bishop of London as their chairman, they could not be entirely ignored, especially when they seemed to have support in the press. There was collective outrage, for example, over Coward's play *Fallen Angels*, which was licensed in 1925 with only minor cuts.[64] PMC members were delegated to attend the performance and their report was submitted to the Lord Chamberlain, complaining that the play

> must have a demoralising tendency upon the minds particularly of young people . . . if it represents real life, then moral restraints and marital fidelity are really boring and unnatural and that to profess chastity before marriage

58 *Hansard* HC Deb, 15 May 1900, vol.83 cc.276–308, 278.
59 Johnson, *The Lord Chamberlain's Blue Pencil*, 39.
60 Stephens, *The Censorship of English Drama 1824–1901*, 150–1.
61 *The Times*, 5 September 1902.
62 *Hansard* HL Deb, 10 June 1926, vol.64 cc.365–92, 368.
63 Shellard *et al.*, *The Lord Chamberlain Regrets*, 103.
64 Removal of references to illegitimacy, and 'rampant adultery' for example.

and fidelity afterwards is sheer hypocrisy. The whole play is full of innuendos and suggestive remarks.[65]

The Bishop of London then followed up with a letter to the Lord Chamberlain, prompting him to go and see the offending play and negotiate further modifications.[66] The PMC were equally incensed by Coward's *Design for Living* in 1939 (which featured a ménage à trois as well as deeply disguised homosexual themes). Howard Tyrer, who as Secretary of the PMC until 1940 was also one of its most energetic campaigners, complained: 'The moral, if you can call it such, seems to be that there are certain people who cannot fit into ordinary conventions of life and that they must therefore be free to live as they choose.'[67] Earlier, in 1926, the Bishop of London had no doubts about the influence of the PMC:

> As Chairman of the PMC I dare say I have been a trouble to successive Lords Chamberlain, and I have found them all courteous and attentive and none more so than the present Lord Chamberlain. Again and again he has listened to representations that I have made to him; again and again I know that plays have been modified as the result of our representation.[68]

By the 1920s the indecency campaigners were being seen as a distinct moral minority, and at times, something of an irritant. Public taste was changing following more than four devastating years of war. Cromer, as Lord Chamberlain in 1926, commented wearily after hearing the catalogue of complaints from Lord Morris and the Bishop of London:

> I should be failing in my duty if I did not at once take steps to suppress what is indecent, and I venture to challenge the allegation that at the present moment there is on the British stage anything which is indecent. As to 'objectionable,' the word 'objectionable' is one that is interpreted by different people in different ways.[69]

In the same debate, Lord Buckmaster, one of the original members of the Advisory Committee, argued: 'It is not fair to an author to turn down a play merely because it deals with . . . an unpleasant subject. If you are to turn down plays on that ground many of the greatest masterpieces of literature would be incapable of being performed.'[70] Within the Lord Chamberlain's Office there was also dissent. In 1934, Reader Henry Game, responding to the PMC's complaints about Rattigan's play *First Episode*, suggested in exasperation that its members were

---

65 See facsimile copy of the report in Shellard *et al., The Lord Chamberlain Regrets*, Plate 7.
66 Ibid., 103–4.
67 Jongh, *Politics, Prudery and Perversions*, 65.
68 *Hansard* HL Deb, 10 June 1926, vol.64 cc.365–92, 370.
69 *Hansard* HL Deb, 10 June 1926, vol.64 cc.365–92, 383.
70 *Hansard* HL Deb, 10 June 1926, vol.64 cc.365–92, 375.

confused 'between the functions of the Theatre and a Sunday School'.[71] After a meeting with Howard Tyrer, Assistant Comptroller Gwatkin wrote:

> As usual he was unconstructive except in the sense of complete destruction, and rebuilding on a standard of nursery rhymes and red flannel bloomers . . . I pointed out to him that one could not arrange entertainments designed only for those who are weak-minded and impressionable at the expense of the larger majority which is reasonable in its outlook.[72]

The strongest force against the indecency campaigners was an increasingly assertive liberal opposition driven by a growing sense that the repressiveness of the British approach was culturally damaging. In 1909 actor/manager Granville-Barker, whose tenure at the Royal Court theatre ensured that most of Shaw's work at least found a home, stated in evidence to the Committee: 'I regard the extreme narrowness of the field in English drama as being distinctly influenced and brought about by the operation of the censorship.'[73] Barrie, whose work caused no offence to anyone, nevertheless argued that 'it makes our drama a more puerile thing in the life of the nation than it ought to be, and is a stigma on all who write plays.'[74] Theatre critic William Archer summed up the attitude of many:

> I think it [censorship] has been entirely ineffective in keeping off the stage plays which are very offensive to the feelings of people who have any at all keen sense of decency or of what is fitting; whereas it has been entirely effective in keeping off the stage several plays of very considerable intellectual power and of very stern morality.[75]

These voices would not succeed in effecting legislative change until 1968, but there is no doubt that by the 1930s the censors were aware of the criticisms and were licensing plays which they knew would cause controversy. The impact of groups such as the PMC, although never negligible, was being weighed against more nuanced moral sensibilities.

'Salacious scenes': Indecency in films

Film censorship is often treated as a separate issue from censorship of theatre,[76] but there are many parallels and legal interconnections rooted in the concept of

71 February 1934 LCO CORR:1934/12646: *First Episode* in Shellard *et al.*, *The Lord Chamberlain Regrets*, 104.
72 19 April 1939 LCP CORR: 1938/1778: *Design for Living* in Shellard *et al.*, *The Lord Chamberlain Regrets*, 104.
73 *Report from the Joint Select Committee on the Stage Plays*, 1,224.
74 Ibid., 1,764.
75 Ibid., 707.
76 A rare exception being A. Aldgate and J.C. Robertson, *Censorship in Theatre and Cinema* (Edinburgh: Edinburgh University Press, 2005).

indecency. The debates and pressures which helped form the legal framework of British cinema were familiar ones and there was even an overlap of personnel in the early years of the twentieth century. However, there was a significant additional dimension to censorship of films: issues of social purity and public morality were by no means confined to Britain (although a detailed examination of the wider international context lies beyond the scope of this book).[77]

In the United States, censorship at the state level was rife in the early years of cinema, with many states following the pattern of the Pennsylvania Board of Censors in eliminating 'immorality and lust and indecency of all kinds'.[78] One of the earliest of Edison Manufacturing Company's films, the imaginatively titled *The Kiss between May Irvin and John C. Rice* (1896) lasted a mere 47 seconds, recreating a scene between the two well-known stage stars from a theatrical production *The Widow Jones*, but caused moral outrage when screened in June of that year. The June 1896 issue of *The Chap-Book* (a short-lived literary magazine which ran from May 1894 to July 1898) reported that 'the life-size view, bestial enough in itself, was nothing compared to this. Their unbridled kissing, magnified to gargantuan proportions and repeated thrice, is absolutely loathsome.' Subsequently, the growth of the Motion Picture Producers and Distributors of America under the presidency of Will H. Hays (former Chairman of the Republican National Committee and dedicated Presbyterian), of powerful pressure groups such as the Legion of Decency (backed by the Catholic Church), and a series of very public scandals, resulted in a period of rigid self-regulation.[79] As approximately 60 per cent of films shown in Britain after 1914 were made in the United States, much of the driving force behind content control lay in indecency debates in that country.[80] However, this merely added momentum to the indecency campaigners' agenda in Britain. Cinema, like theatre, became a fiercely contested moral ground despite the prior restraint exercised by regulators and the industry itself.

Cinema – the end of old England?

Despite Edison's best efforts to be remembered as the 'Father of Cinematography', the moving picture was not in fact a US invention, being first developed by a French émigré to England, Louis Aime Augustin Le Prince. The first moving images in the world were recorded on paper film in and around Leeds in 1888, almost half a decade before Edison's and the Lumière brothers' more

---

77 See also N.J. Rosenbloom, 'Between reform and regulation: The struggle over film censorship in progressive America, 1909–1922', *Film History* 1 (1987): 307–25.

78 R.J. Klein, 'Film censorship: The American and British experience', *Villanova Law Review* 12, no. 3 (Spring 1967): 419.

79 The trials of Roscoe 'Fatty' Arbuckle between 1921–1922 for the rape and homicide of actress Virginia Rappe; the (unsolved) murder of actor/director William Desmond Taylor in 1922; the death of actor Wallace Reid as a result of morphine addiction in 1922. All resulted in sensationalist newspaper coverage; see A.H. Petersen, *Scandals of Classic Cinema: Sex, Deviance and Drama from the Golden Age of American Cinema* (New York: Plume Books, 2014).

80 Aldgate and Robertson, *Censorship in Theatre and Cinema*, 2.

famous demonstrations.[81] The new technology evolved swiftly into a usable commercial form.

An early and popular (although short-lived) form of moving images in the shape of mutoscopes first appeared in the United States in 1895. These devices used simple flip-book technology to project a series of images which simulated motion to the individual viewer through what became known in England as 'What the Butler Saw' machines'.[82] Although these proved to be something of a technological dead end, rapidly being succeeded by developments in cinematography, they certainly caused consternation among the self-appointed moral guardians of late Victorian England. On 3 August 1899 under the title 'Demoralizing Moving Pictures', *The Times* published a letter from Samuel Smith MP, in which he complained about 'a new source of evil which has recently sprung up at our popular watering places'. He went on to state that he had visited 'out of curiosity', a penny-in-the-slot booth at Southport, where he was 'astounded that the Southport authorities permitted such viciously suggestive pictures to be publicly exhibited'. Smith was convinced that such devices were a great danger to public morals and was particularly incensed that 'two or three girls were going round' the exhibition (on which he expended 'three or four pennyworths'). Rather intriguingly, he goes on to state that similar exhibitions had previously taken place in the gentlemen's lavatories in Rhyl. Patriotically xenophobic, he considered that unless steps were taken to ban such machines, 'we shall see a rapid decline of English morals to the level of Paris' – clearly a fate worse than death even for a true-born Scotsman (Smith was born in Galloway).

These prior concerns about the decency of mutoscopic slot machines showing animated scenes (usually of women in various stages of undress) were merely the start: cinema posed an entirely new scale of problem.[83] The first time a film was projected to a paying audience in London was in 1896. The new technology quickly caught on: 'By the early Edwardian era, projected film was already a major part of the culture of the working classes, who went to see it in music halls, fairgrounds, unused shops and other temporarily rented premises.'[84]

The nascent industry of the later nineteenth century grew from its first purpose-built venue in 1906 to about 1,600 cinemas in 1910, and 3,500 by 1916.[85] By 1927, Lord Danesfort could assert confidently in the House of Lords that

81 Le Prince mysteriously disappeared from a moving train bound for Dijon on 16 September 1890 and remained for many years an unsung innovator. For a detailed account of his numerous achievements in cinematography, see R. Howells, 'Louis Le Prince; the body of evidence', *Screen* 47, no. 2 (2006): 179–200.

82 For an interesting short article about the presence of mutoscopes in James Joyce's *Ulysses*, see K. Mullin, 'Gerty through the mutoscope', *James Joyce Broadsheet* no. 49 (February 1998): 1–2.

83 See Samuel Smith MP, *Hansard* HC Deb, 13 July 1900, vol.85 cc.1475–1572, 1548–9.

84 D. Rapp, 'The British Salvation Army, the early film industry and urban working-class adolescents, 1897–1918', *Twentieth Century History* 7, no. 2 (1996): 157.

85 J. Robertson, *The Hidden Cinema: British Film Censorship in Action 1913–1975* (London: Routledge, 1989), 1.

It is estimated that something like twenty million people a week in this country attend film exhibitions and those twenty millions include a very large
number of children. Indeed, I am informed on what I believe is trustworthy
authority that about ninety per cent of all the children between eight and
fourteen who attend the elementary schools of this country attend these film
exhibitions more or less regularly.[86]

Cinema thus became a defining cultural phenomenon in Britain in the first half of
the twentieth century. According to A.J.P. Taylor:

> Cinema changed the pattern of English life, particularly for the lower middle
> class. It took people from their homes; eclipsed both church and public house;
> spread romantic, but by no means trivial values. Women joined their husbands
> in enjoyment, as they had never done at football matches or other public pleas-
> ures. The cinema was the greatest educative force of the early twentieth century.
> Yet highly educated people saw in it only vulgarity and the end of old England.[87]

Between the late 1920s through to the 1950s, 'cinema was the most popular leisure activity in Britain.'[88] By 1943, the Wartime Social Survey found that 70 per
cent of the British population regularly went to a cinema.[89] The popularity of
cinema, particularly amongst the young, would be a continued explicit theme in
the legal debates that followed, while the fact that this new medium of entertainment appealed so strongly to the working classes informed the implicit agendas
of censorship.

Film censorship: Tightening the self-regulatory bond

Parliament was quick to intervene in the British film industry. The driving force
behind legislation was pressure about public safety in view of the fact that many
of the early film exhibitions were taking place in completely unlicensed premises, and 'The Home Secretary was bombarded by a volley of petitions issued
by indignant local bodies.'[90] The response was the passing of the Cinematograph Act 1909. Much as regional theatres were licensed by local authorities,
so now the cinemas became subject to the same form of oversight. The primary
and explicit purpose of the 1909 Act was to ensure a safe regulatory framework

---

86 *Hansard* HL Deb, 18 May 1927, vol.67 cc.345–66, 345.

87 A J. P. Taylor, *English History 1914–1945* (Harmondsworth: Penguin Books, 1970), 237.

88 R. James, 'The people's amusement: Cinemagoing and the BBFC, 1928–48', in E. Lamberti (ed.),
   Behind the Scenes at the BBFC: Film Classification from the Silver Screen to the Digital Age
   (London, Palgrave Macmillan, 2012), 16.

89 Ibid.

90 T. Matthews, *Censored: What They Didn't Allow You to See and Why. The Story of Film Censorship in Britain* (London, Chatto and Windus, 1994), 8.

for the buildings themselves, particularly in view of the volatile nature of cellu-lose nitrate film in a projection booth. Under section 1 it was unlawful to hold a 'cinematograph exhibition' except on licensed premises.[91] But by giving licens-ing powers to local authorities, the Act also gave them indirect powers over the content of films shown, since scope of the terms of licences was not defined in the legislation.[92] Section 2(1) simply authorized local authorities to require 'such terms and conditions' as they deemed necessary and the courts agreed that this did not limit them to safety concerns.[93] Thus, these powers would remain a matter for dispute[94] and moral activists, by democratic participation in local politics, had an effective means of exerting influence: 'It did not take long for some local authori-ties to add to any licence the condition that the films shown must not be improper or indecent.'[95]

As with theatre, the campaigners against indecency found much to complain about despite the efforts of the censors, and had a variety of outlets for activism; not only were the films shown a matter for moral consideration, but the whole physical setting of sitting in a darkened room provided temptations to indulge in immoral thoughts and deeds. The most effective strategy was undoubtedly to gain influence in the local councils themselves, ideally by actually winning seats, but if not by pressure through meetings and correspondence. It is unlikely to be coin-cidence that in 'its early days the British Board of Film Censors (later renamed the British Board of Film Classification and hereafter BBFC) was often criticized by local authorities for being too liberal'.[96] Supportive journalists and newspa-per correspondence pages provided another valuable means of being heard, just as they did with theatre: 'The English press, goaded by the industry's frequent offenses against good taste, had begun to agitate against "Filth in the Film".'[97] Clearly, sufficient pressure was exerted to have effect. By 1912, 'local author-ity pressure upon film content was sufficiently strong for all sections of the film industry – distributors, exhibitors, and producers – to fear an imposed central government censorship'.[98] To pre-empt this, the British film industry approached

---

91 The first prosecution in Crewe occurred on 3 December 1912, when Frank W. O. Smith, proprietor of the Queen's Hall cinema, was fined the then considerable sum of £5 for not keeping passages clear in his establishment.

92 See further D. Williams, 'The "Cinematograph Act" of 1909: An introduction to the impetus behind the legislation and some early effects', *Film History* 9, no. 4, 'International Cinema of the 1910s' (1997): 341–50.

93 *London County Council v Bermondsey Bioscope Co., Ltd.* [1911] 1 KB 445.

94 In *Theatre de Luxe (Halifax) Ltd v Gledhill* [1915] 2 KB 49 the majority judgment somewhat lim-ited the scope of local authority power to make regulations under the 1909 Act. The most famous case on the issue, *Associated Provincial Picture Houses Ltd v Wednesbury Corporation* [1947] 1 KB 223, dealt with a narrower point under section 1(1) of the Sunday Entertainments Act 1932.

95 S. Brown, 'Censorship under siege: The BBFC in the Silent Era', in E. Lamberti (ed.), *Behind the Scenes at the BBFC: Film Classification from the Silver Screen to the Digital Age* (London: Palgrave Macmillan, 2012), 5.

96 Robertson, *The Hidden Cinema*, 3.

97 Low, 'History of the British Film 1906–14, 85–86 (1949)', in Klein, 'Film Censorship', 440.

98 Robertson, *The Hidden Cinema*, 1.

the Home Office for permission to create their own regulatory body. The BBFC, funded from an industry levy, was established in 1912 and, as the British Board of Film Classification,[99] continues to be the primary regulator of British film today. The BBFC's first president was George Redford, the former Examiner of plays. Developing its own working method, the BBFC would either refuse to classify a film completely, which was tantamount to an outright ban, or, more commonly, require cuts to be made in order to meet one of the age-related classifications.[100]

By 1916 more than sixty films had been refused a classification,[101] prompting the BBFC to publish its draft 'model conditions' which proposed to censor not only 'any film likely to be injurious to morality' but also any 'poster, advertisement, sketch, synopsis or programme, displayed, supplied or sold, either inside or outside the [film] premises which is likely to be injurious to morality'.[102] In this respect, the BBFC clearly shared the nebulous moral perspective of groups such as the PMC, at least in the formative years of its existence. Early cinema gave plenty of fuel for their concerns and, like the Lord Chamberlain's Office, the BBFC soon found it was unable to keep everyone happy. It was attacked by parties on all sides of the political spectrum for its tendency to reject anything that might be considered politically controversial or would lead to social protest.[103] As discussed in more detail later, fear that cinematic representations would lead to an increase in juvenile crime was a pervasive concern. The social appeal of darkened venues for young people, the experimental nature of the medium, and the commercial reality that 'contemporary taste, as one exhibitor put it, ran towards 'the hot and the strong' ensured that cinemas would never meet the moral standards of some.[104]

The 'growing evil' on film

Moral campaigners were divided on the subject of cinema. The first secretary of the NCPM (founded in 1904), the Reverend James Marchant, had previously worked for the NVA alongside Coote. In 1917, the Cinematograph Trade Council, representing a number of interested parties, asked the NCPM to undertake an inquiry into the physical and moral influences of the cinema. The NCPM's president, the Bishop of Birmingham, led the review with the Reverend Alfred

---

99 The name was changed in 1984.
100 The original classifications were limited to 'A' (adults only) and 'U' (universal). 'H' (horrific) was introduced in 1932 and converted into the more general and familiar 'X' certificate in 1951. History of the age ratings symbols: www.bbfc.co.uk/education-resources/student-guide/bbfc-history/history-age-ratings-symbols Political films could also feel the wrath of the censor; Sergei Eisenstein's masterpiece Battleship Potemkin was not issued with a certificate (X) until 1954 for fear it would incite British troops to mutiny.
101 Robertson, *The Hidden Cinema*, 2.
102 *The Times*, 9 November 1916.
103 Eisenstein's *Potemkin*, for example, was refused a classification for fear it would incite British troops to mutiny. See Matthews, *Censored*, 3–47.
104 Ibid., 2.

Garvie (its vice-president), Marchant, and T.P. O'Connor MP, now President of the BBFC. Although the subsequent 400-page report suggested that stricter censorship was needed, it nevertheless concluded that in general, cinema was not a threat to public morality and in fact had informally educated millions of people.[105] Some five years earlier the *Chelmsford Chronicle* of 20 September 1912 reported that the governor of Newcastle prison attributed a drop in crime rates to attendance at cinemas; he was of the opinion that cinema gave potential offenders an outlet from pressures to commit crime.

Conversely, many people thought that films could encourage and stimulate bad behaviour; on 29 October 1915 the *Sheffield Evening Telegraph* reported that an 11-year-old old boy had been bound over for shop breaking and theft in the city: 'The boy told the Bench he had seen it done at picture palaces and the Chairman said it was remarkable the amount of crime that was traceable to lads attending picture palaces. Something would have to be done to combat this influence.' Many magistrates' benches were clearly of a similar mind and began to impose specific conditions on the probation of juveniles who were found guilty of petty offences (mainly larceny). On 20 June 1916, a 12-year-old boy who had been found guilty of breaking and entering and stealing a watch and chain worth 30s was sentenced at Crewe Magistrates Court to be put on probation for twelve months with the condition of 'not attending a picture palace or similar venue'. The boy was to be only the first of several dozen children in Crewe who were convicted of larceny and were subject to similar probation orders, curfews, and banning orders from the perceived baleful influence of the 'moving picture'. In the same month, the Exeter Head Teachers' Association called for children under a certain age to be banned from entering picture palaces unless accompanied by an adult.[106]

Since the NCPM was 'oriented to work in close alliance with Parliament and state institutions' this (relatively) clean bill of health for cinema may have helped ward off further attempts to impose statutory censorship.[107] Similarly, compared to their critical perspectives on theatre, the press adopted a more positive and constructive approach to film reviews and production and were now less willing to align themselves with the disapproval of the more censorious moral campaigners. Notably, *The Times* was praised for its responsible and constructive film and cinema critiques, which in turn helped 'raise the tone' of the whole genre.[108] This more accommodating approach reflected a perception that it was better to seek to control such a powerful medium and use it to promote moral values, rather than indulge in 'indiscriminate denunciation'.[109]

In March 1920, the Commission reconvened at the NCPM's offices extending its religious representation and, demonstrating a more progressive approach,

---

105 National Council of Public Morals, *The Cinema: Its Present Position and Future Possibilities* (London: Williams and Norgate, 1917b), in Brown, 'Censorship under siege', 11.

106 'Cinema and the child', *Western Times*, 2 June 1916.

107 Hunt, *Governing Morals*, 182.

108 *The Times*, 6 March 1920, and see 'Film censorship', 27 October 1920.

109 'Film censorship', *The Times*, 27 October 1920.

included the feminist Marie Stopes, whose play *Vectia* based on her marriage to Ruggles Gates had been banned. In addition, there was also now a female examiner at the BBFC. The new remit was to explore the educational value of cinema, recruiting distinguished psychologists to conduct experiments and Board of Education inspectors to report on cinematic influence and enhance cinema's educational standing amongst both children and adults. Acknowledging that 'vigilance was still necessary', this second phase was presented as a more 'happily constructive' review.[110] The Bishop of Birmingham sought to allay the concerns of groups such as the PMC and the Manchester Purity League about the susceptibilities of working-class audiences to outside influences. In his view, the removal or censorship of the cheapest and most accessible form of entertainment, and one that had great social value, could only be counterproductive. It would make the lives of the working classes 'more drab than ever and cause the public house or the revolutionary lecture in some open place to be the only refuge of the working man'.[111]

Despite such endorsement, the Association of Municipal Corporations and the national Police Watch Committee became increasingly frustrated with the BBFC, particularly as US films fell outside their remit, and called on the Government to step in and appoint a State board of censors. The BBFC sent a weekly circular to local authorities listing the films passed, but it was left to the discretion of the local watch committees to decide whether to permit the screening of those not listed inevitably resulting in inconsistent decisions. On behalf of the two authorities, the Mayor of Eastbourne pleaded, 'We want security against the exhibition of films which are calculated in any way to demoralize the people upon which some cinema films are exercising a harmful influence.'[112] O'Connor felt compelled to explain and defend the operation of the BBFC in a lengthy article, 'The Censorship: how the work is done. Guiding Principles'. He listed sixty-seven reasons justifying the rejection of particular films, including the specific 'indecorous and inexpedient titles, nude figures, improper exhibition of feminine underclothing, indecorous dancing, excessive drunkenness, murder, cruelty and torture etc.,' and the more general 'scenes dealing with or suggestive of immorality, indelicate sexual situations, salacious wit and deliberately taking up a life of immorality'.[113] He also stressed that film censorship could be stricter than theatre censorship as film was thought less able to convey the real-life human depth of emotion in some cases, thereby justifying the prohibition of the subsequent film version of a play. Finally, responding to the constant demands from morality organizations and other groups for additional advisory bodies, O'Connor emphasized the 'absolute independence' of the BBFC, albeit appointed and paid for by the film trade. In January 1923 he was again forced to make a defensive statement (after a minor excision to the film *Oliver Twist*), pleading that moralists and creatives

110 *The Times*, 6 March 1920.
111 *The Times*, 21 February 1922.
112 *The Times*, 11 October 1921.
113 *The Times*, 21 February 1922.

alike should have faith in the general judgment of the BBFC to balance the public preservation of decency with the freedom of artistic expression.[114]

By 1925, following something of a running legal battle between cinema owners and the licensing authorities, the nature of the relationship between local councils and the BBFC was reasonably clear. So long as the local authority retained the legal power to ignore BBFC decisions,[115] it could impose licence conditions concerning general compliance with BBFC classifications.[116] The BBFC remained entirely without legal force or sanction, but its classification decisions became the de facto standard with which film-makers were forced to comply. Parliamentary discussion of the 1925 report of the BBFC throws some light on its concerns:

> The Board, for instance, say that they deprecate what seems to be a growing habit with actors of both sexes of divesting themselves of their clothing on slight or no provocation. Again they say that some of the dances, especially in cabaret or similar scenes, are of a nature that cannot be considered decorous or even decent. Further on they say regarding the all-important question of sex, that they wish to call attention to the increasing difficulties caused by the growing tendency shown to treat the subject with a lightness which formerly would not have been countenanced.[117]

Some influential figures were unconvinced that the BBFC was going far enough. The former chair of the Theatres Committee at London County Council commented: 'The average film, especially as shown in the poorer houses, was deplorable, and it was precisely the worst films that were being shown to the most impressionable public.'[118] By the late 1920s the BBFC were examining in excess of 6 million feet of cinematograph film a year and sending back hundreds for 'drastic alteration on the ground that they would offend the religious, political or moral susceptibilities of British audiences'.[119] In 1926 four films were banned for the reasons of Bolshevist propaganda, drugging and ruining of young girls, scenes in a lunatic asylum, and the typically ambiguous 'showing scenes of habitual immorality'.[120]

Such concern over the influence of cinema on the working classes continued to be voiced throughout the 1930s. The *Nottingham Evening Post* of 11 January 1935

---

114 *The Times*, 29 January 1923.
115 An absolute deference to the BBFC was rejected as *ultra vires* by the courts *Ellis v Dubowski* [1921] 3 KB 621.
116 For example, 'No film which has not been passed for universal exhibition by the [BBFC] shall be exhibited in the premises without the express consent of the Council.' See *Mills v London County Council* [1925] 1 KB 213.
117 Lord Danefort, *Hansard* HL Deb, 18 May 1927, vol.67 cc.345–66, 348.
118 Speech by Lieutenant-Colonel Cecil Levita, former chair of the Theatres Committee at London County Council, *The Times*, 7 January 1926.
119 *The Times*, 19 March 1929.
120 Ibid.

reported that Mr Theodore Komisarjevsky (a Russian theatrical producer) had recently complained that on being 'lured into kine-palaces . . . people cannot help becoming shallow-pates . . . cannot help developing the complexes of sexual maniacs and gangsters'. Komisarjevsky may of course have had commercial as well as moral reasons for condemning the infantilizing influence of the cinema; the quote in the newspaper was reproduced from his recently published book *The Theatre and a changing civilization*.[121] However, during a speech to the Devon National Union of Teachers Annual Conference in 1937, Mr Frederick Jones (the President) made a claim for a more nuanced and rational response to the relatively new media; he 'refuted every charge laid against the modern child, and said for gangsters and cinemas today they could substitute Red Indians and music halls for the child of yesterday'.[122]

The debate as to the moral influences of cinema continued post-war, with the appointment of a Departmental Committee on Children and the Cinema (the Wheare Committee) in 1950, charged with looking into the effect of cinemagoing on juveniles. The Committee made several recommendations in its report, published in May 1950, which led to the creation of the Children's Film Foundation in 1951, an organization that produced films specifically for young persons.[123] Mary Field, in her report to the Carnegie United Kingdom Trust, stated that the Wheare Report 'marks a decisive change of attitude towards the whole question of children and films. The old negative view that all commercial films are inherently bad and that children should, at all costs, be shielded from their influence was rejected in favour of the opinion that films are a part of our modern culture and, as such, can be used for the profit and pleasure of young audiences'.[124]

Radio and television

The inter-war era ushered in further technological advances and for the moralists yet another area of concern. Although a nineteenth-century invention, radio did not achieve widespread public success in Britain until the creation of the British Broadcasting Company (now Corporation) in 1922.[125] From its founding under the first Director General, the Scottish Calvinist John Reith (later Lord Reith), the BBC was conscious of its unique role as an arbiter and reflector of national 'taste' and 'decency'; Reith ensured that on Sundays the BBC did not begin broadcasts

---

121 *Nottingham Evening Post*, 11 January 1935.

122 *North Devon Journal*, 17 June 1937.

123 For a detailed account of the legislation surrounding the showing of films in British cinemas, see S. Hanson, *From Silent Screen to Multi-Screen: A History of Cinema Exhibition in Britain Since 1896* (Manchester, Manchester University Press, 2007).

124 M. Field, *Children and Films: A Study of Boys and Girls in the Cinema* (Dunfermline: Carnegie United Kingdom Trust, 1954).

125 For a history of the BBC and its role in creating national identities, see T. Hajkowski, *The BBC and National Identity in Britain, 1922–53*, (Manchester: Manchester University Press, 2010).

until 12.30pm in order to allow churchgoers time to return from services. Within six months of its foundation, the BBC had established a Central Religious Advisory Committee, which met for the first time on 18 May 1923.[126] Under Reith's leadership the BBC followed a self-imposed censorship of its radio output and this continued after the war, with the production in 1949 of what became known as the 'Green Book', its full title being *BBC Variety Programmes Policy Guide For Writers and Producers*.[127] This contained innumerable pitfalls to avoid at all costs, including any references to immorality of any kind, especially with regard to comedians' sketches or risqué and antique aural jokes such as 'Winter Draws On'.

Despite such measures, the BBC did not escape the gaze and censure of the moral minority. In 1941 it faced a barrage of criticism for its decision to commission a series of twelve radio plays from Dorothy L. Sayers, to be broadcast over a number of months under the overall title of *The Man Born to Be King*. These plays, written by a noted novelist, were intended to dramatize the life of Christ. Sayers, despite now being best remembered for her Lord Peter Wimsey series of detective novels (as well as coining the slogan, 'Guinness Is Good For You'), was also a respected Anglican theologian, who refused a Lambeth Doctorate in Divinity, offered to her by the Archbishop of Canterbury. The first of the plays, *Kings in Judea*, was scheduled to be broadcast on 21 December 1941. News of this aural portrayal of Jesus rapidly reached the moralists, and they stirred into action. The *Aberdeen Journal* of 20 December 1941 reported:

> Members of Northern Presbytery, Free Presbyterian Church of Scotland, solemnly protest against BBC arrangement to broadcast series of plays 'The Man Born to be King', including impersonation of Christ, as breach of divine law, gross profanation of most sacred events, and of blasphemous character.

The *Lincolnshire Echo* of 22 December 1941 similarly reported that the Lord's Day Observance Society Secretary H.H. Martin had stated of the cycle of plays, 'It is the BBC's crowing shame and perilously close to blasphemy.' The chief complaint of the moralists was that an actor, Robert Speaight (himself a devout Catholic convert) spoke the words of Jesus, and by doing so, thereby committing blasphemy by daring to impersonate the son of God.

In the event, despite such criticism, the plays were considered something of a broadcasting triumph and were published in 1943, perhaps reflecting changes in the moral mood of a country at war: the population in general had more pressing matters to think about than debate the thoughts of a vocal, though increasingly out of touch, moral minority. Radio (unlike television) has never had an official

---

126 R. S. Fortner, *Radio, Morality and Culture, Britain, Canada and the United States 1919–45*, (Carbondale: Southern Illinois University, 2005), 42.

127 The book was originally designed specifically for internal reference at the BBC, but in 1976 was published in an edited format as a quaint relic of British society's mores: B. Took, *Laughter in the Air* (London: Robson Books/BBC, 1976).

'watershed'; this is probably a reflection of its perceived more limited audience (especially with regard to its age demographic).[128]

It is significant that the first moral campaign group to monitor the output of the visual medium of television was not created until 1965, when the National Viewers' and Listeners' Association was formed as a direct result of a 1963 'Clean up TV' campaign launched by Mary Whitehouse.[129] From the moment of its inception with the BBC's first television broadcast in 1932 (with regular broadcasts following in 1936), British television, in a similar way to radio, was subject to firm regulation and self-administered prior restraint. The BBC was created and governed by the terms of its Charter and License Agreement while independent television, which began in 1955, was a statutory framework introduced by broadcasting Acts and overseen by statutory regulators. Crucially, the regulatory framework of both BBC and independent TV, which continues in modified form to the present time, created explicit requirements to comply with standards of 'good taste and decency', enforceable by a range of regulatory bodies and coercive measures. 'Good taste and decency' were not defined by Parliament. In many ways, therefore, the indecency concerns of the most fervent moral campaigners were incorporated almost by default into the regime of broadcasting law, and the boundaries of restraint would be seriously tested only long after the end of the period covered in this book.

Conclusion

There can be little doubt that the concept of indecency was an underpinning influence in the stringent censorship of both theatre and film, and later broadcasting, in the early twentieth century. Moral campaigners contributed to the environment in which censorship operated by means of a variety of direct and indirect strategies. Where they could influence local councils, their impact was certainly significant: the passing of the Cinematograph Act 1909 and the creation of the BBFC are at least partly attributable to local authority pressure. The campaigners repeatedly failed to achieve additional legislation over content or state control. Governments distanced themselves from the decision making process of censorship, probably because successive Home Secretaries saw the dangers of facing parliamentary interrogation over the banning of specific plays or films. But the drum beat of

---

128 BBC Guidelines, Section 5 'Harm and Offence, The Watershed and Scheduling for TV, Radio and Online': www.bbc.co.uk/editorialguidelines/page/guidelines-harm-watershed/#Radio Scheduling section 5.4.12. Outrage over radio output and the BBC's self-censorship can still occasionally make the headlines: witness the controversy over the Corporation's decision only to play a short extract of the song 'Ding Dong the Witch is Dead' from the Wizard of Oz when it briefly reached Number 2 in the charts following the death of Lady Thatcher in April 2013.

129 Now Mediawatch UK. For details of the organization's campaigns in the first decade of its existence, see R. Wallis, 'Moral indignation and the media: An analysis of the NVALA',' *Sociology* 10 (May 1976): 271–95.

indecency was maintained through newspapers, petitions, and correspondence, ensuring that those responsible for censorship were never in any doubt about the objections, and those who sought to write and produce innovative work could do so only by the employment of evasive tactics. The net effect on British dramatic and cinematic arts of the twentieth century is impossible to quantify but the impact is hard to deny. Both British theatre and British film struggled to deal with the profound social issues and conundrums of the times, being widely regarded as superficial and shallow when compared with their continental counterparts. Censorship may also account for the emergence of the arch and innuendo-filled style of humour that is often regarded as peculiarly British. Attitudes changed, especially in the post-war period, and the 'indecent' faded into the innocuous, but precedents had been set for legal constraints on tone and taste that continued throughout the twentieth century.

6 Indecency in practice
The policing and judicial response

Introduction

Previous chapters of this book have outlined how public indecency was defined during the period under discussion, and how individuals, organizations, and (to a lesser extent) governments attempted to stem the perceived ever-swelling tide of public indecency by an often disjointed series of campaigns and legislation. However, indecency was (and remains) not just a theoretical construct. It is therefore necessary also to investigate how indecency was dealt with in practice by the executive and judicial authorities in England. To what extent was the loudness with which concerned individuals and groups vocalized about the 'serious and growing evil' reflected in either recorded crime figures or the response of the police, magistrates, and judges? Did they listen intently, or did they exhibit selective deafness?

The following two chapters, using data extrapolated from officially published annual *JS* 1857–1960 (renamed *CS* from 1928), together with a survey of almost 50,000 cases that came before the magistrates' bench in Crewe, Cheshire, between 1880 and 1940, will attempt to show how such public indecency was practically viewed and dealt with by the police and the judiciary both on a national and provincial level.[1]

This chapter will focus on non-drink-related public indecencies such as profane or obscene language, indecent exposure, sacrilege, etc., whereas Chapter Seven will concentrate exclusively on drunkenness and drink-related offences (though it is recognized both that drink often played a considerable role in precipitating other forms of public indecency and that some cases involved more than one type of public indecency). It will look briefly at nationwide indictable offences and then in more detail at summary proceedings in Crewe.[2]

---

1 The Crewe database was originally constructed as part of a Leverhulme Trust–funded research project carried out by Barry Godfrey, Stephen Farrall, and David J. Cox; see Godfrey *et al., Criminal Lives* and *Serious Offenders* for further details.
2 All figures for indictable offences are given for England and Wales; the statistics did not readily separate the two countries as they shared a common policing and judicial system. Scottish figures were published separately.

Nationwide indictable indecency

From 1856 the Secretary of State for the Home Department requested detailed criminal statistical reports to be compiled annually and printed by the Criminal Registrar. Limited criminal statistics for indictable offences had been first officially recorded by clerks of the courts in 1810, but it was not until the 1850s that they were systematically organized by Samuel Redgrave (first Criminal Registrar, and a statistician to the very core of his soul) into the various categories that were used in the annual *CS*.[3] These categories remained largely unchanged throughout the period under discussion, although there were numerous tweaks to titles, etc. These annual publications contain a vast array of information concerning recorded criminal activity throughout England and Wales garnered from police forces and courts. Much has been written regarding their limitations as an accurate source of information for historians and criminologists, and it is recognized that the series does have severe limitations.[4] However, they *were* a triumph of Victorian bureaucracy in their ambition, scope, and detail, and, as Robert Morris has pointed out, 'incontestably the most profuse and the most accessible data available. They are, therefore, to be taken seriously for what they are, that is artefacts of contemporary social processes'.[5] They are admittedly flawed but have the benefit of being largely consistent in such flaws. If they are approached as such, with all the necessary caveats, as recent studies have demonstrated, they can be of considerable use to historians of criminal justice history.[6]

For the purposes of this study, six indictable offences were selected as being most representative of public indecency: 'attempted illegal abortion/procuring a miscarriage', 'unnatural acts' (both practised and attempted), 'indecency with males', 'sacrilege', 'keeping a disorderly house', and 'indecent exposure'. Several of these offences changed title during the course of 1857–1960 (for example, attempted 'illegal abortion' was first described as an 'attempt to procure miscarriage') but the recording methodology remained largely consistent, thereby enabling statistical comparisons to be made. 'Indecency with males' was first recorded as a category in 1893, whilst the categories 'keeping a disorderly

---

3 For an overview of the historical development of criminal statistics, see B. Godfrey, *Crime in England 1880–1945*, Chapter Three.

4 For criticism of the recorded *Criminal Statistics* see V.A.C. Gatrell and T.B. Hadden, 'Criminal statistics and their interpretation' in E.A. Wrigley (ed.), *Nineteenth Century Society: Essays in the Use of Quantitative Methods for the Study of Social Data* (London, Cambridge University Press, 1972): 336–96; H. Taylor, 'Rationing crime: The political economy of the criminal statistics since the 1850s', *Economic History Review*, 51, no. 3 (1998): 569–90; R. M. Morris, 'Lies, damned lies and criminal statistics: Reinterpreting the criminal statistics in England and Wales', *Crime, Histoire & Sociétés / Crime, History & Societies* 5, no. 1 (2001): 111–27. Contemporaries were also aware of the publications' limitations; several attempts were made to improve them, most notably in 1893, when there was a radical overhaul of the ways in which their raw data was gathered. No figures are available for 1939 due to the outbreak of war.

5 Morris, 'Lies, damned lies and criminal statistics', 125.

6 See for example Godfrey *et al.*, *Serious Offenders*, and D.J. Cox, '"Trying to get a good one": Bigamy offences in England and Wales 1850–1950', *Plymouth Law & Criminal Justice Review* 4 (Autumn 2011): 1–32.

house' and 'indecent exposure' were not listed separately post-1930. Figures for all of the other categories are complete for the entire period with the exception of 1939, when no figures were recorded due to the outbreak of war. Major changes in recording indictable offences as known to the police occurred in 1893, when indictable offences that could be tried summarily were also included. This had the effect of greatly increasing the recorded figures; consequently all statistical analysis in this and the following chapter refer to the two periods of 1857–1892 and 1893–1960 separately. Sexual indecency in the form of rape/attempted rape/ indecent assault are not included in these figures; such acts of serious interpersonal violence lie outside the purview of this book.

These offences were all listed under a table entitled 'Indictable Offences: Nature of the Crimes Committed in Each Police District (as Known to the Police) in the Year ended . . .'[7] It is not the intention to provide a definitive and detailed account of the legal history of each of these offences in this chapter but rather to give an account of how many offences in each category were reported to the police in each year, allowing an overview of the extent to which indictable public indecency featured in the higher courts of the criminal justice system. The figures for 1857–1960 are reproduced in Table 6.1.

What is immediately apparent is that despite the frequent cries of concern from the moralists at the 'serious and growing evil' of public indecency, such matters appear to have rarely troubled the higher courts of England: less than 1 in 80 indictable crimes known to the police fell into the six categories under consideration. Although moralists considered public indecency to be a serious and growing problem, the majority of public indecency offences were regarded as relatively trivial and therefore tried as summary misdemeanours rather than indictable felonies. If we look at the number of reported offences in the six categories as a total of all reported offences, we see that between 1857 and the outbreak of World War Two, the percentages remained largely static overall. For the period 1857–1938 the average percentage of the six categories as a total of all recorded indictable offences was just under 0.9 per cent, and this figure never varied by more than 0.5 per cent. Indeed, for 1857–1892 the figure remained remarkably consistent, notwithstanding minor yearly fluctuations. Similarly, the drop from 1893 onward remained similarly consistent, suggesting that it had more to do with changes in reporting practices than an actual drop in offending – although the clear decrease to an average of just over 0.69 per cent for the period 1893–1913 is somewhat surprising given that from 1893 onwards the figures include all indictable offences tried summarily. It is only from the post–World War Two period that reported offending rates rise consistently, with a clear increase in the mid-1950s (perhaps reflecting something of what appears to have been a minor moral panic resulting from post-war uncertainty as indicated earlier in the resurgence of interest in the prosecution of publishers for 'saucy' postcards), but by the end of the period, the rate had begun to fall again.

7 This particular table was chosen as police returns show *all* reported offences rather than simply those that reached trial at either petty/quarter sessions or assizes.

Table 6.1 Selected indictable offences abstracted from *JS* 1857–1960 table entitled 'Nature of the crimes committed in each police district (as known to the police)'

Year	Attempt to procure miscarriage	Unnatural acts	Attempted unnatural acts	Total unnatural acts	Indecency with males	Sacrilege	Keeping disorderly house	Indecent exposure	Total of categories	Total recorded indictable offences	% of total recorded indictable offences
1857	16	31	117	148		97	106	81	596	57,273	1.04
1858	12	115	65	180		63	155	48	638	57,868	1.10
1859	14	135	47	182		76	132	42	628	52,018	1.21
1860	15	102	40	142		55	141	8	503	50,405	1.00
1861	10	116	34	150		54	97	31	492	50,809	0.97
1862	10	103	47	150		73	119	23	525	53,225	0.99
1863	9	126	49	175		76	100	36	571	52,211	1.09
1864	11	139	65	204		100	42	24	585	51,058	1.15
1865	10	109	52	161		100	116	22	570	52,250	1.09
1866	8	118	37	155		92	61	23	494	50,549	0.98
1867	8	93	31	124		131	59	23	469	55,538	0.84
1868	15	97	43	140		71	58	18	442	59,080	0.75
1869	7	126	41	167		106	48	24	519	58,441	0.89
1870	19	100	71	171		93	82	20	556	51,972	1.07
1871	8	93	44	137		55	118	21	476	45,149	1.05
1872	8	102	41	143		64	86	13	457	44,191	1.03
1873	9	88	38	126		75	97	28	461	45,214	1.02
1874	4	85	47	132		73	88	32	461	47,824	0.96
1875	9	86	48	134		71	69	18	435	47,045	0.92
1876	4	106	49	155		72	62	14	462	49,320	0.94
1877	8	123	31	154		97	69	37	519	50,843	1.02
1878	13	96	44	140		125	109	38	565	54,065	1.05
1879	7	94	35	129		103	83	38	489	52,147	0.94
1880	8	80	47	127		170	61	53	546	52,427	1.04

Year											
1881	12	79	40	119		166	81	40	537	51,193	1.05
1882	10	96	44	140		177	69	64	600	52,180	1.15
1883	12	73	38	111		120	81	47	482	49,534	0.97
1884	10	87	45	132		168	90	61	593	47,089	1.26
1885	11	90	66	156		150	89	54	616	43,962	1.40
1886	14	83	38	121		111	54	54	475	44,925	1.06
1887	11	80	51	131		129	67	26	495	42,391	1.17
1888	15	74	47	121		153	39	34	483	43,336	1.11
1889	23	95	58	153		152	16	41	538	41,285	1.30
1890	20	80	58	138		172	21	27	516	38,650	1.34
1891	5	85	74	159		120	7	31	481	37,252	1.29
1892	13	84	53	137		29	11	28	355	39,021	0.91
1893[8]	14	82	73	155	73	152	20	34	603	86,396	0.70
1894	21	66	55	121	71	153	42	23	552	86,052	0.64
1895	29	70	54	124	108	200	12	7	604	81,323	0.74
1896	10	59	56	115	89	153	19	13	514	78,614	0.65
1897	22	44	54	98	66	201	57	10	552	78,905	0.70
1898	15	72	49	121	102	223	20	26	628	82,426	0.76
1899	6	52	54	106	92	226	25	18	579	76,025	0.76
1900	9	49	63	112	77	155	16	9	490	77,934	0.63
1901	4	75	59	134	110	154	33	7	576	80,962	0.71
1902	13	59	51	110	93	174	19	13	532	83,260	0.64
1903	16	60	51	111	126	124	24	9	521	86,172	0.60
1904	20	54	40	94	112	159	31	16	526	92,907	0.57
1905	21	60	46	106	118	212	17	11	591	94,654	0.62
1906	47	56	63	119	127	250	21	15	698	91,665	0.76
1907	32	56	69	125	148	206	32	12	680	98,822	0.69
1908	31	56	65	121	137	272	45	9	736	105,279	0.70
1909	28	66	61	127	127	235	59	9	712	105,287	0.68
1910	18	66	96	162	139	209	19	36	745	103,132	0.72

(Continued)

Table 6.1 Continued

Year	Attempt to procure miscarriage	Unnatural acts	Attempted unnatural acts	Total unnatural acts	Indecency with males	Sacrilege	Keeping disorderly house	Indecent exposure	Total of categories	Total recorded indictable offences	% of total recorded indictable offences
1911	42	45	69	114	161	163	25	6	625	97,171	0.64
1912	47	75	111	186	132	167	46	13	777	101,997	0.76
1913	50	57	145	202	157	210	63	9	893	97,933	0.91
1914	44	61	143	204	133	146	14	9	754	89,387	0.84
1915	34	69	112	181	141	126	15	10	688	77,972	0.88
1916	72	51	116	167	149	104	18	3	680	80,653	0.84
1917	55	33	94	127	86	120	10	9	534	88,864	0.60
1918	90	75	82	157	79	112	9	3	607	87,762	0.69
1919	75	47	92	139	138	150	13	6	660	87,827	0.75
1920	58	71	192	263	156	163	46	14	963	100,827	0.96
1921	57	43	187	230	168	177	20	18	900	103,258	0.87
1922	31	59	221	280	170	247	31	18	1,057	107,320	0.98
1923	54	63	211	274	201	197	26	21	1,047	110,206	0.95
1924	39	70	265	335	185	188	30	16	1,128	112,574	1.00
1925	86	67	258	325	166	151	39	15	1,107	113,986	0.97
1926	55	91	354	445	155	155	25	7	1,287	133,460	0.96
1927	74	67	345	412	197	139	85	7	1,326	125,703	1.05
1928[9]	113	58	336	394	147	154	91	3	1,296	130,469	0.99
1929	84	102	364	466	191	101	17	2	1,327	134,581	0.99
1930	98	47	398	445	203	163	31	2	1,387	147,031	0.94
1931[10]	98	73	371	444	178	123			1,287	159,278	0.81
1932[11]	78	46	487	533	258	143			1,545	208,175	0.74
1933	55	82	554	636	210	111			1,648	227,285	0.73
1934	73	64	581	645	192	106			1,661	233,359	0.71
1935	116	78	535	613	227	109			1,678	234,372	0.72
1936	141	125	690	815	352	104			2,227	248,803	0.90

Year											
1937	197	102	703	805	316	121			2,244	266,265	0.84
1938	172	134	822	956	320	133			2,537	283,220	0.90
1939	No figures are available for this year due to outbreak of World War Two										
1940	110	97	808	905	251	128			2,299	305,114	0.75
1941	171	177	757	934	390	159			2,588	358,655	0.72
1942	344	208	998	1,206	582	157			3,495	364,889	0.96
1943	461	245	1,208	1,453	623	175			4,165	372,760	1.12
1944	649	277	1,186	1,463	449	223			4,247	415,010	1.02
1945	464	223	1,318	1,541	459	306			4,311	478,394	0.90
1946	286	247	1,523	1,770	561	368			4,755	472,489	1.01
1947	178	255	1,839	2,094	690	333			5,389	498,576	1.08
1948	197	258	2,216	2,474	660	394			6,199	522,684	1.19
1949	228	562	2,409	2,971	852	357			7,379	459,869	1.60
1950	251	534	2,893	3,427	989	333			8,427	461,435	1.83
1951	237	452	3,272	3,724	1,152	353			9,190	524,506	1.75
1952	233	670	3,087	3,757	1,686	334			9,767	513,559	1.90
1953	243	700	3,305	4,005	1,675	286			10,214	472,989	2.16
1954	257	1,043	3,280	4,323	2,034	284			11,221	434,327	2.58
1955	179	766	3,556	4,322	2,322	245			11,390	438,085	2.60
1956	187	907	3,355	4,262	1,934	342			10,987	479,710	2.29
1957	159	803	3,605	4,408	1,919	379			11,273	545,562	2.07
1958	140	625	2,969	3,594	1,877	468			9,673	626,509	1.54
1959	154	706	3,420	4,126	1,606	442			10,454	675,626	1.55
1960	221	641	3,095	3,736	1,504	476			9,673	743,713	1.30
Totals[12]	8,291	16,922	61,771	78,693	31,298	17,822	3,948	1,690	220,435	17,515,754	1.26

8 New category of 'indecency with males' introduced. Figures for indictable offences from 1893 onward include all indictable offences tried summarily.

9 Title changed from *JS* to *CS*.

10 Keeping disorderly house and indecent exposure no longer listed separately (recategorized under 'other' offences).

11 Overall figures are inflated due to the abolition of the Metropolitan Police's 'Suspected Stolen' book (a list of all suspected larcenies within the Metropolitan Police area), henceforth including all such figures in total.

12 Figures abstracted and compiled from *JS* (later *CS*) 1857–1960, available online at http://parlipapers.chadwyck.co.uk/marketing/index.jsp.

Attempted illegal abortion/procuration of miscarriage

Although as Lord Reid stated in 1973, 'indecency is not confined to sexual indecency: indeed it is difficult to find any limit short of saying that it includes anything which an ordinary decent man or woman would find to be shocking, disgusting and revolting,' several of the categories of indictable indecency were related to sexual activity of one sort or another and its consequences.[13]

Abortion was an indictable felony in Britain from 1803 until 1967. The maximum penalty until the early nineteenth century was death, eventually being replaced in 1861 (Offences Against the Person Act) by penal servitude for between three years and life for self-administration, or a lengthy term for 'whosoever shall unlawfully supply or procure any poison or other noxious thing, or any instrument or thing whatsoever, knowing that the same is intended to be unlawfully used or employed with intent to procure the miscarriage of any woman, whether she be or be not with child'.[14] This category of indictable offence remained low, only in double figures annually until 1928, peaking (perhaps unsurprisingly) during World War One at 90 reported offences in 1918. The number of offences then rose sharply from the mid-1930s, peaking again during World War Two, before reducing to an average of 210 offences per year in the post-war period. The total number of reported offences between 1857 and 1960 was 8,291.[15]

This figure undoubtedly greatly under-represents the actual number of abortions (both attempted and successful) carried out illegally; as Patricia Knight has stated, 'the exact extent of abortion . . . is impossible to estimate, since only a small percentage of cases came to the attention of doctors and an even smaller number before the courts.'[16]

From the late nineteenth century, as we have seen in Chapter Four, increasing concern was manifested over illegal termination (and it is interesting that these worries were seemingly more often directed to the medical problems that illegal abortion could lead to, rather than religious or moral scruples over the termination of unborn life). The *British Medical Journal* on 7 February 1920 reported that:

> Between 1893 and 1905 the attention of the profession was repeatedly drawn in this Journal to the prevalence in the Midland counties of cases of plumbism [lead-poisoning] in women, caused by the ingestion of diachylon (lead oleate), with the object of procuring abortion. Hundreds of cases of lead poisoning from

---

13 *R v Knuller (Publishing etc.)* [1973] AC 435, 457–8.

14 Offences against the Person Act 1861, Section 59.

15 All figures with regard to the indictable statistics are absolutes; they take no account of the rise in population in England and Wales during the period being discussed.

16 P. Knight, 'Women and abortion in Victorian and Edwardian England', *History Workshop Journal* 4, no. 1 (1977): 57–69. For an historical overview of abortion in England and the western hemisphere, see J. Riddle, *Eve's Herbs: A History of Contraception and Abortion in the West* (Harvard: Harvard University Press, 1997).

this cause were then occurring every year, so much so that in the out-patient rooms of the Nottingham and Sheffield hospitals it became a routine practice to examine the gums of women patients.[17]

The Infant Life Preservation Act 1929 allowed abortion to be practised by a doctor if 'done in good faith for the purpose only of preserving the life of the mother'.[18]

During the early 1930s further concern showed itself over the perceived rise in the number of abortions being attempted:

> At a meeting of the City Division, held at the Metropolitan Hospital, Kingsland Road, on December 6th, Dr L.A. Parry of Hove delivered a British Medical Association lecture on criminal abortion . . . All authorities were agreed that criminal abortion was frequent and increasing . . . nearly all criminal abortions were produced by instrumental interference. Various instruments had been used, provided they were long and pointed, such as sounds, catheters, stylets, lead pencils, quill pens. These were very dangerous on account of the readiness with which the point might be wrongly directed and the walls of the uterus pierced. The dangers from puncture of the membranes were principally sepsis, haemorrhage, and shock, of which sepsis was the most common. Criminal abortion was, as a rule, performed by those who belonged to the dregs of their profession – the dissolute nurse, doctor, or chemist.[19]

Abortion in England was effectively legalized in 1967 following the passing of the Abortion Act, which allowed abortions of foetuses under twenty-eight weeks to be carried out with the permission of two doctors.

Unnatural acts, attempted and achieved

This category refers to buggery or sodomy (both de facto gender-specific offences, as lesbianism has never been a criminal offence in England), and bestiality (a criminal offence which could involve all genders).[20] Between 1857 and 1960, a total of 78,693 cases of unnatural acts (attempted and achieved) were reported to the police in England and Wales. Such cases averaged around 140 per year until the 1920s, when the number of reported attempted unnatural acts rose sharply, averaging 394 cases per year until the outbreak of World War Two. The post-war average of attempted unnatural acts stood at 2,739 per year, suggesting that concern over such

---

17 *BMJ* 1, no. 3,084 (7 February 1920), 192.

18 Infant Life (Preservation) Act 1929 c.34, 1.1.

19 *BMJ* 2, no. 3,756 (31 December 1932), 1190–1.

20 There is unfortunately no way of separating bestiality offences from other unnatural offences, as the annual *CS* do not differentiate between buggery/sodomy and bestiality. This in itself is perhaps an interesting comment on contemporary views of homosexuality. For an excellent and thought-provoking overview of historically condemned sexual activities (including homosexuality and bestiality) throughout Europe, see Peakman, *The Pleasure's All Mine*.

behaviour was increasing in the nervous Cold War atmosphere 'as homosexuals became increasingly equated by the Establishment with depravity and betrayal'.[21] The 'Lavender Scare' of early 1950s America (itself a result of the McCarthy witch hunts) had suggested that gay men were much more likely to be blackmailed into betraying State secrets, and this paranoia rapidly spread to England.[22] The shameful persecution and subsequent suicide of men such as Alan Turing, whose work had played an almost incalculable role in winning the war, was the result of an anti-homosexual directive by Home Secretary Sir David Maxwell Fyfe issued to the Home Office. Virulently homophobic, he held the view that 'homosexuals in general are exhibitionists and proselytisers and are a danger to others, especially the young'.[23]

Buggery had been a felony in England since 1533, following the passing of 'an act for the punishment of the vice of buggery'. This Act included bestiality under the term *buggery* as well as anal sex with either a man or a woman (though not with an animal). For practical purposes the term *buggery* was interchangeable with *sodomy*.[24] The Offences against the Person Act 1828 re-enacted the death penalty for the offence, and the Offences against the Person Act 1861 reduced the sentence to penal servitude for between ten years and life.[25] Following the Wolfenden Report of 1957, which recommended that 'homosexual behaviour between consenting adults [i.e. over the age of 21] in private should no longer be a criminal offence', the Sexual Offences Act 1967 finally removed the offence of buggery in private between consenting adults over the age of 21 (with the exception of members of the armed forces) from the statute book.[26] The Sexual Offences Act 1993 reduced the age of consent to 16 (now 18 if the adult involved is in a position of trust by virtue of section 16 Sexual Offences Act 2003). Both buggery with animals and bestiality remain criminal offences under section 69 Sexual Offences Act 2003.

Indecency with males

The Criminal Law Amendment Act 1885 strengthened the laws against buggery to include any act of sexual activity between males, thereby providing a 'catch-all' for all forms of homosexual activity, bringing cases of fellatio and other intimate sexual practices between males into the purlieu of the law. However, it was not until 1893 that a separate offence of 'indecency with males' appeared in the *CS*.[27]

---

21 *Independent*, 27 December 2013. See also M.E. Vargo, *Scandal: Infamous Gay Controversies of the Twentieth Century* (Abingdon: Routledge, 2013).
22 D.K. Johnson, *The Lavender Scare* (Chicago: University of Chicago Press, 2004).
23 *Hansard* HC Deb, 03 December 1953, vol. 521 cc.1295–9, 1296.
24 See for example the Offences against the Person Act 1828, section 15, where *sodomy* is used interchangeably with *buggery*.
25 The last persons hanged for sodomy in England were James Smith and John Pratt, who were executed at Newgate on 27 November 1835; see OBP t18350921–1934.
26 Parliamentary Papers, *Report of the Departmental Committee on Homosexual Offences and Prostitution* (London: HMSO, 1957), para 62, 25.
27 There is often a disjoint between changes in legal practice and statistical recording in the *CS*.

A total of 31,298 cases of indecency with males were reported to police between 1893 and 1960, with the annual total reaching four figures (1,152) in the 1950s, reflecting the febrile atmosphere engendered by the government of the time and discussed earlier.

Sacrilege

This offence (which largely, though not exclusively, related to breaking and entering a church) was theoretically punishable by death until the Larceny Act 1861, which replaced the death penalty with imprisonment with or without hard labour for up to two years, or penal servitude for between three years and life.[28] The last recorded execution for sacrilege appears to have been that of Thomas Newbury, who was condemned to death at Hampshire Summer Assizes in 1812 for stealing the Gosport minister's surplice, two bottles of sacramental wine, and two pounds of church candles.[29]

The number of indictable sacrilege offences reported to the police remained low throughout the entire 1857–1960 period, with an average of 171 offences per year. Some cases, despite the serious nature of the offence, could elicit a degree of humour. On 4 November 1904 William Holt (aka Arthur Desmond), a prolific offender well-known to the Cheshire constabulary, was sentenced to four years' penal servitude at Chester Assizes for the offence of sacrilege as a result of being caught red-handed breaking and entering Broadheath Wesleyan Chapel and stealing communion plates to the value of £5 10s. The case was widely reported in the press, as Holt apparently left the following note in the vestry (he obviously knew his Bible): 'Wine is a mocker; strong drink is raging. But nevertheless your port wine has been a treat. If thy brother sin seven times forgive.'[30] The prison sentence had little apparent effect on him; after being released from prison on licence, in 1908 he was sentenced to another four years' penal servitude and the remainder of his previous sentence for further sacrilege in a Church of England Mission Hall in Manchester. *The Guardian* of 21 April 1908 reported that 'the judge said this man had pursued a career of crime since 1901 and between that date and 1904 he was hardly ever out of gaol.'

Indecent exposure and keeping a disorderly house

These two categories of indictable offences never featured prominently in the annual *JS* and indeed the annual figures were so low (an annual average of 53 reported offences for keeping a disorderly house and only 23 for indecent exposure between 1857 and 1930) that they were no longer recorded as separate offences post-1930.

28 Larceny Act 1861, section 50.
29 Letter entitled 'Executions in Hampshire' from Mr Henry Moody, curator of Winchester Museum, *The Times*, 24 December 1856.
30 *The Inter-Ocean*, 23 October 1904, the Biblical quotations are from Proverbs 20:1 and Luke 17:3 and 4 respectively.

Although theoretically indictable offences, both keeping a disorderly house and indecent exposure were often dealt with as purely summary offences (as will be shown in Chapter Seven in the discussion of summary offences heard by the Crewe magistrates' bench between 1880 and 1940).

The keeping of disorderly houses had first reached the statute books as an offence following the passing of the Disorderly Houses Act 1751. Despite this attempt to formalize the offence, in practice it was often extremely difficult to precisely identify the offender in such cases, and consequently, suspects were often charged with lesser, summary offences.

With regard to indecent exposure, the offence was gender specific, referring overwhelmingly to the unrequested exhibition of male genitalia to unsuspecting females or public masturbation. Section 4 of the Vagrancy Act 1824 required the offender to 'wilfully, openly, lewdly and obscene expose his person with intent to insult any female' which in practice required a statement from the female complainant that she saw his penis erect and was thereby insulted. The offence was punishable with three months' imprisonment or a fine. A similar offence could also be found under the Town Police Clauses Act 1847 of 'wilfully or indecently exposing the person in a street to the obstruction, annoyance or danger of the residents and passers-by'. This offence could be committed by both males and females but was only punishable with a fine or a maximum fourteen days' imprisonment. The offence was often a difficult one to prove, as many suspects stated that they were unwittingly caught short and were merely in the act of impromptu and unavoidable urination rather than deliberately exposing their private parts. Both provisions were repealed by section 66 Sexual Offences Act 2003, which is gender neutral and requires a person to intentionally expose the genitals with the intention that someone will see them and be caused alarm or distress.

Everyday indecency in Crewe 1880–1940

As discussed public indecency did not feature heavily with regard to reported indictable offences within England during the period under discussion, the vast majority of indecency offences being instead heard by borough magistrates in petty sessions. The discussion now turns to the ways in which it was dealt with at a summary level by investigating the offences that came before Crewe Magistrates' Bench 1880–1940.[31]

Crewe was created by a decision of the Grand Junction Railway (precursor to the more famous London & North Western Railway [hereafter L&NWR], one of the 'Big Four' pre-nationalization railway companies) to site a railway station

---

31 The source is a transcribed machine-readable database of all 49,203 cases that came before Crewe Borough Petty Sessions 1880–1940. The database includes details of the date of the court appearance, defendants' and complainants' names, gender (and occasionally age and address), synopsis of offences (sometimes with details of location), verdict, and punishment.

near the tiny settlement of Monks Coppenhall, Cheshire, in 1837. In 1843 the area became the hub of a major railway works and engine sheds complex, and the town continued to grow rapidly throughout the remainder of the nineteenth century. It was incorporated as a borough in 1877 and a borough police force followed shortly after, with a divisional petty sessions being created in 1881 (during 1877–1881 Crewe magistrates usually sat at nearby Nantwich and Willaston).[32] By the beginning of the twentieth century, Crewe's population exceeded 40,000, almost 8,000 of whom were employed by the L&NWR.

Crewe was unusual in that despite being an artificially created single-industry settlement akin to the Cadbury brothers' Bournville, William Lever's Port Sunlight, or Titus Salt's Saltaire, it was not an overtly paternalistic venture; although the L&NWR provided schools and hospitals, there was no overweening or concerted and deterministic attempt to control all aspects of the inhabitants' lives. For example, there was not an over-representation of the railway company on the magistrates' bench, and it is significant that most offences committed within the confines of the railway works were dealt with by a system of fines, demerits, and dismissals.[33] Railway companies such as the L&NWR also had legal authority to enact and institute their own private by-laws including ones prohibiting indecency on their trains and property such as By-law no. 9 of the Mid-Wales Railway, passed by the Board of Trade, 24 July 1875:

> Any person found in a Carriage, or elsewhere upon the Company's premises, in a state of Intoxication, or using Obscene or Abusive Language, or writing Obscene or Offensive words on any part of the Company's Stations or Carriages, or committing any Nuisance, or otherwise wilfully interfering with the Comfort of other Passengers, is hereby subject to a Penalty not exceeding Forty Shillings, and shall immediately, or if a Passenger, at the first Opportunity, be removed from the Company's Premises.[34]

Crewe can therefore be regarded as a typically provincial town in terms of demographic and socio-economic composition (albeit it was one that experienced more rapid than average growth through the nineteenth century), whose unusually complete surviving petty sessions records can provide us with an invaluable insight into exactly how public indecency was perceived and prosecuted in the late-Victorian to the pre–World War Two period.

---

32 Although a Borough force was created, Crewe never appointed its own Chief Constable. Their most senior officer was a Superintendent who was responsible to the Cheshire Chief Constable. For a brief history of the Cheshire Constabulary (founded 1856–1857), see R. W. James, *To the Best of Our Skill and Knowledge: A Short History of the Cheshire Constabulary 1857–1957*, second edition (Warrington: Museum of Policing in Cheshire, 2005).

33 See Godfrey *et al., Criminal Lives,* for further details of the socio-economic composition of the Crewe Magistrates' Bench and the internal disciplinary measures favoured by the L&NWR in their Railway Works.

34 TNA Rail 1001/206 By-laws and regulations: railway companies (n.d.).

Categories of offences

For the purposes of this study, the database was interrogated and the following five categories analyzed:

- Sexual indecency: this category includes indecent exposure, indecent assault, brothel-keeping, aiding and abetting prostitution, buggery, conspiring to produce miscarriage, living on immoral earnings, and other sexually related forms of indecent behaviour.
- Religious indecency: this category includes profanity (usually the issuing of profane oaths), riotous behaviour in a place of public worship, sacrilege, Lord's Day Observance offences, etc.[35]
- Behavioural indecency: this category comprises using obscene language, exposing indecent prints for sale, abusive conduct and behaviour, public urination, distribution of obscene photographs, etc.
- Gambling indecency: this category includes playing pitch and toss, street gambling, betting without a licence, keeping a lottery, permitting gambling on public premises, telling fortunes, etc.
- Vagrant indecency: this category includes vagrancy, causing children to beg, illegal hawking, etc.

During the period 1880–1940 there was a total of 5,994 cases in the five categories under discussion that came before Crewe magistrates (12.2 per cent of all cases heard by the Bench). Of these, 5,079 (84.7 per cent) were male defendants, with 915 (15.3 per cent) of defendants being female. This gender split is broadly in line with the gender split of the total number of 49,203 cases brought before the magistrates in the period (males accounting for 87.6 per cent of defendants, females accounting for 12.4 per cent of the total), although the percentage difference does suggest that females were somewhat more likely to be brought before the magistracy for indecency offences than for other types of offence.

The overall (male and female) average dismissal rate for indecency cases was 12.2 per cent. This is considerably higher than the overall dismissal rate (7.5 per cent) for all cases during the period, suggesting that such types of offence could often be difficult to prove in court. However, there is a significant gender discrepancy: while the dismissal rate for female indecency cases (12.8 per cent) is similar to the overall dismissal rate for all female cases (11.4 per cent), the dismissal rate for male indecency cases was 12.1 per cent compared to an overall dismissal rate for all male cases of only 7 per cent. This discrepancy is most likely accounted for by the high rate of dismissal in vagrancy cases (almost 25 per cent): males accounted for 88 per cent of all those brought before the Crewe magistrates for this offence (1,549 out of 1,761 cases). In most of the other indecency categories (with the exception of

---

35   It is recognized that profane and obscene language could be viewed as similar indecent behaviour, but the Crewe petty sessions records maintain a clear distinction between the two offences of using profane language and obscene language; in the cases where both obscene and profane language are recorded as having been used by the same defendant, these have been placed in the behavioural category.

Table 6.2 Public indecency offences heard by Crewe Magistrates, 1880–1940

	M	F
Total indecency offences 5,994	5,079	915
Non-dismissal rate[36] 87.8	87.9	87.2
Sexual indecency offences 421	265	156
Non-dismissal rate 88.1	82.6	97.4
Religious indecency offences 298	207	91
Non-dismissal rate 95.0	95.7	93.4
Gambling indecency offences 17,47	1,729	18
Non-dismissal rate 93.1	93.1	94.4
Behavioural indecency offences 1,767	1,329	438
Non-dismissal rate 93.8	95.4	89.0
Vagrant indecency offences 1,761	1,549	212
Non-dismissal rate 75.1	75.4	72.6
Total offences 49,203	43,105	6,098
Non-dismissal rate 92.5	93.0	88.6

sexual indecency), the dismissal rate for males is much closer to the overall average rate, as shown in Table 6.2.

It can be seen that with regard to indecency offences, there are some significant differentials in conviction rates with regard to gender. This is most notable in sexual indecency offences, in which females were far more likely to receive a 'guilty' verdict than males; only 2.6 per cent of cases involving female defendants were dismissed, compared with 11.9 per cent of cases with male defendants. Conversely, female defendants were less likely to be convicted of behavioural indecency: 11 per cent of cases with female defendants were dismissed, compared

---

36 Non-dismissal rate includes all cases that were either disposed of by magistrates with either a custodial sentence, fine, bind over, supervision order, or other punitive sentence, and these figures also include a very small number of cases (72) that were committed to a higher court.

Table 6.3 Verdicts in public indecency cases heard by Crewe Magistrates, 1880–1940

	Total	Male	Female
Total convictions	5,260	4,462	798
Behavioural indecency	1,658	1,268	390
Gambling indecency	1,626	1,609	17
Vagrant indecency	1,322	1,168	154
Sexual indecency	371	219	152
Religious indecency	283	198	85

to only 6.2 per cent of cases with male defendants. In addition, 46 per cent of dismissals of females had female complainants, compared to an average of 19.7 per cent for all indecency offences, suggesting that the magistrates (who until 1920 were all male) may have been less inclined to believe the evidence of female complainants than their male counterparts.

Turning to the verdicts given to those offenders whose cases were not dismissed, Table 6.3 shows that just over 5,000 defendants were convicted.

The table shows that (by a very small margin) behavioural indecency was the most prevalent type of indecency prosecuted in Crewe 1880–1940, with gambling indecency being a close second. Both of these categories also had a high overall conviction rate (93.8 per cent and 93.1 per cent respectively), whilst the next highest category of vagrant indecency had a low overall conviction rate of 75.1 per cent, despite being numerically the second most commonly prosecuted type of indecency. Both religious indecency offences and sexual indecency offences were relatively low in number, reflecting the national picture.

Disposal of offenders

In respect of the sentences those convicted of public indecency offences received, most notable is the very small number of indecency offences that were not dealt with summarily by the Crewe bench: only 72 of the 5,994 cases (1.2 per cent) were refused a hearing at the petty sessions and were committed to a higher court (usually quarter sessions, though a handful of cases did proceed further to the Cheshire Assizes). Of these, all but two were sexual indecency offences involving serious sexual abuse, buggery, and incest. Table 6.4 shows that in total 5,260 cases resulted in a non-dismissal disposal.

Table 6.5 shows exactly what disposals these offenders received.[37]

These figures throw up some interesting findings both in terms of gender sentencing and the perceived seriousness of different types of public indecency. The most heavily penalized offence is perhaps unsurprisingly sexual indecency, as this category includes some of the more serious offences that took place in Crewe

---

37 Total percentages in this and other tables may not add up to exactly 100 due to the effect of rounding on individual figures.

Table 6.4 Number of non-dismissal disposals of public indecency cases, Crewe Magistrates, 1880–1940

	Total	*Male*	*Female*
Total number of non-dismissal disposals for indecency offences	5,260	4,462	798
Behavioural indecency	1,658	1,268	390
Gambling indecency	1,626	1,609	17
Vagrant indecency	1,322	1,168	154
Sexual indecency	371	219	152
Religious indecency	283	198	85

Table 6.5 Disposal of offenders in public indecency cases, Crewe Magistrates, 1880–1940
Behavioural indecency

	Up to £1 fine/1 month[38]	*Over £1 fine/1 month*	*Bound over*	*Supervision*	*Other*
Total	1,331	83	224	4	16
% of total disposals	80.3	5.0	13.5	0.2	1.0
M	1,016	64	173	3	12
% of total M disposals	80.1	5.0	13.6	0.2	0.9
F	315	19	51	1	4
% of total F disposals	80.8	4.9	13.1	0.3	1.0

Gambling indecency

	Up to £1 fine/1 month	*Over £1 fine/1 month*	*Bound over*	*Supervision*	*Other*
Total	1,189	102	328	3	4
% of total disposals	73.1	6.3	20.2	0.2	0.2
M	1,182	99	324	1	3
% of total M disposals	73.5	6.2	20.1	0.1	0.2
F	7	3	4	2	1
% of total F disposals	41.2	17.6	23.5	11.8	5.9

Vagrant indecency

	Up to £1 fine/1 month	*Over £1 fine/1 month*	*Bound over*	*Supervision*	*Other*
Total	1,103	41	140	21	17
% of total disposals	83.4	3.1	10.6	1.6	1.3
M	983	33	119	19	14
% of total M disposals	84.2	2.8	10.2	1.6	1.2
F	120	8	21	2	3
% of total F disposals	77.9	5.2	13.6	1.3	1.9

(Continued)

38 It must be borne in mind that these fines (both above and below £1) do not include any associated costs that the magistrates may have also awarded against the defendant. On occasion these costs could be considerably more than the amount of any fine imposed.

Table 6.5 Continued
Sexual indecency

	Up to £1 fine/1 month	Over £1 fine/1 month	Bound over	Supervision	Other
Total	145	92	42	12	80
% of total disposals	39.1	24.8	11.3	3.2	21.6
M	65	69	34	11	40
% of total M disposals	29.7	31.5	15.5	5.0	18.3
F	80	23	8	1	40
% of total F disposals	52.6	15.1	5.3	0.7	26.3

Religious indecency

	Up to £1 fine/1 month	Over £1 fine/1 month	Bound over	Supervision	Other
Total	262	1	20	0	0
% of total disposals	92.6	0.4	7.1	0.0	0.0
M	182	1	15	0	0
% of total M disposals	91.9	0.5	7.6	0.0	0.0
F	80	0	5	0	0
% of total F disposals	94.1	0.0	5.9	0.0	0.0

All offences

	Up to £1 fine/1 month	Over £1 fine/1 month	Bound over	Supervision	Other
Total	23,811	2,226	8,177	334	10,948
% of total disposals	52.3	4.9	18.0	0.7	24.1
M	21,064	1,862	7,310	273	9,582
% of total M disposals	52.5	4.6	18.2	0.7	23.9
F	2,747	364	867	61	1,366
% of total F disposals	50.8	6.7	16.0	1.1	25.3

during the period; both male and female sexual offenders were much more likely either to receive a heavy fine or gaol sentence or to have their cases committed to a higher court. However, within this category, females were much more likely to receive a smaller penalty than males: over half of the female defendants received a fine of less than £1 or under 1 month in gaol, compared to less than a third of male defendants. This is most probably due to the type of sexual indecency that males committed, which was violent, non-consensual assault, compared with the sexual indecency committed by females, mainly prostitution-related offences such as brothel keeping.

The following account of a police raid on a brothel was reported in the *Crewe Chronicle*, 24 April 1916.

Police Raid a Crewe House

Young Widow Sent to Prison

A Sordid Story

'The story reveals a terrible state of human depravity'. Such were the words used by Supt Thompson at Crewe Police Court on Monday, when Emily Dytor, a young widow, residing at 34 Orchard Place, Crewe, was charged on a warrant with keeping and using her house as a disorderly house between May 15th and June 17th. She was further charged with allowing her five children, under the ages of 12 years, to reside in such a house. Mrs Netta Titley, also a young widow, was charged with aiding and abetting the above accused, and a similar charge was preferred against Mrs Alice Dutton, a married woman residing in Lincoln Street. Two young men stood by the accused women charged with aiding and abetting Mrs Dytor. They were William Dawes, a fitter, of Remer Street, and James Lewis Evans, a painter residing in Earle Street, Crewe. All were very respectably dressed. Mrs Dytor wearing a light raincoat over a gown of light coloured muslin.

Supt Thompson, who prosecuted, said the accused Mrs Dytor was the occupier of 34 Orchard Place, off West Street, and she was charged with keeping a disorderly house. The four other accused were charged with aiding and abetting her. There was also another charge against Mrs Dytor of allowing her five children to dwell in the house. They were resident in the house, but were not all there when the arrests were made. The story revealed a terrible state of human depravity, and when the magistrates had heard the evidence, he felt sure that they would be satisfied that the case was one which required very serious treatment. . . . It was absolutely necessary in the interests of the public that [such cases] should be brought, and he appealed to the Bench to inflict such punishment as would act as a deterrent to others. Two of the female prisoners had patrolled the streets of Crewe for some time, and the evidence would show that they had taken men – some married – to Orchard Place for a certain purpose. Some of the men were sons of very respectable parents, and the accused and other women had been the means of causing constant and terrible anxiety in many homes in the town. What was more deplorable than anything else was the fact that one of the young women was the mother of seven children, five of whom resided under the roof where acts of immorality were practiced. He did not say that the acts were performed in the presence of the young children, but men and women could not possibly visit a house for such purposes without the children having some idea and it was bound to act and have a most shameful influence upon their lives and morals. . . .

Decision of the Bench

After a short consultation, the Chairman said that Mrs Dytor would have to go to gaol for 14 days on the two charges. Mrs Titley would be fined £3 or 21 days; Mrs Dutton £1 or 14 days; and the two men £3 each or 21 days' hard labour.

What perhaps is most revealing about this rather sorry tale is the evidence of Superintendent Thompson (a long-serving police officer in Crewe Borough Police); he stated that 'he felt it his bounden duty to bring those cases into court from time to time in order to try and stamp out the evil. They were very difficult cases to prepare, and in many instances it took weeks of trouble and anxiety to bring them before the court.' It is clear that Superintendent Thompson did not view such matter as high on the list of priorities of his duties, and that, quite apart from the implied request for greater resources (often present in police statements to the court), he did not think that this type of offence merited the time and man-power involved in bringing a successful prosecution. The relative leniency of the sentence appears to suggest that he had a point.

Many of the offences that we have categorized as public indecency were offences under the Town Police Clauses Act 1847, notably section 28, which was a catch-all for all sorts of offending, ranging from indecent exposure, throwing fireworks, flying a kite, or using profane or obscene language. This Act made it incumbent on a police officer to arrest any such offender regardless or not of whether prosecution costs would be met by the local authority. However, it is clear that this requirement often did not filter down to the police constable on the beat, as is illustrated by the following case which took place over half a century after the passing of the Act.

On 2 December 1898, William Thomas, a labourer of Sevenoaks, Kent, was observed by PC 330, William Cutting, in the high street to be in a verbal altera-tion with another individual. Thomas was heard by PC Cutting to say, 'Come out here if you want to fucking well fight you fucker, you fucking bastard.'[39] PC Cutting did not arrest Thomas there and then, but instead reported his behaviour to the Urban District Council, as he believed that an offence had been commit-ted under a local by-law rather than under the Town Police Clauses Act, and that therefore the council should prepare a prosecution. The Clerk to the Sevenoaks Urban District Council, Mr H. Thompson, declined to prosecute under the by-law, returning the onus of prosecution to the police under the Act. This prompted the Chief Constable of Kent, Lt. Col. H. M. A. Warde, to write to the Home Office, asking for clarification about who should prosecute in such matters, informing the Secretary of State that he (the Chief Constable) had received legal advice that his constable's view of the matter was correct. This request initiated a flurry of activity and consternation from the Home Office, who on 20 January 1899 replied to Warde, making it clear in no uncertain terms that 'a constable is bound to take into custody and convey before a Justice any person who within his view com-mits certain offences, *whether or not any expenses which may be incurred have been guaranteed by the Urban District Council.*' [emphasis added][40] The letter goes on to point out that 'a constable would fail in his duty if he did not proceed to prosecute the offender whom he had conveyed before the Justice.'[41] Cutting is

39 TNA HO 45 22607 Police: Powers of police under Town Police Clauses Act (1888–1949).
40 Ibid.
41 Ibid.

also indirectly reprimanded for not having arrested the offender at the time of the offence. An internal Home Office memo makes clear that the police have acted unlawfully: 'the Police would hardly be more justified legally not first demanding their expenses in such a case than they would be in a case of burglary or murder.'[42]

Although this appears to have been one of the few occasions on which this situation reached the eyes of the Home Secretary, it is apparent that the police could be reluctant to prosecute if their expenses in bringing such a case were not guaranteed to be reimbursed by the local authority. There appears to have been a constant battle between the police and those responsible for their finance with regard to resources: in Chief Constables' annual *Reports* of the period there is often an implicit (and occasionally explicit) request for more money to finance their operations, and this may have had an effect on prosecution rates of minor offences such as profane and obscene language.

In all of the other categories of the offences that came before the Crewe Bench, the vast majority of offenders similarly received a relatively minor penalty of either a fine up to £1 or a gaol sentence of up to one month, or were bound over to keep the peace.[43] This suggests that despite the fact that such offences had a high conviction rate, the Crewe magistrates regarded such offences as of relatively limited importance. Although they were happy to find defendants guilty, it was rare that a very punitive sentence was imposed.

Somewhat surprisingly, religious indecency is by far the most leniently treated of all indecency offences; despite profanely offending against the Almighty in an avowedly Christian State, almost without exception offenders (male and female) were either given sentences of less than £1 fine or under one month in gaol, or were bound over to keep the peace. Only two individuals (both male) were given fines of more than £1 or a gaol sentence of over one month.

The uttering of profane oaths had been a criminal offence since the seventeenth century, and in the following century the Profane Oaths Act 1746 introduced a stratified and hierarchical level of fines: labourers and rank-and-file soldiers and sailors could be fined 1s, those below the (largely undefined) rank of gentleman could receive a fine of 2s, whilst gentlemen and the aristocracy could be fined up to 5s.[44]

The extent to which this Act was actually used is debatable. A brief survey with regard to an earlier period (where statistical information is severely limited due to the lack of transcription of court records) suggests that the Act was in fact rarely invoked. An investigation of Irene Wyatt's invaluable work in collating the

---

42 Ibid.
43 For the majority of cases, it is unfortunately not possible to ascertain whether or not the offender paid the fine or went to prison, as the records do not register this information.
44 The Act, which also contained an order that it was to be read publicly in every church or chapel on the first Sunday after each quarter day (with a fine of £5 if the minister did not comply) was not formally repealed until 1967. The offence of swearing now potentially falls under s.5 Public Order Act 1986 if there is an intention to cause harassment, alarm, or distress and there are other circumstances present. Blasphemy has existed as a crime for over 2,000 years, but was never listed in the *CS* as a separate crime. For an excellent introduction to its history, see D. Nash, *Blasphemy in the Christian World: A History* (Oxford: Oxford University Press, 2010).

Calendars of Summary Convictions at Petty Sessions 1781–1837 for Gloucestershire shows that of the 6,439 cases recorded as appearing before magistrates
only 160 of these were for swearing or cursing (2.5 per cent of the total number
of offences).[45] Further examination of these 160 cases shows that the number
of such cases peaked during the first two years of the 1790s: there were a total
of 74 cases in 1790–1791, and only eight convictions for swearing or cursing
post-1815. These findings suggest two possible options: that swearing and cursing was rather more tolerated in the early decades of the nineteenth century than
the latter decades of the eighteenth, or conversely, that society (including the
lower classes, who predominate in the court records) had become more polite and
showed greater self-restraint.

No mention was made in the 1746 Act of women who offended in this way.
During a 1960 Lords' discussion on the subject, Lord Swaythling rather gallantly
mused that 'perhaps it was unthinkable for a woman to offend that Act in those
days.'[46] This was patently not in fact the case by the early twentieth century; as the
following example shows. The *Crewe Chronicle* of 2 July 1910 carried a report
of a case heard before Crewe Borough Magistrates. Under the title 'A Disgrace to
Her Sex', the report stated:

> Jane Cookson was charged on a warrant with having used obscene language.
> There were two informations against the accused. Fanny Pearsons, 6 Orchard
> Street, said she heard the accused use terrible language. She was a pest to the
> neighbourhood, and several people had threatened to leave the neighbour-
> hood on account of her conduct. Louise Leech, Orchard Street, also gave
> evidence. She had never heard such bad language. Elizabeth Walley said the
> accused was swearing all day. It was very desirable in the interests of the
> children that the accused should be removed from the district. Superinten-
> dent Pearson said the accused had a very bad record, having been before the
> magistrates eleven times for using profane language, the last penalty being
> 40s and costs. She was summoned to appear at the last sessions, but did not
> appear, and a warrant was issued for her arrest. She was a disgrace to her sex.
> She was fined £1 and costs on both charges.

Despite the gender-specific remarks of the newspaper report – 'a disgrace to her
sex' – there was in fact very little differential between the sentencing of males and
females with regard to behavioural indecency. The figures provided earlier for all
types of punishment meted out by the magistrates are remarkably similar for both
sexes, and this pattern is also evident in the sentencing of vagrant indecency. This
is somewhat surprising: if one adheres to Zedner's view that women offenders

---

45 I. Wyatt, *Calendar of Summary Convictions at Petty Sessions 1781–1837*, Gloucestershire Record
 Series, vol. 22 (Gloucester: Bristol and Gloucestershire Archaeological Society, 2008). The returns
 which Wyatt utilizes are unfortunately not complete (and are not presented in a machine-readable
 database), but still give an invaluable insight into the functioning of the late eighteenth and early
 nineteenth century proceedings of the lower magisterial courts.
46 *Hansard* HL Deb, 14 March 1960, vol.221 cc.1073–87.

were seen as 'doubly deviant' in that they not only broke the law but also did not adhere to contemporary perceptions as 'the guardian of the domestic hearth' or 'angel of the home', one might expect there to be less tolerance of indecent behaviour by females during the period and consequently a harsher punishment.[47] However, Zedner's analysis of the treatment of 'deviant' women has been challenged more recently, and it is obvious that there was more to sentencing than a simple gender divide: class, social status, and knowledge of prior offending behaviour clearly also often played a major part in the sentencing process.[48] If one looks at the figures for all 45,000+ cases that resulted in a disposal during the period under discussion, this lack of a gender bias in sentencing patterns appears to be largely consistent. There is a broad similarity in sentencing patterns for both males and females, with only a few minor differences – women, for example, were slightly less likely to be bound over and slightly more likely to receive fines of over £1 or imprisonment for more than one month.

Gambling indecency is the only category that at first sight bucks this trend: female offenders were more likely to receive a harsher sentence than males, with 1 in 6 women being given a fine in excess of £1 or a gaol sentence of over one month, compared to 1 in 16 men. However, the actual number of female offenders in this category is extremely small – only 17 out of a total of over 1,600 offenders were women, and these anomalies can be further explained by the fact that the majority of female offending involved women offenders allowing domestic or commercial premises to be used for gambling purposes rather than being caught gambling in the street at games such as pitch and toss.

Conclusion

One of the most obvious and striking conclusions to the above analysis is that reported indecency cases did not form a significant percentage of the total number of reported indictable cases at any time during the period under discussion, even during the post–World War Two period when figures were somewhat skewed in the early mid-1950s by the anti-homosexual campaigns described earlier; the average dropped back to 1.30 per cent by 1960. The rise in the 1950s was clearly largely comprised of an increase in the number of reported cases of unnatural acts and indecency with males. There were no significant changes in the method of recording such figures during the 1950–1959 period, and no suggested explanations for the rise are given in any of the Introductory Notes that appear at the beginning of each annual volume of *Judicial Statistics*. Two possible explanations are that either there was simply a real rise in such offences, perhaps as a corollary to a more permissive society (but this seems unlikely), or conversely (and more probably) that more prudish post-war attitudes on behalf of both the

47 L. Zedner, *Women, Crime and Custody in Victorian England* (Oxford: Oxford University Press, 1991).

48 See for example, B. Godfrey, *et al.,* 'Explaining Gendered Sentencing Patterns for Violent Men and Women in the Late-Victorian and Edwardian Period', *British Journal of Criminology* 45(5) (September 2005): 696–720.

police and the government led to an increase in the recording of such actions. Various forms of larceny remained by far the largest category of reported indictable offences throughout the entire period, with indecency offences accounting for only around 1 in 100 indictable offences (220,435 reported offences out of a total of 17,515,754).

Turning to summary offences (by far the most numerous level of offences throughout the period), public indecency accounted for only 12.2 per cent of total recorded summary offences in Crewe in 1880–1940, roughly 1 in 8 offences. It seems that despite the claims of the numerous concerned pressure groups and organizations, in reality public indecency (with the exception of drunkenness, as will be seen in the next chapter) played a relatively small part in the overall recorded criminal behaviour of the populace at large. Whether this was due to the continuation of Wilson's 'robust view of the vulgarity of British life', in which the majority of the English populace accepted a degree of indecency on an almost daily basis, and therefore ignored it, preferring this to the 'moralising cant of the nineteenth century' is certainly open to debate.

Samuel Redgrave, Criminal Registrar 1834–1860, stated the ideal in his introduction to the 1857 *JS* that a full-time and professional police (created throughout England and Wales by statute following the 1856 County Borough Police Act) 'will care for the removal of all demoralising influences, for the better maintenance of public order and decorum, for the suppression of habitual vagrancy, for the supervision of places of low resort and common lodging houses'.[49] Redgrave voiced the hope that the introduction of uniformed law enforcement officers who patrolled the streets of England's towns and cities would have a dramatic effect on public morals, and that the constables (all male until 1919) would suppress all forms of indecency on the street.

The reality was often very different. As Joanne Klein has recently remarked, 'once on the streets, recruits realized that policemen could not be the ideal described in their [training] classes. Enforcing every law and regulation was not only physically impossible, it was not appropriate in every situation.'[50] Then as now, there was clearly a degree of discretion employed by police officers when dealing with putative criminal behaviour. On many occasions it was the long-suffering neighbours of persistent offenders that insisted the matter be dealt with by the police, as exemplified in the following newspaper report from the *Crewe Chronicle*, 4 August 1934:

Kept the Police Busy

'Linguist' Complains of 'Interference'

Sarah Mellor, 36 Stafford Street, Crewe, was summoned for using obscene language on July 14th. The Police evidence showed that defendant attracted a crowd of people in Stafford Street as a result of her conduct.

49 *JS* 1857, *Introductory and Explanatory Report*, vi.
50 Klein, *Invisible Men*, 26.

A copy of the language she was alleged to have used was handed to the Bench, but when it was shown to the defendant she denied using the words complained of.

'The house is always surrounded by police!' exclaimed defendant.

Mr H. Bullock (one of the magistrates): Why is that?

Defendant: You are not allowed to fall out with your own husband. You cannot have a few 'words' in your own house without the Police interfering!

Supt. Cash: The Police have been sent for to this house more than the average. Defendant is addicted to this sort of thing. She carries on, and the neighbours run for the Police. Sometimes she desists before they arrive, but on this occasion she didn't.

Defendant was bound over for 12 months.

Did a decline in State religion play a part in such tolerance? Some historians have questioned any decline in organized religion during the nineteenth century; for example, in a 2011 Gresham Lecture, Richard Evans opined that the Victorian period was a time of genuine concern and interest in religion, and went on to quote J.A. Froude's 1883 view that 'an established religion . . . is the sanction of moral obligation; it gives authority to the commandments, creates a fear of doing wrong, and a sense of responsibility for doing it . . . to raise a doubt about a creed established by general acceptance is a direct injury to the general welfare.'[51] However, in spite of the Reverend Charles William Stubb's 1887 exhortation for members of the Church of England to follow 'the wider mission of the Church of England herself, spiritualising all national life, leading her people through a sense of duty to righteousness, kindling morality into enthusiasm',[52] it would appear that then, as now, a significant percentage of the population paid little more than lip service to religious practice and teaching. Furthermore, there *was* a definite shift from spiritual to secular oversight of morality and decency throughout the nineteenth and twentieth centuries; witness the proliferation of local government officials to police many aspects of daily life, from market inspectors to weights and measures inspectors, from education/truancy officers to sanitary inspectors. There is also obviously a discussion to be had concerning why moral and behavioural decency *has* to be linked to any form of religious observance – the Sermon on the Mount does not have exclusive tenancy of the moral high ground.

51 Quoted in R.J. Evans, 'The Victorians: Religion and Science', Gresham Lecture, 14 March 2011: www.gresham.ac.uk/lectures-and-events/the-victorians-religion-and-science.

52 C.W. Stubbs, *The church in the villages: principles and ideal : an address to the Church Council and Wardens of the United Parishes of Stokenham, Chivelstone, and Sherford* (Cranford's Library, Dartmouth, 1887), 16.

7   Intoxicated indecency

How the drink problem was resolved

Introduction

This chapter investigates by far the most prevalent and most troublesome to the authorities of all forms of public indecency: drunkenness and drink-related offending. Much has been written about drunkenness in the Victorian and subsequent periods; this chapter therefore does not intend to step too heavily on previously trodden ground, although it will discuss historical developments with regard to the ways in which organizations and government attempted to control and limit the perceived problem of the 'demon drink'.[1] Drunkenness was undoubtedly seen by many in the late Victorian period as a major evil, and one to be scourged from the shores of England at all costs, but by the end of World War One national prosecutions for drunkenness had begun to decrease dramatically, and as is shown later, this decrease continued almost without exception during the interwar period.

The main body of this chapter examines the policing and judicial response to drink-related offences both nationally and again with specific regard to Crewe as an exemplar of a provincial town. How did the respective bodies who came across drunks and their often very public affronts to decency actually behave? To what extent did the frequently hyperbolic rhetoric match up to the practice? How were pragmatic or punitive measures utilized by both the executive (in the form of police prosecutions) and the judiciary (primarily in the form of magistrates, and, much less frequently, by judges) in order to attempt to control the problem?

The following letter, published on 2 August 1879 in the *Crewe Chronicle* is typical of many such apparent 'cries from the heart' of concerned individuals regarding the state of the perceived often-inebriated nation that appeared regularly in the provincial and regional press:

'Letter to the Editor

Drunkenness at Crewe

The increase of drunkenness has become very noticeable in our town, so much so that it is utterly unsafe for any respectable individual to pass certain

---

1 For an excellent recent synthesis of the available literature, see H. Yeomans, *Alcohol and Moral Regulation: Public Attitudes, Spirited Measures and Victorian Hangovers* (Bristol: Policy Press, 2014), in which he also investigates contemporary attitudes to drink and the current moral panic over binge drinking, and relates present-day concerns to an historical study of the problem.

public houses about the hour of eleven on Saturday nights. It is pitiable to see poor wretches, maddened by their libations, endeavouring to complete each other's misery by spoiling each other's faces; then staggering home with the blissful prospects of black eyes, aching heads, and empty pockets to greet them on the Sunday morning. But what astonishes me is how this sort of thing comes about. According to our laws 'no intoxicated persons shall be supplied with drink', thus effectively preventing drunkenness. Yet how is it we see such a vast number of men, aye, and women too, in a most beastly state of intoxication. How have they got so very drunk? To satisfy ourselves we have only to visit the different gin palaces of our town, where it is astonishing to see how openly and unreservedly the law must be violated. Yet we rarely hear of a publican being summoned. I ask; how is it that this sort of thing is allowed to proceed? Our police are most vigilant in most things; why not so in this? I hear a most excellent character of our new Inspector, and I hope he will give this matter his special attention, thus being the means not only of clearing our streets of intoxicants, but also of rendering many miserable homes happy. ANTI-BOT[2]

Contrast this serious concern over the levels of drunkenness and lack of prosecution of landlords for permitting drunkenness with the following rather frivolous report that appeared a few years later in the same publication on 25 October 1884 concerning the annual dinner of the Crewe and Coppenhall Association for the Prosecution of Felons.[3] In his response to a toast to the 'Trade of the Town', a Mr Flack stated:

> He did not know much about the trade of Crewe except his own – he believed there was only one honest trade, and that was keeping a public house (Laughter). They had to bear such a good character to get a license [*sic*], and they were fined for getting men drunk, and they were fined for not keeping proper stuff for making them drunk (more laughter).

---

2 Of course, as with similar pseudonymic letters that made frequent appearances in such publications, there is always the possibility that the letter was in fact written by the editor or other member of staff in order to drum up debate, controversy, and circulation figures for the following week's newspaper – but even if this was the case, it still illustrates that this matter was a bone of contention.

3 Associations for the Prosecution of Felons were privately funded subscription societies in which members paid an annual subscription as an insurance against the cost of private prosecutions that they may incur during the year. For further details of the activities of such societies, see D. Phillips, 'Good men to associate and bad men to conspire: Associations for the prosecution of felons in England 1760–1860', in D. Hay and F. Snyder (eds.), *Policing and Prosecution in Britain, 1750–1850,* (Oxford: Oxford University Press, 1989): 113–70; B. Godfrey, and D. J. Cox, *Policing the Factory: Theft, Private Policing and the Law in Modern England* (London: Bloomsbury, 2013), 102–3; and Cox, D. J., *Crime in England 1688–1815* (Abingdon: Routledge, 2014), 29–30. By the late nineteenth century most (as was the case with the association at Crewe) were little more than an excuse for an annual multi-course dinner at a local hostelry. The 1884 newspaper report substantiated this by later stating that the chairman of the association remarked that 'there had only been ten cases before their notice in the past four years'.

In the 1881 census George T. Flack is listed as 'Licensed Victualler, The Crown, Earle Street, Crewe'.[4] Perhaps mindful of his position with the Association, Mr Flack appears to have been careful not to fall foul of the law in his role as licensee: he makes no appearance in the court records for any drink-related offences (but he was bound over in March 1887 for having an unmuzzled dog at large in a public place by Samuel Stockton, Borough Nuisance Inspector).

Permitting drunkenness on licensed premises is not included within the following figures, as although clearly drink-related, it was more of a regulatory offence rather than one of public indecency, in the same category as the watering-down of beer obliquely referred to by Flack.[5] In total, only 80 such cases came before the magistrates in the period 1880–1940, a surprisingly low number considering the prevalence of public houses in Crewe. On 3 February 1936 the *Crewe Chronicle* carried a report from Superintendent Cash who stated that there were 87 licences in Crewe, which at that time had a population of some 46,000 therefore equating to one licence for every 648 persons; and this ratio had risen considerably over the past few decades, it was 1:259 in 1871.[6] Of the 80 cases, 58 defendants were male and 22 female (reflecting the high number of female licensees in the drinks trade; many male publicans often had other full-time jobs and left the daytime running of the public house to their wives).[7] Well over a third of these cases (36.3 per cent) were dismissed, with all but eight of convicted licensees being sentenced to up to £1 fine or under one month in gaol.

As well as being a railway town, Crewe was also a mercantile centre with a high percentage of merchants and shopkeepers taking an active role on the Crewe bench. A survey of the 1902 Crewe Bench reveals that over 50 per cent of serving magistrates were shopkeepers of one sort or another (including the Mayor, who was a pawnbroker).[8] This may go some way to explaining both the lack of prosecutions and the low level of sentencing with regard to permitting drunkenness. It also appears that publicans were allowed to continue to ply their trade despite frequent brushes with the law. This is exemplified by examining the offending career of Crewe publican Thomas Richardson (1841–1911), who appeared before the Bench on almost a dozen occasions during his life, charged with a variety of public nuisance and drink-related offences.

Despite numerous appearances on charges of permitting drunkenness, he remained licensee of the same public house for over 30 years. Richardson originally worked as an engine fitter in the railway works at Wolverton, Buckinghamshire,

4 TNA RG 11/3541 1881 Census Registration Sub-District 1C Wybunbury. Civil Parish, Township or Place: Coppenhall.

5 For a succinct account of licensing and its policing in Victorian England, see P. Jennings, 'Policing public houses in Victorian England', *Law, Crime and History* 3, no. 1 (2013): 52–75.

6 Godfrey *et al., Criminal Lives*, 42.

7 For example, one of the authors' maternal great-grandfather kept various public houses in the Black Country during the late-Victorian period, but also had a number of simultaneous occupations whilst he was a licensee.

8 See Godfrey *et al., Criminal Lives*, 18.

but like many others transferred to Crewe in 1862 when the manufacture of engines ceased at the Wolverton factory. Married with four children, he worked as an engine fitter for several years, but 1874–1909 was also landlord of the Prince of Wales public house in West Street, Crewe (which also appears to have operated as a theatre at least 1868–1883). In 1874 he made his first appearance before the Bench when he was dismissed with a caution for selling alcohol to drunks on licensed premises. He appeared on the same charge again in 1885, and once more in 1892 (when a charge of selling drink to his drunken wife was dismissed). In 1903 he was fined 2 shillings and 6 pence or 2 days hard labour for being drunk in charge of a horse and cart, and two years later he was fined £1 for selling drink in false measure. He makes his final appearance before the court in 1909, fined 10 shillings and costs or 14 days' hard labour for permitting drunkenness on his premises.[9]

The national picture of intoxicated indecency

Turning to the national picture, the problem of public intoxicated indecency was clearly seen as a significant one throughout at least the first half of the period under discussion. Much of the problem with drink-related offences was often blamed by contemporaries on the relative cheapness and availability of beer. The Beer Act 1830 allowed any ratepayer, on payment of a fee of 2 guineas to the Excise, a licence to brew and sell beer from their premises. Prior to the introduction of this Act, magistrates exercised control over the issuing of licences.[10] The Act had been introduced partially in an attempt to stem the problem of increasing consumption of stronger alcohol, most notably in the form of gin or wine (both regarded by many as dangerously Continental), with beer being regarded (literally) as home-grown and more nutritious. For example, milk stout (also known as 'invalid stout') was often given on a daily basis to post-operative hospital patients as it was thought to contain high concentrations of iron and other B-group vitamins.[11] Similarly, as seen earlier, thanks to Dorothy L. Sayers, in the early 1930s Guinness was being promoted as being 'Good For You' with seven beneficial effects: 'strength, nerves, digestion, exhaustion, sleeplessness, its tonic effects and the blood'.[12] As the brewing process includes the boiling of water, in the Victorian period beer was also often considered as a safe alternative to publicly available water, which until the latter decades of the nineteenth century remained

9 Data abstracted from Crewe Borough Petty Sessions records held at Chester Archives, QPCr/3863/1–34.
10 For an investigation into how this Act affected public drinking, see N. Mason, "The sovereign people are in a beastly state": The Beer Act of 1830 and Victorian discourse on working-class drunkenness', *Victorian Literature and Culture*, 29 (2001): 109–27.
11 See D. Hughes, *"A Bottle of Guinness Please" – the Colourful History of Guinness* (Wokingham: Phimboy, 2006) for a history of milk stout and its consumption in hospitals.
12 See 'A Guinness a Day,' www.guinness.com/en-au/Adsdetails.html?adid=?22 for further details of the 'Guinness Is Good For You' advertising campaign.

largely untreated. However, there had been considerable opposition to the introduction of the Act (especially among the upper and middle-classes); as Nicholas Mason remarks, 'Even after the growth rate of beer shops began to decline in the early 1840s, the beer shop remained a prominent symbol of working-class degeneracy in the discourse of the privileged classes.'[13]

By 1872 this pressure resulted in the issuing of beer licences reverting to the overwhelmingly middle-class magistracy.[14] Zangerl, in his study of the social composition of the magistracy 1831–1837 has shown that in the mid-1880s, the borough magistracies were dominated by the middle classes: in the 74 boroughs from which he was able to extrapolate figures, over 71 per cent of magistrates were recorded by the contemporary Clerks of the Peace as middle class.[15] With regard to the composition of the county magistracies the picture was similar, with the 'squirearchy' of landed gentry accounting for over two-thirds of the magistrates' bench.[16]

Despite this reactive measure, as can be seen from the figures abstracted from the annual *JS*, prosecutions for drunkenness continued to rise overall for the next 40 years, albeit with a brief and limited respite during the 1880s, with numbers peaking in the Edwardian period. It must also be remembered that these figures are for those cases that reached the courts: the 'dark' figure of occurrences of intoxicated indecency that was either not brought to the police's attention, together with the number of incidents in which the police simply moved drunks on without initiating proceedings remains unknown, but is likely to have been considerable. Table 7.1 shows five-yearly average rates of summary proceedings in England and Wales against all offenders for drunkenness and aggravated drunkenness 1860–1960.[17]

These are raw data and no account has been taken of population growth over the period. There is a clear downward trend in the post-Edwardian period, which continued almost unabated until the post–World War Two period (the rise in the latter half of the 1930s may arguably be attributable to the effects of the Great Depression), when figures began to rise again, but to nowhere near their Victorian and Edwardian heights (or depths). A considerable amount of research has been carried out into the possibility of establishing conclusive links between economic downturns and drinking patterns, but many of the findings have been contradictory or inconclusive. It is therefore impossible to categorically state that

13 N. Mason, '"The sovereign people are in a beastly state", 109–27, 121.
14 Wine and Beerhouse Act 1869; Licensing Act 1872.
15 C. Zangerl, 'The social composition of the county magistracy in England and Wales, 1831–1887', *Journal of British Studies* 6 (November 1971): 115.
16 Ibid. For further research about the social composition of the provincial magistracy (including property qualifications) see Cox and Godfrey, *Cinderellas and Packhorses*, and H. Johnston, 'The Shropshire magistracy and local imprisonment: Networks of power in the nineteenth century', *Midland History* 30, no. 1 (2005): 67–91.
17 Data extrapolated from *JS* 1860–1960. The figures include totals for the Metropolitan Police districts, together with all provincial counties.

Table 7.1 Five-yearly average rates of summary proceedings in England and Wales against all offenders for drunkenness and aggravated drunkenness, 1860–1960

1860–64	92,055
1865–69	108,762
1870–74	158,974
1875–79	196,544
1880–84	185,643
1885–89	170,366
1890–94	179,723
1895–99	199,326
1900–4	216,424
1905–9	205,058
1910–14	193,354
1915–19	76,563
1920–24	85,160
1925–29	68,490
1930–34	44,888
1935–39	51,486
1940–44	31,716
1945–49	25,876
1950–54	50,662
1955–59	60,408

the consistent upward trend in drunkenness offences from the 1870s through to the outbreak of war in 1914 is directly related to the general downward turn in growth during the period.[18] In a recent article, Bor *et al.* found (admittedly with regard to studies based on US statistics for the late 2000s) that whilst the abstinence rate among the adult population reduced due to economic hardship, overall drinking increased, with frequent or binge drinking accounting for much of this rise, revealing a polarization of drinking behaviours.[19] This finding, if it holds true in general terms, would seem to go at least some way to explaining the large increase in prosecutions for drunkenness in the 1870s, a period of considerable economic uncertainty, and may also be a partial explanation of subsequent fluctuations until the outbreak of World War One. Heavy or binge drinking would almost certainly lead to increases in prosecutions for drink-related offences, as such behaviour has public consequences that attract frequent attention from the police.

18 See for example, A. Dingle, 'Drink and working class living standards', *Economic History Review* 25, no. 4 (November 1972): 608–22. The existence or non-existence of a 'Great Depression' in Britain in the last quarter of the nineteenth century has itself been the subject of much debate; see for example F. Crouzet, *The Victorian Economy* (Abingdon: Routledge, 2006), especially Chapter Three; also see S. B. Saul, *The Myth of the Great Depression, 1873–1896* (Basingstoke: Palgrave Macmillan, 1985).

19 J. Bor, S. Basu, A. Coutts, M. McKee, and D. Stuckler, 'Alcohol use during the Great Recession of 2008–2009', *Alcohol and Alcoholism* 38, no. 3 (May/June 2013): 343–8.

Responses to intoxicated indecency

Public reaction to such a perceived increase in public drunkenness during the last quarter of the nineteenth century was notable. Many of the larger temperance movements (which often shared areas of common cause with the Liberal Party, whilst the drinks trade was largely supported by the Conservatives) began in the 1870s in response to this challenge, although smaller-scale teetotal or temperance organizations with a missionary role, aimed more at individual reform rather than political and judicial change, had existed since at least the early 1830s, one of the earliest such societies being founded in Preston, Lancashire, in 1832.[20] Temperance societies had the avowed aim of their members pledging to refrain from drinking spirits or other strong liquor, whereas teetotal societies promoted complete abstinence from all forms of alcohol, although in practice there often seems to have been a conflation of the two objectives in the mind of the public.[21]

Such organizations often relied on religious support, for example, the Church of England Temperance Society was founded in Lambeth in 1873 (developing from an abortive existence in 1862 as the Church Teetotal Society), whilst the Catholic equivalent, known as the League of the Cross, was founded in Liverpool 1872–1873. The Blue Ribbon Movement, a Gospel temperance society which originated in New England, first appeared in England 1880 and enjoyed considerable success with regards to its membership levels in the following decade. By the mid-1880s it was well known enough in the English provinces to feature in a case appearing at Crewe Bench, when the daughter of Ann Belfield, who had been summonsed on an assault charge, was asked if both herself and her mother were drunk at the time of the incident. She replied that 'she was not in the habit of getting drunk', but admitted that 'she was not in the Blue Ribbon Army'.[22] This remark elicited laughter from the public gallery of the magistrates' court.[23]

Other temperance societies had specific objectives and membership, for example, the British Women's Temperance Association (founded in Newcastle 1876), or the Band of Hope (founded in 1847 as an adjunct of the Leeds Temperance Society and now known as Hope UK), concentrated on preventing future alcoholism by recruiting children to its ranks. As the Reverend G.W. McCree (a Baptist minister and social reformer) stated, 'the boys of our Sunday School are tempted to drink on the first day they enter the workshop. Unless trained to total abstinence, it is almost a moral certainty that they are at the very outset overcome.'[24]

---

20 For a detailed history of the numerous temperance and teetotal societies that sprang up in the United Kingdom during the nineteenth century, see J. Blocker, D.M. Fahey, and I.R. Tyrrell, eds., *Alcohol and Temperance in Modern History: An International Encyclopedia*, vol. 1 (Santa Barbara: ABC Clio, 2003).

21 For a succinct overview of the impact of temperance societies on past and present governmental policy, see V. Berridge, *Temperance: Its History and Impact on Current and Future Alcohol Policy* (York: Joseph Rowntree Foundation, 2005).

22 *Crewe Chronicle*, 6 November 1886.

23 It is noticeable in many such contemporary newspaper reports that the public gallery of magistrates' courts always seemed to be well-attended.

24 G.W. McCree, ed., *The Band of Hope Record*, vols. 1 and 2 (April 1861–December 1862), 3.

The indefatigable McCree also pronounced widely and frequently on other forms of public indecency apart from drunkenness; his commentaries on Matthew 5:13 ('You are the salt of the earth: but if the salt have lost his flavour, with which shall it be salted? It is thereafter good for nothing') state that 'The disciples of Jesus Christ should seek to prevent the corruption of literature' and also that 'they should seek to prevent the corruption of public amusements.'[25]

The Band of Hope flourished throughout the remainder of the nineteenth century, and by Victoria's Diamond Jubilee in 1897 (when the Queen became Patron of the Society), membership reportedly stood at over 3 million.[26] Until 1901, children could legally purchase alcohol for their own consumption, and the Intoxicating Liquors (Sale to Children) Act 1901 only imposed the restriction that children under the age of 14 now had to purchase alcohol in corked and sealed containers. It was not until the passing of the Children and Young Persons Act 1909 that children under the age of 16 were prohibited from purchasing alcohol.[27]

Intoxicated indecency in Crewe

Turning to the Crewe database, drunkenness and drink-related offences were by far the most prevalent types of public indecency prosecuted by the police and other bodies 1880–1940, a total of 5,774 offences (almost 12 per cent of the total number of cases heard by the magistrates). Once again, the number of male defendants greatly outnumbered female defendants: 83 per cent of defendants were male. Similar to other public indecency offences, the overall non-dismissal rate was high (93 per cent of defendants received some form of punishment), but males were more likely to be convicted than females (93.7 per cent of males received a penalty, compared to 89.5 per cent of females).

The *Crewe Chronicle* of Saturday 28 August 1886 carried the following typical report of a drink-related offence.

Crewe Borough Sessions – A Disgraceful Case

Margaret May, who had the appearance of a tramping woman, was charged with being drunk and guilty of disorderly conduct in Nantwich Road, on the 24th inst. PC Watkinson stated that early that (Tuesday) morning he found the prisoner drunk. She was almost naked and there was a crowd around her. With assistance he brought her as far as the police station. PS Wynne said he found the prisoner in the custody of the last witness. There was a crowd of about twenty young men standing round the prisoner, who had nothing on.

25 G.W. McCree, 'The Purification of Society': http://biblehub.com/sermons/auth/mccree/the_purification_of_society.htm.

26 History of Hope UK: www.hopeuk.org/wp-content/uploads/History.pdf.

27 Children over the age of five can still legally drink alcohol at home with their parents' consent; see Drinkaware, 'The law on alcohol and under-18s': www.drinkaware.co.uk/check-the-facts/alcohol-and-the-law/the-law-on-alcohol-and-under-18s.

Witness asked her to put her clothes on, which were lying near her on the ground, but she declined to do so. She stripped her chemise clean off her back, and stood completely naked in the street. In this condition she had to be carried to the police station. For the defence, Michael May said he was the husband of the prisoner. Just after 11 o clock the previous evening he accused his wife of having been drinking, and chased her out of the house. She had some clothes on at the time. He (witness) was in drink at the time. It was entirely his fault that the prisoner left the house. He took her clothes to the police station. Cross-examined by Supt Leah: He brought two shawls and a jacket to the police station. The prisoner had had drink. The prisoner was fined 10s and costs, or, in default of payment, 14 days' imprisonment with hard labour.[28]

As can be seen from Table 7.2, straightforward drunkenness was, by a very small margin, the most common charge, although drunk and disorderly charges ran a close second.[29] Other much less frequently heard charges were those of being drunk and incapable, drunk in charge of a vehicle (both mechanical and animal-powered), and a small number of prosecutions for being drunk in charge of a child. The latter offence was highlighted in the *Crewe Chronicle* of 10 January 1893 under the headline 'First Cheshire Case under the new Act: a warning to mothers', where it went on to report that 'to be drunk in charge of a child was now an offence against the law, and three appearances in a court rendered a person liable to be put on the black list', which could lead to a prison sentence of up to three years. It is interesting to note the gender-specific nature of the warning: in fact, fathers could also be charged with the same offence, and the Crewe database contains half a dozen such cases.

Overall sentencing patterns (see Table 7.3) reveal a low level of punitiveness: over 98 per cent of all sentences resulted in either a fine of less than £1, a gaol

Table 7.2 Categories of drink-related public indecency, Crewe Magistrates, 1880–1940

Overall categories	T	M		F	
Drunk	2,724	2,254	82.7%	470	17.3%
Drunk and disorderly	2,633	2,193	83.3%	440	16.7%
Drunk and incapable	262	212	80.9%	50	19.1%
Drunk in charge of vehicle	126	125	99.2%	1	0.8%
Drunk in charge of child	29	6	20.7%	23	79.3%

28 A search of both the 1881 and 1891 censuses for Crewe and environs failed to find either Mary or Michael, suggesting that they were temporarily lodging in the town, rather than residents.

29 'Drunk and disorderly' refers to creating a public nuisance whilst being drunk, whereas 'drunk and incapable' refers to being so drunk that one is either unable to stand, walk, or comprehend what is being said.

Table 7.3 Overall sentencing of offenders in drink-related public indecency cases, Crewe Magistrates, 1880–1940

Up to £1		Over £1		Bound over		Supervision		Other		
4,848	90.3%	27	0.5%	467	8.7%	1	0.0%	27	0.5%	T
4,041	90.0%	24	0.5%	405	9.0%	0	0.0%	19	0.4%	M
807	91.6%	3	0.3%	62	7.0%	1	0.1%	8	0.9%	F

Table 7.4 Disposals of offenders in each of the drink-related public indecency categories, Crewe Magistrates, 1880–1940

		Up to £1/month	Over £1/ month	Bound over	Supervision	Other
Drunk	T	2,202 (89.0%)	6 (0.2%)	250 (10.1%)	1 (0.0%)	14 (0.6%)
	M	1,833 (88.7%)	4 (0.2%)	217 (10.5%)	0 (0.0%)	12 (0.5%)
	F	369 (90.7%)	2 (0.5%)	33 (8.1%)	1 (0.2%)	2 (0.5%)
D & D	T	2,327 (92.6%)	17 (0.7%)	158 (6.3%)	0 (0.0%)	11 (0.4%)
	M	1,943 (92.3%)	16 (0.8%)	141 (6.7%)	0 (0.0%)	6 (0.3%)
	F	384 (94.3%)	1 (0.2%)	17 (4.2%)	0 (0.0%)	5 (1.2%)
D & I	T	193 (82.5%)	0 (0.0%)	41 (17.5%)	0 (0.0%)	0 0.0%
	M	155 (81.2%)	0 (0.0%)	36 (18.8%)	0 (0.0%)	0 (0.0%)
	F	38 (88.2%)	0 (0.0%)	5 (1.6%)	0 (0.0%)	0 (0.0%)
DICV	T	107 (87.0%)	4 (3.3%)	11 (8.9%)	0 (0.0%)	1 (0.8%)
	M	106 (86.9%)	4 (3.3%)	12 (9.8%)	0 (0.0%)	1 (0.8%)
	F	1 (100.0%)	0 (0.0%)	0 (0.0%)	0 (0.0%)	0 (0.0%)
DICC	T	19 (70.4%)	0 (0.0%)	7 (25.9%)	0 (0.0%)	1 (3.7%)
	M	4 (100.0%)	0 (0.0%)	0 (0.0%)	0 (0.0%)	0 (0.0%)
	F	15 (65.2%)	0 (0.0%)	7 (30.4%)	0 (0.0%)	1 (4.3%)

term under one month, or being bound over to keep the peace, with women receiving a slightly higher percentage of less-punitive sentences (and females were also less likely to receive a bind over).

Examining the sentencing patterns for each of the drink-related categories, Table 7.4 reveals the following figures.[30]

Somewhat surprisingly, the offence of being drunk and disorderly appears to have been the most leniently treated of all drink-related indecency offences, with

30 D & D – Drunk and Disorderly; D & I – Drunk and Incapable; DICV – Drunk in Charge of Vehicle; DICC – Drunk in Charge of Child(ren).

over 90 per cent of proven charges attracting a sentence of only up to £1 or one month in gaol. However, conversely, magistrates appear to have been much less likely to bind over a drunk and disorderly defendant than a simply drunk defendant, presumably because of the added public nuisance that the defendant had caused and the thought that a bind-over may well not act as a suitable deterrent from breaching the peace in future. In all of the drink-related offences, magistrates were clearly reluctant to impose any more punitive sentences than either a fine of up to £1/one month in gaol or a bind over (but it must be remembered that these are all summary rather than indictable offences).

The following report from the *Crewe Chronicle* of 20 December 1890 illustrates that drunkenness in the street or public house was often accompanied by other forms of public indecency.

Crewe Borough Sessions

Rowdy Neighbours in Chetwode Street

William Dean, Elizabeth Dean, Mary Dean, and John Humphries were charged with being drunk in Chetwode Street on the 5th December. The defendant Humphries did not appear. PC Hughes stated that on the 5th instant he was off duty at his lodgings in Chetwode Street. About twelve o'clock midnight he was awoke by someone calling 'Murder'. He got up, and having partly dressed he went downstairs into the street. Witness then saw a great crowd, the four defendants being amongst them. They were drunk and quarrelling with each other. They were also making use of most disgraceful language. Witness requested them to go into the house, but they replied they would not go in the house for any – – policeman in Crewe. Elizabeth Dean struck witness on the face, and Mary Dean also assaulted him. The defendant William Dean said he would knock his brains out. In reply to William Dean the constable denied that he struck Elizabeth Dean on the back. Mary Dean: 'Did my mother strike you'? Witness: 'Yes'. Mary Dean: 'No, I struck you'. (Laughter) PC Kinsey corroborated. Superintendent Leah: Have you any doubt about the defendants being drunk? Witness: No, sir. William Dean (excitedly): But I have. George Bourne said he was disturbed in his sleep by a noise in the street and on going to the bedroom window he saw the defendants making a disturbance. They all appeared to be drunk and were in the street for twenty minutes. In reply to William Dean the witness said he saw him take his coat off to challenge the policeman to fight. William Dean: 'I had no coat on'. (Laughter). William Dean denied that they were drunk, and alleged that PC Hughes knocked his wife against the door. Mrs Dean denied that she struck the constable, and charged the officer with having encouraged her daughter to stay out all night. Annie Dean, the daughter of the first-named defendants, having given evidence for the defence, Mary Dean and Elizabeth Dean were next charged with assaulting PC Hughes whilst in the execution of his duty. PC Hughes said he put the defendant Elizabeth Dean in the house, but she rushed out again and struck him in the face with her hand. Mary Dean also struck him in the face three times, and kicked him on the leg. Her father stood close by and encouraged her to do it. Witness got hold of her intending to take her to the police station, when she fell on her back and pretended to faint. Mary Dean said she did not kick the witness, she merely smacked his face. PC Kinsey and George Bourne gave corroborative evidence. The defendants were each fined 2s 6d and costs.

Similarly, some two years earlier, on 9 June 1888, the newspaper had reported on a case of 'Hard Swearing', when at Crewe Borough Sessions, a married woman named Mary Ann Owen was summonsed for being drunk in Hope Street on 22 May. The prosecution's chief witness, P.C. Poole, stated that about 8pm, he was called to Hope Street, where he saw a crowd of people. The officer saw the defendant there drunk. She had apparently been throwing 'dirty water' (probably the contents of a chamber pot) out of her bedroom window, much to the chagrin of the neighbourhood. He asked her to return to her house but she refused until he threatened to arrest her. The newspaper report stated that 'there was some water about the street, and the defendant's door was wide open. The defendant was the cause of the crowd in the street.' Mary Owen denied being drunk at the time of the incident, stating that 'she had not had drink that day'. William Owen, her husband, was cross-examined and stated that his wife had not been drunk. Another witness, Elizabeth Rowledge, (no stranger to Crewe Magistrates on account of her own persistent drunkenness) stated 'She could not say whether the defendant was quite sober. She [Rowledge] was not drunk. As long as a person did not require carrying to bed after having had drink she did not consider him or her drunk (laughter).' Mary Owen was fined 2s 6d and costs.

Although many of the defendants' statements and drunken antics as reported in the local newspapers were often reported with something of a comical tinge, drink-related offences often revealed extremely serious underlying problems, as can be seen from the case of Eva Bebbington. On 15 July 1916 the *Crewe Chronicle* carried the following headline: 'Sordid Story at Crewe – Young Girl's Serious Plight'.

The report went on to recount the shocking circumstances of 15-year-old Eva Bebbington, daughter of William and Sarah Bebbington, who was charged with soliciting for the purposes of prostitution. She had been apprehended whilst approaching soldiers on Gresty Road, Crewe. Her parents were both charged with conducing the commission of the offence by neglect. This was a sad story of drunkenness, neglect, and failure on the part of her parents. Eva had already been in trouble with the law; at the age of 7 in 1908 she had stolen a stores book valued at 5s and had been sent to a reformatory school. By 1911 she was reunited with her parents. Her mother appears to have suffered from mental illness, as she had been temporarily admitted to Upton Lunatic Asylum during 1907. Eva's father Thomas was a skilled labourer, being a master slater, but had been in trouble with the law since his early twenties; his was a mixed offending pattern of being prosecuted under the Education Act for not sending his children to school, failure to pay his general domestic rates, neglecting his children, and being arrested on numerous occasions for drink-related offences. In 1911 Sarah Bebbington served three months in gaol for neglect of two of her children. Three of Eva's siblings had also spent time in either reformatory or industrial schools; their home life was clearly not a happy or stable one. The *Crewe Chronicle* of 12 July 1916 carried a report of Eva's arrest, stating that the magistrates were told by the police that 'the parents had drunken habits and at the house there were frequently drunken carousals day and night.' In the report of 15 July, Superintendent Thompson said that Eva had pleaded guilty, and had been on remand 'with a view to her being got into a suitable home. . . . They wished to save her if possible, and give her a chance of leading a new life'. The report further stated that Eva's parents had been found guilty of conducing their daughter's offence 'by their negligence and drunken habits. The police had found it necessary to go to the house and warn them. This young girl (Eva Bebbington) was out at night as late as 12 o'clock and 2 o'clock in the morning, and the parents were of such drunken habits that they could not possibly exercise proper care over her'.

Another witness, PC Hardy, stated that he had frequently seen Eva Bebbington out late at night, and on passing her parents' house 'had heard drunken rows and disorderliness'. He did not think they exercised reasonable care over their child. He had seen the girl at the railway station. When he served the summons, the mother said 'I will go on my holidays after this' [i.e. be sent to prison]. Eva was sent to stay at Miss Wright's Rescue Home for Girls in Chester for three years, and each of her parents were fined £2, with a week to pay. Eva's life seemed to settle down after she returned: she married Evan Edwards in 1922 and did not appear before Crewe magistrates again.

Habitual drunkenness

On 11 June 1887, under a strapline 'Excessive drinking in Crewe', the *Crewe Chronicle* gave a brief account of the death of a 45-year-old female resident of the town who, according to the coroner's inquest, had died from chronic alcoholism. Such occurrences were not unusual; excessive and prolonged imbibing was seen as a major problem during the latter half of the nineteenth century. Whilst many people made the occasional appearance in magistrates' courts for drunken behaviour, the authorities and the various burgeoning temperance societies were most concerned about the repeat offender, whom they categorized as an 'habitual drunkard'. Many such individuals, both male and female, amassed an impressive number of court appearances. John Nield, a widowed butcher residing in Crewe, made almost 50 appearances for drunkenness in a ten-year period between 1882 and 1891 (his offending career appears to have been initiated by the death of his wife and two of his seven children within the space of just over a year), whilst Catherine Mayo, who was born in Manchester c.1840 had, by the time of her appearance for theft at Liverpool Assizes in May 1889, also racked up 57 recorded charges of drunkenness. But for the fact that her habitual drunkenness was accompanied by an equally habitual ineptitude at larceny (at least a dozen recorded offences, for which she received sentences of up to three years' penal servitude),

Mayo would have been a prime recipient for receiving the full force of habitual drunkard legislation.[31]

The Habitual Drunkards Act 1879 viewed habitual drunkenness very much along the lines of Dr R.B. Grindrod's 1839 definition that 'Drunkenness may correctly be considered as a species of voluntary insanity,' and consequently permitted habitual drunkards to voluntarily place themselves in an inebriates' retreat for up to twelve months.[32] This primarily appealed to middle- and upper-class offenders, who could afford to retreat from the world for up to a year, as they or their family had to pay the costs of staying at such institutions. As such, the Act did little if anything to deal with the problem of lower-class habitual drunkards, although it was recognized that repeated short sentencing of offenders such as Catherine Mayo had little if any deterrent effect; as a prominent Church of England Temperance Society member Reverend G.P. Merrick wrote in 1878, 'short [prison] sentences are wholly inoperative to correct the moral tastes and physical inclination of the habitual drunkard.'[33]

The 1879 Act was not a success, with only half a dozen or so institutions being created in the decade following the legislation. In 1888 there were only 66 patients in total in eight institutions.[34] The Act was clearly not making any major inroads into the problem of habitual drunkenness, although it was renewed in the Inebriates Act 1888. Debate continued throughout the next decade: in June 1895 the Lord Chancellor, Lord Herschell, stated in a Lords' Debate on the passage of an Inebriates' Bill that 'he doubted whether anyone could be found to say that our present method of dealing with those who were convicted of habitual drunkenness was satisfactory. It appeared that out of 33,000 women who were every year on average sent to prison for drunkenness, 11,000 of them had not less than ten convictions recorded against them; and of the men 16,000 of them had each undergone the same number of imprisonments.'[35]

In 1898 a further Inebriates Act was passed, providing for the detention in a State inebriate reformatory of anyone summarily convicted of drunkenness on three previous occasions for a period not less than one year or exceeding three

---

31 Despite spending many years of her life in prison, Mayo did not reform; her drunkenness and larceny offending continued to within a year of her death in an Upton workhouse in 1911.

32 Grindrod (1839: 506). Inebriates' retreats were to be licensed and not to be run by anyone who also kept an asylum. One of the first such retreats was Dalrymple House, Rickmansworth, which operated 1884–1935 and housed male inebriates only. For details of the development of such retreats, see S.S. Alford, *A paper read before the Social Sciences Association, on the Habitual Drunkards' Act of 1879, with an account of a visit to the American Inebriate Homes, February 2 1880* (London: H.K. Lewis, 1880).

33 Quoted in S. Auerbach, 'Missionaries, moral advocacy, and the transformation of police court procedure in London, 1876–1930' (available online at www.web.law.columbia.edu/sites/default/files/microsites/law-culture/files/2010-files/Auerbach-paper-revised.pdf).

34 *The Times*, 5 September 1888.

35 *The Times*, 22 June 1895. The Liberal government under Lord Roseberry suffered a crushing defeat in the General Election shortly after this speech, leading to this debate being kicked into the long grass for a while.

years. The Act also allowed for the detention of those convicted of an indictable offence who also either admitted to being, or was found by the jury to be a habitual drunkard. The prosecuting police authority was to be responsible for conveying the offender to the reformatory, and the inmate could be forced to contribute to the cost of their stay if they had 'any real or personal property more than sufficient to maintain his family'.[36] Drink-related offences covered by the Act included being found drunk in a highway or other public place, being guilty while drunk of riotous or disorderly behaviour, being drunk in charge of a vehicle or loaded firearm, or refusing to quit licensed premises when drunk. The introduction of these State-run reformatories had a much greater effect on working-class drunkards (especially females); Table 7.5 shows the number of men and women committed to them in the first ten years of their operation.[37]

It is clear from these figures that female habitual drunkards were much more likely to be sent to such institutions; females outnumbered males by a ratio of 6:1. This suggests that either female habitual drunkards were considered more capable of reform than their male counterparts, or that the authorities considered the spectacle of a habitually drunk woman more concerning to society and consequently were more likely to try and remove them from public view for a period of time. This gender discrepancy is marked when compared to sentencing patterns for drink-related offending in Crewe, as discussed later.

Despite the backing of several bodies such as the Howard Association (which praised the legislation as at least providing that 'the worst class of this description will be treated in a more rational manner'), these reformatories rapidly fell out of favour as a means of controlling habitual drunkenness due to the baulking of local authorities in paying for their construction and maintenance: such institutions could cost over £150 per person per year.[38] There were also concerns about the moral legality of forcibly separating individuals from their families for such

Table 7.5 Admission figures for State-run reformatories, 1899–1908

Year	Males	Females	Total
1899	0	88	88
1900	16	128	144
1901	35	169	204
1902	46	232	278
1903	38	259	297
1904	38	380	418
1905	91	352	443
1906	110	294	404
1907	65	428	493
1908	44	218	262

36 Inebriates' Act 1898, section 12.
37 *JS* 1909.
38 *The Times*, 4 October 1898; *Crewe Chronicle*, 26 September 1904.

an extended period. Contemporary reports suggested that magistrates were reluctant to commit people to the reformatories through what one exasperated editorial in *The Times* classed as 'mistaken kindness'. The same article (which exhibits a passionate support for Francis Galton's 'ideas as to improving the human race') goes on to state that 'so far we have been dealing only with the fringes of a large evil. There is room not merely for 22 such institutions, which is the present number, but for several times as many.'[39] However, opposition to the creation of such edifices continued, as did magistrates' seeming reluctance to send offenders to such places. *The Times* stated in an editorial of 12 January 1909 that

> The Inebriates Act has now been for nine years upon the Statute Book, but we read in the [annual] report that the total number of persons committed to reformatories under its provisions has been less than 2,600, although, during the same period . . . the offenders who have been convicted and sentenced for drunkenness in courts of summary jurisdiction have been somewhat in excess of a million and three-quarters. It is manifest that proceedings conducted on this scale can have no real influence . . . as far as the national welfare is concerned the Acts might almost as well have been non-existent.

By 1921 even the President of the Inebriates Reformation and Aftercare Association was forced to admit that 'practically no cases have been sent to reformatories for some years,' and in 1962 a letter to *The Times* regarded the provision of such reformatories as 'moribund beyond recovery'.[40]

The reformatories' effect on stemming the long-term drinking habits of habitual drunkards was also questionable, as is illustrated by the following case. One of Crewe's most prolific female offenders was Ellen Owen, who had amassed over fifty summary offences for drunkenness and petty larceny before being sentenced to one year's detention in the Royal Victoria Home for Inebriates in 1901. Upon release from the home, she returned to Crewe, where she almost immediately offended again, appearing before the Bench on a charge of larceny (she was found drunk in a public house, attempting to hide a foot-long stolen cigar by sitting on it). The *Crewe Chronicle* of 22 March 1902 reported that the Chairman of the Bench stated (upon hearing Ellen's extremely disingenuous plea for mitigation that she had been teetotal for a year) that 'You told us when we sent you to the Inebriates home twelve months ago that it would do you no good. You have proved your statement beyond doubt.'

There are surprisingly few mentions of habitual drunkards in the Crewe database; only four cases refer specifically to a habitual drunkard (and none of them result in the individual being sent to a reformatory). It is perhaps significant that a John Evans was prosecuted on two charges on 4 November 1904, one charge of being drunk in Market Street (for which he received a 10s fine) and one charge of

39 *The Times*, 1 November 1901.
40 *The Times*, 22 July 1921 and 19 February 1962.

being a habitual drunkard buying alcohol in the Cumberland Arms, less than a half mile from Market Street (for which he was fined £1). The magistrates were clearly aware that Evans had a drink problem (there are ten appearances by defendants named John Evans between 1896 and 1904, but unfortunately it is impossible to definitively state that they are all the same individual), but were clearly reluctant to formally categorize and sentence him as such. Similarly, an Emily Bebbington made almost two dozen appearances before the Crewe Bench 1906–1921 for drunkenness and obscene language.[41] Under the headline 'Mrs Bebbington Again', the *Crewe Chronicle* of 16 August 1919 reported that she 'made her 23rd appearance before the Crewe magistrates on Tuesday, charged with drunkenness and disorderly conduct. Acting Sergeant Taylor said the accused was behaving abominably, and he had to convey her to the police station on a cart. . . . There were fifteen convictions against her for drunkenness, and seven for obscene language'. Again, despite her frequent appearances and obvious problems with alcohol, there appears to have been no attempt by magistrates to commit her to an inebriates' reformatory.

On 3 February 1936 the *Crewe Chronicle* carried a report headed 'Crewe a Sober Town', in which Sir William Hodgson, Chairman of the Borough Licensing Sessions (and also Chairman of Cheshire County Council), in reply to Superintendent Cash's report on the state of licensed premises and drink-related offences in Crewe, stated that 'it is gratifying to find that Crewe remains a sober town.' Superintendent Cash had reported that in the past year 'five persons have been proceeded against for drunkenness, none of whom were convicted, compared with four proceeded against and three convicted in the previous year.' Whilst Cash's figures do not exactly tally with the petty sessions records (which show six cases involving four male and two female defendants in 1935 and only three cases in 1934), they serve to illustrate the extent to which public indecency in the form of drink-related offences had largely disappeared from sight in the courts of a large provincial town. In 1880 there were 164 appearances by defendants on drink-related charges heard by the Crewe magistrates, and it is interesting to compare the five-year averages for the entire period shown in Table 7.6.

There were over five times as many prosecutions for intoxicated indecency in the first half of the sixty-year period than in the latter half. This is a striking statistic, but was it for some reason unique to Crewe? Compared to the five-year averages for Crewe against the national (England & Wales) totals, Table 7.7 shows the following.

With the exception of the five-year period 1890–1894 (when there was an inexplicable drop in intoxicated indecency offences for three consecutive years) the ratio of drunkenness offences in Crewe are broadly consistent with national trends. However, from 1910 onward, the ratio of such offences in Crewe drops

41 Emily Amanda Bebbington (née Thorley) does not appear to have been any relation of Eva Bebbington mentioned earlier; Bebbington (or Bebington) was and remains a fairly common surname in Cheshire, due to there being two settlements known as Higher Bebington and Lower Bebington in the Wirral.

Table 7.6 Five-year averages of appearances on drink-related public indecency charges, Crewe Magistrates, 1880–1939

1880–84	711
1885–89	799
1890–94	507
1895–99	903
1900–4	1,026
1905–9	915
1910–14	520
1915–19	173
1920–24	43
1925–29	73
1930–34	26
1935–39	56

Table 7.7 Comparison of five-year averages for drink-related public indecency offences, England & Wales and Crewe Magistrates, 1880–1939

5-year average Alcoholic offences	England & Wales	Crewe	Ratio as %
1880–84	185,643	711	0.38
1885–89	170,366	799	0.47
1890–94	179,723	507	0.28
1895–99	199,326	903	0.45
1900–4	216,424	1026	0.47
1905–9	205,058	915	0.45
1910–14	193,354	520	0.27
1915–19	76,563	173	0.23
1920–24	85,160	43	0.06
1925–29	68,490	73	0.11
1930–34	44,888	26	0.06
1935–39	51,486	56	0.11

dramatically in comparison with the national total. Godfrey *et al.* suggest that (in relation to Crewe), this was due to:

> a very notable shift in policing and prosecution focus around World War One, when public order offences (i.e. drunkenness) decline steeply, and are over-taken by vehicular (predominantly motoring) offences . . . It was not just the increase in car and motorcycle ownership, but a substantial shift in police attention after 1918 from offences of public order to vehicular offences of all kinds (including bicycles and horse-drawn vehicles) that caused this situation to occur.[42]

42 Godfrey *et al., Criminal Lives,* 32.

Conclusion

Prosecuting agencies in Crewe (i.e. largely the police) appear to have undoubtedly decided for one reason or another to focus more on driving-related offences than drink-related offences in the years around World War One. It appears that the police grew concerned with mobility in public space as much as or even more so than with behaviour in public areas. This would support Clive Emsley's view that motoring legislation and the concomitant interest shown by the police in the enforcement of such legislation fits into the model of the 'policeman state' as posited by V. A. C. Gatrell, an hypothesis which argues that the State increasingly encroached upon the lives of its inhabitants, notably in the form of social policy that regarded respect, deference, and obedience (to the laws of the State) as 'at the very foundation of social order and well-being'.[43]

With regard to the national picture, the post–World War One, whilst the concerns of the effects of excessive alcoholic consumption continued to be debated, drunkenness largely dwindled away as a major component of summary charges brought before magistrates for the remainder of our period. The recent and ongoing (though apparently somewhat subsiding) moral panic over binge drinking and other forms of intoxicated indecency is clearly nothing new, but from the 1970s onward until the first decade of the twenty-first century public debate largely switched to concerns over the rise of drug culture rather than the misuse of alcoholic stimulants.

---

43 C. Emsley, 'Mother, what *did* policemen do when there weren't any motors': the law, the police and the regulation of motor traffic in England, 1900–1939', *Historical Journal* 36, no. 2 (1993): 357–81; V.A.C. Gatrell, 'Crime, authority and the policeman state', in F. M. L. Thompson (ed.) *The Cambridge Social History of Britain, 1750–1950*, vol. 3 (Cambridge: Cambridge University Press, 1993), 258.

8   Conclusion

During an extended and transformational period of social-political and cultural change in the years 1857–1960, the concept of indecency ran as an underpinning thread through many of the debates about appropriate legal responses to certain forms of public behaviour. The idea of 'indecency' helped to define boundaries around the fluid central values of the political establishment and the 'comfortable classes' in the face of rising empowerment of working people and the gradual democratization of British society. At the same time, 'indecency' became the battle cry of moral activists, many of them new to the political sphere and empowered by the very changes that caused them to fear the 'other'. During research into the numerous case studies used throughout this book, it has proven remarkable to the authors on just how many occasions 'indecency' was linked to this notion of the 'other' and 'foreignness'. Continental Europe in particular was often referred to in association with moral opprobrium. To some extent in the interwar period the United States (with its seemingly never-ending export of 'gangster' films) replaced Europe for a time as the immoral bogeyman with dangerously foreign tastes.

As a concept, 'indecency' expressed the necessary tribal notion of 'not like us' or 'not to our taste' whilst providing an infinitely flexible legal basis for extending regulation (or demanding such extension) beyond the already established common law and statutory parameters of criminal and civil law relating to sexual offences, public order, and offensive expression. The perception of the 'serious and growing evil' and resultant activism to combat it was thus a manifestation of the notion – simple but highly contentious – that there should be legal regulation of public morality, usually expressed to suggest that by doing so, private morality would consequently be preserved or improved. The campaigners had no doubt that appropriate private morality in individuals would also enhance the collective good of society. The analysis was thus unsophisticated, but essentially consistent.

The identification of indecency as a 'serious and growing evil' led to significant suppressive activity during the period of 1857–1960, not just once but on numerous occasions, from campaigns for new laws to vigilante patrols in the streets and waves of enforcement activity by magistrates and the police (whose hands often appear to have been forced by adverse publicity in the media). By the late nineteenth century, much of the activity would also be channeled through secular local authorities rather than spiritual agencies, and, thanks to technological innovations, there was also an ever-growing range of opportunities to reach a wider audience. In a remarkable number of fields of human behaviour, indecency was an issue and an accusation designed to influence the moral and behavioural terrain within which the English public conducted their lives. From the highbrow expressive arts of literature and serious drama to the lowbrow fun and trivia of postcards and novels, the merest whiff of irreverence, honesty, or explicitness about sexual relationships was enough to result in both legal and extra-legal opposition. Labelling behaviour such as drunkenness as indecent forced the police to take stringent action to repress and contain.

The activists described in this book as 'indecency campaigners' made their voices heard at the grass-roots level and, often resoundingly, in Parliament. Successive governments were cajoled, berated, and at times tormented by parliamentary spokesmen for the activists such as the NVA's Samuel Smith MP and the PMC's Bishop of London; by sections of the newspaper industry, driven by sympathetic editors, the public meetings, and organized letter-writing campaigns of the moral pressure groups; and by direct action from the campaigners themselves. External censors such as the Lord Chamberlain's Office and the British Board of Film Censorship were unable to operate without at least taking notice of the claims of the campaigners. The influence of this outside pressure is found in the records of Select Committees in the early twentieth century, in the Bills presented to Parliament and the questions answered by numerous Home Secretaries, in the correspondence of the LCO and the archives of the BBFC and the Metropolitan Police. The impact of this perception of indecency as a serious and growing evil is hard to quantify but evident.

Impact of the morality campaigners

On behaviour

Closely related to the explicit concerns voiced by the moralists about the existence of perceived public indecency in its myriad forms, there was also an implicit thread running throughout the moralists' campaigns which amounted to 'how can we prevent such indecent behaviour and attitudes from becoming widespread amongst the lower classes?' The rise of literacy among the working classes following the Education Acts of the 1870s was undoubtedly seen as a cause for concern with regard to how the newly literate populace would choose to utilize this new form of recreation and education. Would penny dreadfuls and shocking tales of immorality and sexual infidelity replace classic and morally uplifting literature on the shelves of the ever-growing number of free public libraries? Public libraries (themselves a product of the 1850s following the Public Libraries at 1850) were also the source of much concern among the middle classes with regard to the social agitation and unrest that they might inculcate among those without the vote; as Mr Henry Goulburn, MP for Cambridge University, rather plaintively asked during a debate in the House of Commons concerning the 1850 Act, 'Should there be an unrestricted presentation of all those publications daily emanating from the press, which certainly were not calculated to promote the preservation of either public order or public morals?'[1] Immorality and sedition were often indecently close bedfellows in the eyes of many moral campaigners, but despite their best (and often protracted) efforts, the English public largely stubbornly refused to be deflected from its literary preferences.

Such campaigners, despite their best efforts over the century under discussion, therefore made little real mark on the everyday behaviour of the majority of the English public. Public behaviour was not modified to any great extent despite the occasional success of the moral minority in closing particular venues or banning particular 'indecent' acts or advertising material. Public entertainment remained sharply divided between the highbrow arts such as opera and ballet and the much more popular but often morally censorious lowbrow tastes of the lower classes such as variety acts and music hall turns. The Windmill Theatre's proud (though inaccurate) boast 'We never closed' during World War Two, can also be seen as a maxim for all the numerous variety theatres, music halls, striptease joints, bottle parties, and other 'indecent' forms of entertainment that the moral minority failed to shut down or remove from the public's purlieu.[2]

On public communication

The impact of the indecency campaigns on arts and literature is undeniable. Critics argued that the pervasive censorship stultified English drama and cinema (although the latter was as much due to similar moral campaigns in the United States). The need to avoid any overt perception of indecency – where indecency was so often equated with any reference to sexual matters – is probably the key reason for the establishment of innuendo as perhaps the most typical feature of twentieth-century British humour. The tradition of censorship of the arts and of the wider terrain of public discourse and 'offensive dialogue' has continued to the present day, with TV content regulation overseen by the Office of Communications, the ongoing role of the BBFC in classifying films, and statutory regulation of DVDs and digital games (and the most recent self-censorship of the British music industry with regard to the age classification of music videos), and the complacency with which political calls for regulation of the Internet is met.

On law

Despite the energy and insistence of the claims of indecency, there was surprisingly little new legislation directly attributable to the moral activists. Governments

---

1 *Hansard* HC Deb, 13 March 1850, vol.109 cc.838–50, 842.
2 All theatres were forced to close their doors for a short period following the declaration of war on 3 September 1939, until it was decided that such closure would have a detrimental effect on public morale.

often appeared sympathetic but rarely took positive action. Select Committees were set up in response to campaigns by both the repressive tendency and those who sought liberalization of laws, but the legislative outcome of many of the committees was often negligible. Undoubtedly, some such committees were created as a means of conveniently kicking complaints into the political long grass. Some statute laws followed, such as the Indecent Advertisements Act 1889 and the Indecent Displays Act 1909, but on the whole these tended to be significantly limited and a consequent disappointment to the moral campaigners. The most significant legislative change in the period was the Obscene Publications Act 1959, driven by the liberalizing activism of the creative artists and their supporters in final rebellion against the puritan tendency of the moral minority. There was, as indicated by magistrates' court cases and police activity, more substantial impact on enforcement of existing laws, but in general, despite the pressure of moral campaigners, successive Home Secretaries remained reluctant to introduce bills or reform the law.

The fact that the campaigners were targeting so many diverse activities and areas of human behaviour was ultimately counterproductive, dissipating activist energy, diluting the message, and eventually – as social attitudes began to change – annoying the very power brokers the campaigners sought to influence. The flexibility and fluidity of the central concept of indecency became the greatest weakness of campaigns designed to stamp out indecent behaviour. It was essentially impossible to produce rational proposals for legislative change when the focus was so diffuse and ultimately 'irrational' (in the sense that it was based on emotion and moral perceptions rather than logical calculations of cause and effect). If groups such as the NVA and later the PMC had focussed on one or two more specific activities, they may well have achieved more legislative success, but the inevitable result of their all-encompassing moral vision seems to have resulted in dividing support in unpredictable ways which did not necessarily cleave along party lines. Thus, while the indecency campaigners may have presumed they had a clear agenda, many 'essential others' who were needed to further that campaign in practical and pragmatic ways did not share either the clarity of vision, the moral conviction, or the basic legal assumption that criminal law was the appropriate tool.

The story of public indecency during the period in question is thus in part a narrative about wide-ranging and often extremely high-profile attempts to build both moral and legal consensus around the notion of indecency – that 'serious and growing evil' which required urgent action. But it is also an explanation of the limits of that process and of the impossibility of reaching the necessary unanimity around ill-defined moral concepts of 'indecency' to justify and implement criminal law in the field of public behaviour.

Bibliography

Books

Aeschylus (1952) *Agamemnon*, translated by Richard Lattimore, Chicago: University of Chicago Press.

Aldgate, A. and Robertson, J. C. (2005) *Censorship in Theatre and Cinema*, Edinburgh: Edinburgh University Press.

Alford, S. S. (1880) *A paper read before the Social Sciences Association, on the Habitual Drunkards' Act of 1879, with an account of a visit to the American Inebriate Homes, February 2 1880*, London: H. K. Lewis.

Anon 'Walter' (1888) *My Secret Life* (11 volumes), Amsterdam: Auguste Brancart.

Anon (1887) *Autobiography of a Flea*, London: Edward Avery.

Anon (1773) *The Bow Street Opera in Three Acts: Written on the Plan of The Beggars Opera*, London: T. Mariner.

Aristotle (2002) *Nicomachean Ethics*, translated by J. Sachs, London: Focus Philosophical Library, Pullins Press.

Balzac, H. de (1874) *Droll Stories*, London: William Mitchell.

Barker, M. (1984) *A Haunt of Fears: The Strange History of the British Horror Comics Campaign*, Jackson, MS: University Press of Mississippi.

Barrie, D. G. (2008) *Police in the Age of Improvement: Police Development and the Civic Tradition in Scotland, 1775–1865*, Cullompton: Willan.

Bartley, P. (2000) *Prostitution: Prevention and Reform in England 1860–1914*, London: Routledge.

Beattie, J. M. (2013) *The First English Detectives; the Bow Street Runners and the Policing of London 1750–1840*, Oxford: Oxford University Press.

Beattie, J. M. (2001) *Policing and Punishment in London 1660–1750: Urban Crime and the Limits of Terror*, Oxford: Oxford University Press.

Berridge, V. (2005) *Temperance: Its History and Impact on Current and Future Alcohol Policy*, York: Joseph Rowntree Foundation.

Blackstone, W. (1979a) *Commentaries on the Laws of England*, vol. 4, Chicago: University of Chicago Press.

Blackstone, W. (1979b) *Commentaries on the Laws of England*, vol. 6, Chicago: University of Chicago Press.

Blocker, J., Fahey, D.M., and Tyrrell, I.R., eds. (2003) *Alcohol and Temperance in Modern History: An International Encyclopedia*, vol. 1, Santa Barbara: ABC Clio.

Booth, W. (1890) *In Darkest England and the Way Out*, London: Funk and Wagnalls.

Bristow, E. (1977) *Vice and Vigilance: Purity Movements in Britain Since 1700*, Dublin: Gill and Macmillan.

Brundage, J. (2009) *Law, Sex and Society in Medieval Europe*, Chicago: University of Chicago Press.

Burgess, T. (1828) *A charge delivered to the clergy of the diocese of Salisbury, at the primary visitation of the diocese in August MDCCCXXVI*, London: C. and J. Rivington.

Carey, J. (1992) *The Intellectuals and the Masses: Pride and Prejudice Among the Literary Intelligentsia 1880–1939*, London: Faber and Faber.

Carter Wood, J. (2004) *Violence and Crime in Nineteenth-Century England: The Shadow of Our Refinement*, London: Routledge.

Chaucer, G. (2005) *Canterbury Tales*, London: Penguin Classics.

Cicero, M. T. (1913) *De Officiis*, London: Heinemann.

Clapson, M. (1992) *A Bit of a Flutter: Popular Gambling and English Society c.1823–1961*, Manchester: Manchester University Press.

Claydon, T. (2004) *William III and the Godly Revolution*, Cambridge: Cambridge University Press.

Colley, L. (2005) *Britons: Forging the Nation 1707–1837*, New Haven: Yale University Press.

Connell, V. (1952) *September in Quinze*, New York: The Dial Press.

Cox, D. J. (2014) *Crime in England 1688–1815*, Abingdon: Routledge.

Cox, D. J. (2012) *A Certain Share of Low Cunning: A History of the Bow Street Runners 1792–1839*, London: Routledge.

Cox, D. J. and Godfrey, B. S., eds. (2005) *Cinderellas and Packhorses: A History of the Shropshire Magistracy*, Almeley: Logaston Press.

Cox, E. (1855) *Reports of Criminal Cases Argued and Determined in All the Courts in England and Ireland*, London: Law Times Office.

Crouzet, F. (2006) *The Victorian Economy*, Abington: Routledge.

D'Cruze, S., Avdela, E., and Rowbotham, J., eds. (2010) *Problems of Crime and Violence in Europe 1750–2000*, New York: Edward Mellen Press.

Davis, J., and Emeljanow, V. (2005) *Reflecting the Audience. London Theatregoing 1840–1880*, Iowa City, IA: University of Iowa Press.

Doig, A. (2010) *State Crime*, Cullompton: Willan.

Emsley, C. (2009) *The Great British Bobby*, London: Quercus.

Emsley, C. (1996) *The English Police: A Political and Social History*, 2nd edition, Abingdon: Routledge.

Faulkner, D. (2006) *Crime, State and Citizen: A Field Full of Folk*, Hook: Waterside Press.

Field, M. (1954) *Children and Films: A Study of Boys and Girls in the Cinema*, Dunfermline: Carnegie United Kingdom Trust.

Fortner, R. S. (2005) *Radio, Morality and Culture, Britain, Canada and the United States 1919–45*, Carbondale: Southern Illinois University.

Gibbons, D. (1992) *Society, Crime and Criminal Behavior*, Upper Saddle River, NJ: Prentice Hall.

Godfrey, B. (2013) *Crime in England 1880–1945: The Rough and the Criminal, the Policed and the Incarcerated*, Abingdon: Routledge.

Godfrey, B. and Cox, D. J. (2013) *Policing the Factory: Theft, Private Policing and the Law in Modern England*, London: Bloomsbury.

Godfrey, B., Cox, D.J, and Farrall, S. (2010) *Serious Offenders: A Historical Study of Habitual Criminals*, Clarendon Criminology Series, Oxford: Oxford University Press.

Godfrey, B., Cox, D.J, and Farrall, S. (2007) *Criminal Lives: Family Life, Employment, and Offending*, Clarendon Criminology Series, Oxford: Oxford University Press.

Grindrod, R.B. (1839) *Bacchus, an Essay on the Nature, Causes, Effects, and Cure for Intemperance*, London: J. Pasco.

Hair, P., ed. (1972) *Before the Bawdy Court: Selections from Church Court and Other Records Relating to the Correction of Moral Offences in England, Scotland and New England, 1300–1800*, New York: Barnes & Noble.

Hajkowski, T. (2010) *The BBC and National Identity in Britain, 1922–53*, Manchester: Manchester University Press.

Hall, R. (1928) *The Well of Loneliness*, London: Jonathan Cape.

Hanson, S. (2007) *From Silent Screen to Multi-Screen: A History of Cinema Exhibition in Britain Since 1896*, Manchester: Manchester University Press.

Harris, J. (1994) *Private Lives, Public Spirit: Britain 1870–1914*, London: Penguin Books.

Hearn, M. (2013) *Saucy Postcards: The Bamforth Collection*, London: Constable.

Heath, D. (2014) *Purifying Empire: Obscenity and the Politics of Moral Regulation in Britain, India and Australia*, Cambridge: Cambridge University Press.

Hilton, B. (1988) *The Age of Atonement: The Influence of Evangelicalism on Social and Economic Thought, 1795–1865*, Oxford: Clarendon Press, Oxford University Press.

Hoppen, K.T. (2008) *The Mid-Victorian Generation 1846–1886*, Oxford: Oxford University Press.

Howell, T.B. (1816) *A Complete Collection of State Trials and Proceedings for High Treason, and other Crimes and Misdemeanors from the earliest period to the year 1783*, vol. 5, London: Hansard.

Hughes, D. (2006) *"A Bottle of Guinness Please" – the Colourful History of Guinness*, Wokingham: Phimboy.

Hughes, R. (2003) *The Fatal Shore*, London: Vintage Books.

Hunt, A. (1999) *Governing Morals: A Social History of Moral Regulation*, Cambridge: Cambridge University Press.

Hynes, S. (1968) *The Edwardian Turn of Mind*, Princeton: Princeton University Press.

Ingram, M. (1990) *Church Courts, Sex and Marriage in England, 1570–1640*, Past & Present Series, Cambridge: Cambridge University Press.

James, R.W. (2005) *To the Best of Our Skill and Knowledge: A Short History of the Cheshire Constabulary 1857–1957*, second edition, Warrington: Museum of Policing in Cheshire.

James, E.L. (2012) *Fifty Shades of Grey*, London: Arrow.

Johnson, D.K. (2004) *The Lavender Scare*, Chicago: University of Chicago Press.

Johnson, J. (1990) *The Lord Chamberlain's Blue Pencil*, London: Hodder and Stoughton.

Jongh, N. de (2000) *Politics, Prudery and Perversions: The Censoring of the English Stage 1901–1968*, London: Methuen.

Jung, S., ed. (2013) *British Literature and Print Culture*, Martlesham: Boydell and Brewer.

Karrass, R.M. (1996) *Common Women: Prostitution and Sexuality in England*, Oxford: Oxford University Press.

King, P. (2006) *Crime and Law in England 1750–1840: Remaking Justice from the Margins*, Cambridge: Cambridge University Press.

Klein, J. (2011) *Invisible Men: The Secret Lives of Police Constables in Liverpool, Manchester and Birmingham, 1900–39*, Liverpool: Liverpool University Press.

Lacey, N. (1994) *State Punishment: Political Principles and Community Values*, London: Routledge.

Langford, P. (2000) *Englishness Identified. Manners and Character 1650–1850*, Oxford: Oxford University Press.

Langford, P. (1991) *Public Life and Propertied Englishmen 1689–1798*, Oxford: Oxford University Press.

Lawrence, D.H. (1960) *Lady Chatterley's Lover*, London: Penguin.

Leavis, F. (1930) *Mass Civilisation and Minority Culture*, Cambridge: Minority Press.

Lent, J. (ed.) (1999) *Pulp Demons: International Dimensions of the Post-war Anti-comics Campaign*, Madison NJ: Fairleigh Dickinson University Press.

Love, H. (1998) *The Culture and Commerce of Texts: Scribal Publications in Seventeenth Century England*, Boston: University of Massachusetts Press.

Matthews, T. (1994) *Censored: What They Didn't Allow You to See and Why: The Story of Film Censorship in Britain*, London: Chatto and Windus.

Mayhew, H. (1861) *London Labour and the London Poor*, London: Dover.

McAleer, J. (1999) *Passions Fortune: The Story of Mills and Boon*, Oxford: Oxford University Press.

McCalman, I. (1988) *Radical Underworld: Prophets, Revolutionaries, and Pornographers in London 1795–1840*, Cambridge: Cambridge University Press.

Mill, J. S. (1859) *On Liberty*, London: Longman, Roberts and Green.

Nash, D. (2010) *Blasphemy in the Christian World: A History*, Oxford: Oxford University Press.

Nash, D., and Kilday, A. (2010) *Cultures of Shame: Exploring Crime and Morality in Britain 1600–1900*, London: Palgrave Macmillan.

National Council of Public Morals (1917a) *Commission of Inquiry into the Declining Birthrate*, London: Chapman and Hall.

National Council of Public Morals (1917b) *The Cinema: Its Present Position and Future Possibilities*, London: Williams and Norgate.

Nicholson, S. (2003) *The Censorship of British Drama 1900–1968: Volume 1, 1900–1932*, Exeter Performance Studies, Exeter: University of Exeter Press.

Nicholson, S. (2005a) *The Censorship of British Drama 1900–1968: Volume 2, 1933–1952*, Exeter Performance Studies, Exeter: University of Exeter Press.

Nicholson, S. (2005b) *The Censorship of British Drama 1900–1968, Volume 3, The Fifties*, Exeter Performance Studies, Exeter: University of Exeter Press.

Noll, M. (2003) *The Rise of Evangelicalism: The Age of Edwards, Whitfield and the Wesleys*, Downers Grove, IL: Intervarsity Press.

O'Gorman, F. (ed.) (2005) *A Concise Companion to the Victorian Novel*, Oxford: Blackwell Publishing.

Oldfield, R. (2012) *Popular Politics and British Anti-Slavery: The Mobilisation of Public Opinion*, London: Routledge.

Olson, C., ed. (2007) *Celibacy and Religious Traditions*, Oxford: Oxford University Press.

Ortega-y-Gasset, J. (1932) *The Revolt of the Masses*, New York: W. W. Norton.

Peakman, J. (2013) *The Pleasure's All Mine – A History of Perverse Sex*, London: Reaktion.

Petersen, A. H. (2014) *Scandals of Classic Cinema: Sex, Deviance and Drama from the Golden Age of American Cinema*, New York: Plume Books.

Phillips, J. S. R. (1916) *The Growth of Journalism*, Cambridge History of English Literature, Cambridge: Cambridge University Press.

Pierson, C. (1996) *The Modern State*, London: Routledge.

Quintilian (2012) *Institutio Oratoria*, New York: HardPress Publishing.

Rawlings, P. (2002) *Policing: A Short History*, Cullompton: Willan.

Reilly, J. W. (1989) *An Account of 150 Years of Policing Birmingham*, Birmingham: West Midlands Police.

Reynolds, S., Wooley, B., and Wooley, T. (1911) *Seems So! A Working-Class View of Politics*, London: MacMillan.

Riddle, J. (1997) *Eve's Herbs: A History of Contraception and Abortion in the West*, Harvard: Harvard University Press.

Ringdal, N.J. (2004) *Love for Sale: A World History of Prostitution*, New York: Grove Press.

Roberts, M. (2004) *Making English Morals: Voluntary Association and Moral Reform in England 1787–1886*, Cambridge: Cambridge University Press.

Robertson, J. (1989) *The Hidden Cinema: British Film Censorship in Action 1913–1975*, London: Routledge.

Rowbotham, J., Stevenson, K., and S. Pegg, (2013) *Crime News in Modern Britain: Press Reporting and Responsibility 1820–2010*, London: Palgrave Macmillan.

Ryan, M. (1837) *The Philosophy of Marriage*, London: John Churchill.

Sagar, K.M. (2003) *D. H. Lawrence's Paintings*, London: Chaucer Press.

Saul, S.B. (1985) *The Myth of the Great Depression, 1873–1896*, Basingstroke: Palgrave Macmillan.

Searle, G.R. (2004) *A New England? Peace and War 1886–1918* Oxford: Oxford University Press.

Shellard, D., Nicholson, S., and Handley, M. (2011) *The Lord Chamberlain Regrets . . . A History of British Theatre Censorship*, London: The British Library.

Shoemaker, R. (1991) *Prosecution and Punishment: Petty Crime and the Law in London and Rural Middlesex, c.1660–1725*, Cambridge: Cambridge University Press.

Smartt, U. (2011) *Media and Entertainment Law*, London: Routledge.

Solway, R.A. (1995) *Demography and Degeneration: Eugenics and the Declining Birthrate in Twentieth Century Britain*, Chapel Hill: University of North Carolina Press.

Spurr, J. (2006) *The Post Reformation: Religion, Politics and Society in Britain, 1603–1714*, London: Routledge.

Stephens, J.R. (1980) *The Censorship of English Drama 1824–1901*, Cambridge: Cambridge University Press.

Stubbs, C.W. (1887) *The church in the villages: principles and ideal: an address to the Church Council and Wardens of the United Parishes of Stokenham, Chivelstone, and Sherford*, Dartmouth: Cranford's Library.

Tait, P. (2005) *Circus Bodies: Cultural Identity in Aerial Performance*, London: Routledge.

Tallack, W. (1899) *Penological and Preventive Principles, With Special Reference to Europe and America*, London: Wertheimer, Lea and Co.

Taylor, A.J.P. (1970) *English History 1914–1945*, Harmondsworth: Penguin Books.

Taylor, D. (2010) *Hooligans, Harlots and Hangmen: Crime and Punishment in Victorian Britain*, Oxford: Praeger.

Thompson, F. M. L., ed. (1993) *The Cambridge Social History of Britain, 1750–1950*, vol. 3, Cambridge: Cambridge University Press.

Thompson, F. M. L. (1988) *The Rise of Respectable Society: A Social History of Victorian Britain, 1830–1900*, London: Fontana Press.

Thompson, K. (ed.) (1997) *International Cinema of the 1910s*, New Barnett: J. Libbey.

Tompkins, S. (2010) *The Clapham Sect: How Wilberforce's Circle Transformed Britain*, London: Lion Books.

Took, B. (1976) *Laughter in the Air*, London: Robson Books/BBC.

Travis, A. (2000) *Bound and Gagged: A Secret History of Obscenity in Britain*, London, Profile Books.

Vargo, M.E. (2013) *Scandal: Infamous Gay Controversies of the Twentieth Century*, Abingdon: Routledge.

Vincent, D. (1998) *Literacy and Popular Culture: England 1750–1914*, Cambridge: Cambridge University Press.

Walker-Smith, D. (1938) *The Life of Lord Darling*, London: Cassell.

Walkowitz, J. (2012) *Nights Out: Life in Cosmopolitan London*, New Haven: Yale University Press.

Walkowitz, J. (1992) *City of Dreadful Delight: Narratives of Sexual Danger in Late-Victorian London*, Chicago: University of Chicago Press.

Weeks, J. (2014) *Sex, Politics and Society: The Regulation of Sexuality Since 1800*, third edition, Abingdon: Routledge.

Wells, R. (1893) *The Best Food, and How to Cook It*, London: Vickers.

Wells, R. (1885) *A New Illustrated Hand-Book of Phrenology, Physiology and Physiognomy*, London: Vickers.

Wells, R. (1880) *Woman: Her Diseases, and How to Cure Them*, London: Burns.

Wells, R. (1878) *Vital Force Series*, London: Oldhams.

Wilberforce, R. I. and Wilberforce, S. (1838) *The Life of William Wilberforce*, vol. 1, London: John Murray.

Wilson, B. (2007) *Decency and Disorder 1789–1837*, London: Faber and Faber.

Woodward, J. (1699) *An Account of the Societies for the Reformation of Manners in London and Westminster and other parts of the country*, London: Defoe.

Wyatt, I. (2008) *Calendar of Summary Convictions at Petty Sessions 1781–1837*, Gloucestershire Record Series, vol. 22, Gloucester: Bristol and Gloucestershire Archaeological Society.

Yeomans, H. (2014) *Alcohol and Moral Regulation: Public Attitudes, Spirited Measures and Victorian Hangovers*, Bristol: Policy Press.

Yonge, C. (1853) *The Heir of Redclyffe*, London: Macmillan.

Zedner, L. (1991) *Women, Crime and Custody in Victorian England*, Oxford: Oxford University Press.

Book chapters

Barker, M. (1999) 'Getting a conviction', in J. Lent (ed.) *Pulp Demons: International Dimensions of the Post-war Anti-comics Campaign*, Madison, NJ: Fairleigh Dickinson University Press.

Bland, L. (1985) 'In the name of protection: The policing of women in the First World War', in J. Brophy and C. Smart (eds.), *Women-in-Law: Explorations in Law, Family and Sexuality*, London: Routledge.

Brown, S. (2012) 'Censorship under siege: The BBFC in the Silent Era', in E. Lamberti (ed.), *Behind the Scenes at the BBFC: Film Classification from the Silver Screen to the Digital Age*, London: Palgrave Macmillan.

Froude, J. A. (1883) 'The Oxford Counter-Reformation 1881', in *Short Studies on Great Subjects,* 4th series (London: Longmans, 1883), 231–60.

Gatrell, V.A.C. and Hadden, T.B. (1972) 'Criminal statistics and their interpretation', in E.A. Wrigley (ed.) *Nineteenth Century Society: Essays in the Use of Quantitative Methods for the Study of Social Data*, Cambridge: Cambridge University Press.

James, R. (2012) 'The people's amusement: Cinemagoing and the BBFC, 1928–48', in E. Lamberti (ed.), *Behind the Scenes at the BBFC: Film classification from the Silver Screen to the Digital Age*, London: Palgrave Macmillan.

Lewis, T. (2003) 'Legislating morality; Victorian and modern legal responses to pornography,' in J. Rowbotham and K. Stevenson (eds.), *Behaving Badly: Social Panic and Moral Outrage – Victorian and Modern Parallels*, Ashgate: Aldershot.

Phillips, D. (1989) 'Good men to associate and bad men to conspire: Associations for the prosecution of felons in England 1760–1860', in D. Hay and F. Snyder (eds.) *Policing and Prosecution in Britain, 1750–1850*, Oxford: Oxford University Press.

Rignall, J. (2005) 'One great confederation? Europe in the Victorian novel', in F. O'Gorman (ed.), *A Concise Companion to the Victorian Novel*, Oxford: Blackwell Publishing.

Journal articles

'Abortion, therapeutic and criminal', *British Medical Journal* 2, no. 3,756 (31 December 1932).

Alexander, J. R. (2008) 'Roth at fifty: reconsidering the common law antecedents of American obscenity doctrine', *The John Marshall Law Review* 41: 393–433.

'Anatomical Models', *British Medical Journal* 1, no. 637 (15 March, 1873).

'The Association and Public Morals', *British Medical Journal* 2, no. 3,599 (28 December 1929).

Bates, A. W. (2006) 'Dr Kahn's museum: Obscene anatomy in Victorian London', *Journal of the Royal Society of Medicine* 99, no. 12 (December): 618–24.

Bor, J., Basu, S., Coutts, A., McKee, M., and Stuckler, D. (2013) 'Alcohol use during the Great Recession of 2008–2009', *Alcohol and Alcoholism* 38, no. 3 (May/June): 343–8.

Brown, P. S. (1977) 'Female pills and the reputation of iron as an abortifacient', *Medical History* 21: 291–304.

Coleman, M. (2005) 'A terrible danger to the morals of the country: the Irish hospitals' sweepstake in Great Britain 1930–87', *Proceedings of the Royal Irish Academy. Section C: Archaeology, Celtic Studies, History, Linguistics, Literature* 105C, no. 5: 197–220.

Cox, D. J. (2011) '"Trying to get a good one": Bigamy offences in England and Wales 1850–1950', *Plymouth Law & Criminal Justice Review* 4 (Autumn): 1–32.

Davis, T. (1991) 'The moral sense of the majorities: Indecency and vigilance in late-Victorian music halls', *Popular Music* 10, no. 1, 'The 1890s': 9–52.

Davis, T. (1990) 'Sex in public places: The Zaeo Aquarium scandal and the Victorian moral majority', *Theatre History Studies* 10: 1–13.

Dingle, A. (1972) 'Drink and working class living standards', *The Economic History Review* 25, no. 4 (November): 608–22.

Dinsmor, A. (2000) 'Glasgow police pioneers', *Journal of the Police History Society* 15: 9–11.

Douglas, P. (2004) 'Charles Carrington and the commerce of risqué', *International Journal of the Book*, 4 (2): 63–76.

Dunae, P. (1979) 'Penny dreadfuls: Late nineteenth-century boys' literature and crime', *Victorian Studies*, winter: 133–50.

Emsley, C. (1993) 'Mother, what *did* policemen do when there weren't any motors': The law, the police and the regulation of motor traffic in England, 1900–1939', *Historical Journal* 36, no. 2: 357–81.

Evans, D. (1992) 'Tackling the 'hideous scourge': The creation of the venereal disease treatment centres in early twentieth-century Britain', *Social History of Medicine* 5, no. 3: 413–33.

Froula, C. (2005) 'On French and British freedoms: Early Bloomsbury and the brothels of Modernism', *MODERNISM/modernity* 12, no. 4: 553–80.

Galton, F. (1865) 'Hereditary talent and character', part two, *Macmillan's Magazine* 12: 319–27.

Godfrey, B., et al. (2205) 'Explaining Gendered Sentencing Patterns for Violent Men and Women in the Late-Victorian and Edwardian Period', *British Journal of Criminology* 45(5): 696–720.

Howells, R. (2006) 'Louis Le Prince; the body of evidence', *Screen* 47, no. 2: 179–200.

Jennings, P. (2013) 'Policing public houses in Victorian England', *Law, Crime and History* 3, no. 1: 52–75.

Johnson, S. (1750) *The Rambler* 55 (25 September).

Johnston, H. (2005) 'The Shropshire magistracy and local imprisonment: Networks of power in the nineteenth century', *Midland History* 30, no. 1: 67–91.

Klein, R. J. (1967) 'Film censorship: The American and British experience', *Villanova Law Review* 12, no. 3, Spring: 419–56.

Knight, P. (1977) 'Women and abortion in Victorian and Edwardian England', *History Workshop Journal* 4, no. 1: 57–69.

Mason, N. (2001) '"The sovereign people are in a beastly state": the Beer Act of 1830 and Victorian discourse on working-class drunkenness', *Victorian Literature and Culture*, 29: 109–27.

McCalman, I. (1984) 'Unrespectable radicalism: Infidels and pornography in early nineteenth-century London,' *Past and Present* 104, no. 1: 74–110.

Morris, R. M. (2001) 'Lies, damned lies and criminal statistics': Reinterpreting the criminal statistics in England and Wales, *Crime, Histoire & Sociétés / Crime, History & Societies* 5, no. 1: 111–27.

Mullin, K. (1998) 'Gerty through the mutoscope', *James Joyce Broadsheet* no. 49 (February): 1–2.

'Objectionable Advertisements', *British Medical Journal* 2, no. 1,666 (3 December 1892).

'An Old Maid with a Spyglass', *British Medical Journal* 1, no. 2,478 (27 June 1908).

Orwell, G. (1941) 'The art of Donald McGill', *Horizon Literary Journal 4*, no. 21: 153–63.

Rapp, D. (2002) 'Sex in the cinema: War, moral panic, and the British film industry, 1906–1918', *Albion* 34, no. 3: 422–51.

Rapp, D. (1996) 'The British Salvation Army, the early film industry and urban working-class adolescents, 1897–1918', *Twentieth Century History* 7, no. 2: 157–88.

Rogers, P. (1974) 'The Waltham Blacks and the Black Acts,' *The Historical Journal* 17: 465–86.

Rosenbloom, N. J. (1987) 'Between reform and regulation: The struggle over film censorship in progressive America, 1909–1922', *Film History* 1: 307–25.

'The Sale and Advertisement of Abortifacients', *British Medical Journal* 1, no. 3,084 (7 February 1920).

Scholes, R. (1963) 'Grant Richards to James Joyce', *Studies in Bibliography*, vol. 16: 139–60.

Sigel, L. Z. (2000) 'Filth in the wrong people's hands: Postcards and the expansion of pornography in Britain and the Atlantic World 1880–1914', *Journal of Social History* Autumn: 859–85.

Snape, R. (2002) 'The National Home Reading Union 1889–1930', *Journal of Victorian Culture* 7, no. 1: 86–100.

'Stiggins and Statuary', *British Medical Journal* 2, no. 2,479 (4 July 1908).

Stutfield, H. (1895) 'Tommyrotics', *Blackwood's Magazine* 157: 833–45.

Taylor, H. (1998) 'Rationing crime: The political economy of the criminal statistics since the 1850s', *Economic History Review* 51, no. 3, New Series (August): 569–90.

Tennant, M. (2014) 'Fields of struggle: A Bourdieusian analysis of conflicts over criminal justice in England, c. 1820–50', *Social History*, 39, no. 1: 36–55.

Walkowitz, J. (2003) 'The "Vision of Salome": Cosmopolitanism and erotic dancing in Central London, 1908–1918', *The American Historical Review* 108, no. 2 (April): 337–376.

Wallis, R. (1976) 'Moral indignation and the media: An analysis of the NVALA', *Sociology* 10 (May): 271–95.

Watkins, D. (2008) 'The protection of literature under English law in a post-modern age', *Mountbatten Journal of Legal Studies* 12, no. 2: 3–22.

Williams, D. (1997) 'The "Cinematograph Act" of 1909: An introduction to the impetus behind the legislation and some early effects', *Film History* 9, no. 4, 'International Cinema of the 1910s': 341–50.

Williams, J. M. (1893) 'Woman suffrage', *Bibliotheca Sacra* 50 (April): 331–43.

Zangerl, C. (1971) 'The social composition of the county magistracy in England and Wales, 1831–1887', *Journal of British Studies* 6 (November): 113–25.

Online resources

'A Guinness a Day': www.guinness.com/en-au/Adsdetails.html?adid=?22

American Libraries Association, 'Frequently challenged books of the 21st century': www.ala. org/advocacy/banned/frequentlychallenged/21stcenturychallenged (2010) 'Missionaries, moral advocacy, and the transformation of police court procedure in London, 1876–1930': www.web.law.columbia.edu/sites/default/files/microsites/law-culture/files/2010-files/ Auerbach-paper-revised.pdf

BBC Guidelines, Section 5 'Harm and Offence, The Watershed and Scheduling for TV, Radio and Online': www.bbc.co.uk/editorialguidelines/page/guidelines-harm-watershed/

British Cartoon Archive: www.cartoons.ac.uk/dpps-obscene-postcard-index

Catholic Herald Archive: http://archive.catholicherald.co.uk/

Cummings, A. 'Why Stanley Kauffmann's *Philanderer* still rings a bell', *The Guardian*, 12 March 2010: www.theguardian.com/books/booksblog/2010/mar/11/stanley-kauffmann-law-philanderer, accessed 27 September 2014.

Drinkaware, 'The law on alcohol and under 18s': www.drinkaware.co.uk/check-the-facts/ alcohol-and-the-law/the-law-on-alcohol-and-under-18s

Evans, R. J. 'The Victorians: Religion and Science', Gresham Lecture, 14 March 2011: www.gresham.ac.uk/lectures-and-events/the-victorians-religion-and-science

History of Hope UK: www.hopeuk.org/wp-content/uploads/History.pdf

History of the age ratings symbols: www.bbfc.co.uk/education-resources/student-guide/ bbfc-history/history-age-ratings-symbols

Joyce, J. 'A Letter to Grant Richards May 5 1906': http://everything2.com/title/A+Letter+ to+Grant+Richards%252C+May+5%252C+1906

Joyce, J. 'A Letter to Grant Richards May 20 1906': http://theamericanreader.com/20-may-1906-james-joyce-to-grant-richards/

Law Commission Consultation Paper No 193 (2010) 'Simplification of criminal law: public nuisance and outraging public decency': http://lawcommission.justice.gov.uk/consul tations/public-nuisance-and-outraging-public-decency.htm

Music Hall and Theatre History website: www.arthurlloyd.co.uk/RoyalAquarium.htm

McCree, G. M., 'The Purification of Society': http://biblehub.com/sermons/auth/mccree/the_purification_of_society.htm

Old Bailey Proceedings Online: www.oldbaileyonline.org/

The Guardian, 8 July 2004, www.theguardian.com/politics/2004/jul/08/britishidentity.economy

Victoria and Albert Museum, 'New Drama in the Early 20th Century': www.vam.ac.uk/content/articles/n/new-drama-in-the-early-20th-century

Victoria and Albert Museum, Political Theatre in the Early 20th Century: www.vam.ac.uk/content/articles/p/political-theatre-in-the-early-20th-century

Official publications

House of Commons Accounts and Papers, *Return of the Laws for regulating or restricting the exhibition of posters, bills and advertisements,* 1903 (no. 323).

JS, England and Wales 1906 Part 1. CS, 1908, Cd. 3929.

Minutes of evidence taken before the Select Committee on the Obscene Publications Bill 1956–1957 (1958) (122) London: HMSO.

Parliamentary Papers (1957) *Report of the Departmental Committee on Homosexual Offences and Prostitution* (London: HMSO).

Parliamentary Papers (1911) Arrangements of the Papers of the House of Commons and of the Papers Presented by Command, 348.

Parliamentary Papers (1909) *Report from the Joint Select Committee of the House of Lords and the House of Commons on the Stage Plays (Censorship) together with the proceedings of the Committee, Minutes and Appendices,* session paper no. 303, vol. 8.

Parliamentary Papers (1908) *Report from the Joint Select Committee on Lotteries and Indecent Advertisements, Together With the Proceedings of the Committee, Minutes of Evidence, and Appendices* (London: HMSO).

Parliamentary Papers (1904) Arrangements of the Papers of the House of Commons and of the Papers Presented by Command, 365.

Parliamentary Papers (1901) Arrangements of the Papers of the House of Commons and of the Papers Presented by Command, 373.

Parliamentary Papers (1885) *Royal Commission on the Housing of the Working Classes 1884–5,* vol. 30.

Parliamentary Papers (1821) *Report from the Select Committee on the Existing Laws Relating to Vagrants,* vol. 543.

Post Office Fifty-fourth Report of the Postmaster General, 1908, Cd. 4240.

Report of the Commissioner of the Metropolis for the Year 1906, 1908, Cd. 3771.

Report of the Inter-Departmental Committee on Physical Deterioration, 1904, Cd. 2175.

Royal Commission on the Care and Control of the Feeble-Minded, 1908, vols 1–8, Cd. 4215–4221, 4202. *Royal Commission on the Militia and Volunteers,* 1904, Cd. 2064.

Archival material

National Archives

HO 45/10837/331148 Criminal Law Amendment Bill, 1917 (1916–18).

HO 45 12288 Publications (including Indecent Publications): Unsavoury details of divorce cases, etc: restriction on publication (1924–1926).

HO 45 22607 Police: Powers of police under Town Police Clauses Act (1888–1949).

HO 45/9752/A59329 Indecent Publications etc.: Sending obscene matter through the post. Suggested legislation (1897–1898).

HO 144/192/A466557 Indecent publications, etc: Reports on various publications and questions of prosecutions (1888–99).

MEPO 2/9428 Indecent exhibition of pictures by D.H. Lawrence at The Warren Gallery, 39A Maddox Street, W1 (1929).

MEPO 3/385 So-called indecent statue in Carlos Place W.1 (1908–1930).

MEPO 3/941 Alleged indecent dance act and Bottle Parties at "Paradise" 189, Regent Street (1937).

MH 55/530 Venereal Disease Act, 1917: prohibition of treatment of venereal diseases by unqualified persons, and the advertising of remedies (1917).

Rail 1001/206 Byelaws and regulations: railway companies (n.d.).

RG 11/3541 1881 Census Registration Sub-District 1C Wybunbury. Civil Parish, Township or Place: Coppenhall.

Chester Archives

QPCr/3863/1–34 Petty Sessions court registers, Crewe (1880–1940).

Other material

JS, England and Wales 1906 Part 1. CS, 1908, Cd. 3929.

McCree, G. W. (ed.) *The Band of Hope Record*, vols. 1 and 2 (April 1861–December 1862).

McGowan, J. (1996) 'The emergence of modern civil police in Scotland: A case study of the police and systems of policing in Edinburghshire 1800–1833' (unpublished PhD thesis, Open University).

Tennant, M. (2008) 'An honourable failure? A reassessment of the police of the First Cheshire Constabulary Force within the wider context of 19th century police reform', paper delivered at the European Centre for Policing Studies, Open University, Milton Keynes, October.

Index